SAY "NO!" TO THE NEW WORLD ORDER

D1600189

Other books by Gary Allen

*Jimmy Carter/Jimmy Carter**

Communist Revolution in the Streets

*Ted Kennedy: In Over His Head**

*Kissinger: The Secret Side of the Secretary of State**

*Richard Nixon: The Man Behind The Mask**

Nixon's Palace Guard

*None Dare Call It Conspiracy**

*The Rockefeller File**

*Tax Target: Washington**

(*Currently available from Concord Press)

SAY "NO!" TO THE NEW WORLD ORDER

Gary Allen

Concord Press
Seal Beach, California

Typesetting by Thoburn Press, Tyler, Texas

Dedication

Over the years I have been blessed by knowing so many wonderful compatriots, so many kind and generous colleagues, so many loving and loyal friends and family, that it is impossible to mention them all.

But there are four in particular who must be noted here:

First and foremost, Congressman Larry McDonald, who was the most courageous, the most tireless, and the most effective leader I ever met — and who was murdered by the Communists precisely because of those traits.

Second, my dear friend and editor for more years than either of us wishes to count, Scott Stanley. His vision, drive, and determination are as limitless as his talent, his generosity, and his patience.

Third, the man who taught me the amazing effectiveness and enormous impact of that simple phrase, "Say 'NO!' to the New World Order," Alfred Aaronson. Without him, neither this book nor the American Freedom Movement would exist.

And finally, my longtime research assistant and good friend, Sam Wells. Without him, many of my articles and most of this book would never have been finished.

Thank you all.

Table of Contents

Foreword

Gary Allen, who never shirked a battle in his life, finally lost one on November 29, 1986. After two years of being in and out of hospitals, operating rooms, and therapy centers, he finally succumbed to complications brought about by the worst effects of diabetes.

Although desperately ill for months, and sometimes too weak to even hold a pen, Gary continued to work on the manuscript for this book until he completed it a few weeks before his death. He considered it his most important work yet, in a lifetime marked by monumental accomplishments.

Here, in part, is what Scott Stanley said of his friend and colleague, at a memorial service for Gary Allen last December.

"Gary Allen's eight books on Conservative themes have been translated into half a dozen languages and sold many millions of copies, practically all in sacrificially inexpensive pocketbook editions, to maximize their impact on a nation then retreating from its greatness.

"Nearly six million of his *None Dare Call It Conspiracy* were sold. No single book since *Uncle Tom's Cabin* has been read by so many Americans with such profound effect. And, in the greater tradition of *The Federalist Papers*, that effect was not only powerful, but enlightening to free men throughout the world. Never again would movement Conservatives blindly accept the leadership of the corporate socialists and banking insiders who have betrayed millions into the arctic midnights and equatorial hells of Communist slavery.

"Almost a quarter of a century ago, not long out of Stanford, where he had played tackle on the football team while majoring in history, Gary did his first professional writing at *American Opinion*, on a story that took him into the Watts area of Los Angeles to cover the bloody riots there. Soon he was investigating and reporting the seminal movement of black revolutionaries at Berkeley, a lone white face surrounded by thousands of hate-filled radicals chanting: 'Black Power! White Blood!' He was among those who marched across Mississippi to report on the incendiary efforts of the Kluxes and Martin Luther King; he confronted heavily armed Black Panthers and Weather Underground fanatics, faced down Communists in countless confrontations from Delano to the Vietnik marches on the Pentagon, and covered the terrorist war in Africa.

"The man's moral and physical courage were the stuff of legends.

"But what I shall most remember are Gary's warm loyalty, quiet courage, and the roar of his anger at injustice. And also his gentle side, the sensitive side that wept at the world's horrors and injustices.

"At the end, no one can doubt that Gary Allen knew well that the only estate worth leaving are the quality of your family and friends, and your love and work and character. He knew too that no epitaph is sweeter, no love more satisfying, no friendship more enduring, no example more courageous and ennobling, than one about which it can be said: *semper fidelis*.

"Let it be known of Gary Allen: He was always faithful."

Preface

Since the end of World War II, forty-three nations, representing nearly one-third of the surface of the world, have fallen to Communism. In every single instance, the U.S. State Department was a willing and knowing accomplice to the betrayal. Why?

Can such remarkable consistency be accidental?

The Soviet Union, a backward nation with a grudging population and saddled with an unworkable economic system, has been turned into a fearsome military colossus—thanks to tremendous technical and financial assistance from the West, mainly the United States. Why?

Can such suicidal stupidity really be accidental?

As we will prove in this book, the world's richest capitalists have for decades cooperated with and bankrolled their alleged mortal enemies, the Communists. Why?

Can such treasonous folly be attributed just to greed?

This book will answer these questions. It all has to do with something the would-be Big Brothers call the New World Order.

The New World Order is to be created by the merger of the United States and the Soviet Union into a one-world government. It could never happen, you say. No one would even propose such a monstrosity.

Sorry to disillusion you, but it can happen here. It is happening now. The Power Brokers of the New World Order have been busily promoting just such a scheme for years. In this book, we will present their signed confessions. And we guarantee, you will be shocked at the plan . . . and outraged at the planners.

Prologue

This book is about some of the richest and most politically powerful people in the United States who, quite literally, want to abolish our country. Your first reaction, undoubtedly, is that this is a wild and crazy accusation being made by some hysterical extremist. Actually, we are not accusing anybody of anything. In this book we will present, in their own words, their confession. They do not deny their intention to what is tantamount to repealing the Declaration of Independence and abolishing the Constitution, replacing these documents with something they themselves call the "New World Order."

"What in the world," you are probably asking yourself, "is a New World Order?" One of the best descriptions was contained in a film you have probably seen. In the 1976 movie, "Network," the multi-national corporate chairman, Mr. Jensen, walks TV anchorman Howard Beal into his boardroom and sits him down. He very quietly closes the drapes, moves to the head of the long boardroom table, and proceeds to scream at the top of his voice: "YOU HAVE MEDDLED WITH THE PRIMAL FORCES OF NATURE, MR. BEAL, AND I WON'T HAVE IT! IS THAT CLEAR?"

And he goes on to explain: "You think you have merely stopped a business deal. That is not the case. The Arabs have taken billions of dollars out of this country and now they must put it back. It is ebb and flow, tidal gravity; it is ecological balance."

There is more; but first, as they say in show business, let me "set the scene." In this brilliant Paddy Chayevsky work, a tired old network anchorman, Howard Beal, goes off his rocker and in the process, starts to rant and rave, on camera, about all the things that have been bugging him for the past forty years. At first the executives at UBS (the network) are tearing their hair out. But then the ratings come in, and they find that the nation is fascinated by Howard Beal. People are tuning in by the millions.

The head of network programming, played with devastating effectiveness by Faye Dunaway, convinces her new boss that rather than being a lemon, Howard Beal's craziness can be turned into lemonade for their network, which has been on the bottom of the rating scales. She quickly converts the news hour into television's version of a supermarket tabloid, complete with astrologers, soothsayers, audience participation, studio band . . . the works.

Of course, the show skyrockets in popularity as this poor, burned-out, half-crazed old anchorman keeps saying, "I'm mad as hell and I won't take it anymore!" The audience loves every delightfully demented diatribe.

Then, without warning, the other shoe drops. Beal goes on his show and starts shouting about how the Arabs are buying up everything in this country, including the stock in the parent company of his network, United Broadcasting System. The network is one tentacle of a giant, multi-national corporation, CCA.

Thinking he is doing the right thing, both for his country and the company, he tells his millions of viewers, "Only one thing can stop them—YOU! Send telegrams to the White House! Get up right now and send a telegram to President Ford saying, 'I'm mad as hell and I won't take it anymore. I want the CCA deal stopped, *now.*'"

The predictable happens. The next morning the President is knee-deep in telegrams and phone messages, demanding he stop the Arab buyout of CCA/ UBS. What the anchorman didn't know, nor did the nation, was that the directors, and especially the chairman, of CCA owed the Arabs over $2 billion and that the stock purchase was an ideal solution for all parties involved. So the chairman, Mr. Jensen, called his network Vice President and demanded that Howard Beal be in his office at 10:00 the next morning; then came the scene quoted above.

Immediately prior to this, as they are strolling into the boardroom, the chairman is quietly telling the anchorman how he had started with the company as a salesman, and that now he wanted to sell him "an idea." After his opening burst, Mr. Jensen then sits down to explain to the poor, confused newsman how the world really works. What followed is so good, I am going to quote it at length, for in that one brilliant scene, Paddy Chayevsky almost perfectly captured the mentality of the people working for a New World Order.

In order to give you the flavor of the tone in which the words are spoken, THE SHOUTING IS IN CAPITALS, the normal-speaking parts are in regular type, and *the softer, whispered parts are in italics*. We pick up the scene as Mr. Jensen continues his "explanation:"

"You are an old man who thinks in terms of nations and people. *There are no Russians. There are no nations. There are no people.* There are no Arabs. There are no third worlds. THERE IS NO WEST. There is only one holistic system of systems. One vast, interwoven, interacting, multi-variant, multi-national dominion of dollars. *Petrodollars, electrodollars, multidollars.* Reichmarks, yen, RUBLES, POUNDS, and shekels. It is the international system, the currency, which determines the totality of life on this planet. *That is the natural order of things today.*

"THAT IS THE ATOMIC AND THE SUBATOMIC AND GALACTIC STRUCTURE OF THINGS TODAY. AND YOU HAVE MEDDLED WITH THE PRIMAL

FORCES OF NATURE."

Gritting his teeth and shaking his fist at the awe-struck Beal, Mr. Jensen froths, "AND YOU WILL ATONE!"

Then, in the most natural and calm voice possible, he asks, "Am I getting through to you, Mr. Beal?" Without waiting for an answer, he plunges ahead: "You get up on your little 21-inch screen and howl about America and democracy. There is no America; there is no democracy. There is only IBM and ITT and AT&T and Du-Pont and Dow and Union Carbide and Exxon. *Those are the nations of the world today.*

"What do you think the Russians talk about in their councils of state? Karl Marx? They get out their linear programming charts, statistical decision theories, minimax solutions, and compute the price/cost probabilities of their transactions and investments. *Just like we do.*

"*We no longer live in a world of nations and ideologies, Mr. Beal.* The world is a collage of corporations, inexorably determined by the immuted bylaws vested. The world is a business, Mr. Beal, and it has been since man crawled out of the slime."

Winding down, the chairman is now going to give Howard Beal, and us, his vision of the future: "Our children will live, Mr. Beal, to see that (perfect world) in which there is no war and famine, oppression or brutality." Almost in tears, he concludes in a soft, caressing voice, "*One vast and ecumenical holy cup for whom all men will work to serve a common profit, in which all men will hold a share of stock.*"

Now barely audible, he whispers, "*All necessities provided, all anxieties tranquilized, all boredom amused.*" Then, in a perfectly normal voice, placing his hand gently on the old man's shoulder, and his face shadowed by a gleam of sunlight, he says, "I have chosen you, Mr. Beal, to preach this adventure."

Humbled and with reverent expectation, Beal asks, "Why me?"

And Jensen offers the perfect reply: "Because you're on television, dummy. Sixty million people watch you every night of the week, Monday through Friday."

And Howard Beal, choking back the joyous tears of a convert, looking up at the silhouetted chairman standing above him, responds, "I have seen the face of God." The chairman concludes, "You just might be right, Mr. Beal."

Welcome to the New World Order.

Chapter One

The Name of the Game

> *"The history of the twentieth century can best be understood by coming to the realization that for the first time in the course of human events, the whole world has come under a single idea. This idea, which goes by many names and under many guises, always ends up in some form of collectivism, which crushes the lives and aspirations of individuals in its utopian quest for heaven on earth."*
>
> — Donald McAlvany, June 1980
> *"Gold and Monetary Report"*

From time immemorial, dreamy professorial types have concocted fantasies of a world superstate, quite naturally to be run by intellectuals. The Greek philosopher Plato in his *Republic* advocated an all-powerful superstate headed by philosopher-kings; the intellectuals naturally saw themselves as those philosopher-kings. Thomas Moore penned his *Utopia*, Edward Bellamy scribbled a similar tome called *Looking Backward*, and the English philosopher, Alfred Lord Tennyson, rhapsodized about the day when the flags would be unfurled in the *Parliament of Man*. The English historian-science fiction writer, Herbert George Wells, in his book *The Open Conspiracy*, detailed his plan for a planetary superstate.

For generations, such pipe dreams mesmerized students and served as the basis for discussions long into the night in college dormitories the world over. These Fantasy Land musings were harmless and had no standing in the world of reality. Students graduated, went to work and quickly forgot about grandiose schemes for creating utopias. (Utopia literally means "no such place.")

But when the wealthiest and most politically powerful men in the world realized that a World Government could multiply their wealth and power to unbelievable levels by putting under their control a monopoly of world commerce and finance, the dreams of dreamers became the schemes of schemers. Under the guise of abolishing war and poverty, the world's most gigantic monopolistic trust could be created.

The Megabuck Machiavellians of High Finance began opening their wallets and pouring unending millions of dollars behind the intellectuals advocating a world government. This process has now been going on for nearly seven decades and the Megabuck Mafia has poured literally billions of dollars into the effort. Common sense tells us they didn't do so frivolously. They obviously see it as an investment which has paid and is continuing to pay handsome returns, like a rigged slot machine, by draining taxpayers' pocketbooks for foreign aid and defense spending through a myriad of internationalist programs. This is the scheme of schemes and the scam of scams.

As a justification for the surrender of national sovereignty and the spending of trillions of dollars, it was necessary to have an enemy; and thus the Soviet Union was created and has been maintained by the very men who were supposed to be its arch-enemies. Sound fantastic? The amount of evidence to prove that statement is mountainous and goes unrefuted. It is simply ignored by the Halls of Ivy and the master media manipulators, both of which are largely subservient to the Money Masters.

The New World Order

The name of the game most often used by the Establishment Money Moguls and their bought-and-paid-for intellectual lackeys and media flaks is *New World Order*. This curious phrase repeatedly appears in the titles of numerous organizations, books, studies, and monographs. They make no bones about the fact that New World Order is simply a euphemistic code word for a World Socialist Superstate. While the term *New World Order* may sound vaguely threatening to some, if called by its true name, *World Socialist Superstate*, it would be frightening to practically everyone.

The average American has heard the phrase New World Order many times and has never given it a second thought. If he thinks about it at all, he dismisses it as the typical wind-baggery of politicians or vacuous musings of the pointy head set. *Nobody* sits around the lunch table, the corner bar, or a cocktail party and raps about the New World Order. If you broach the subject under such circumstances, your colleagues would probably look at you as if you had just floated down from the moon. But the subject *is* discussed with great seriousness in the penthouses on Park Avenue and in the halls of the State Department.

The New World Order is promoted under many other aliases, using such buzz words as interdependence, New International Economic Order, convergence, world federation. Opponents sometimes refer to it as the Great Merger. Whatever the aliases and disguises it sometimes uses, in this book we shall refer to it as the New World Order.

The New World Order crowd would have us believe that world government will bring us perpetual peace and prosperity if we will only surrender our sovereignty (both individual and national), consign the Declaration of Independence to the dust bin of history, scrap our Constitution, and establish a World Court, world tax system, and world army.

The initial reaction of many people is that such a goal is idealistic but impractical and unattainable; however, a little thought will show that it is *anything* but idealistic. We know that government is very difficult to deal with at the City Hall level and more complicated at the county level. Solving problems at the state level is an absolute pail of snails, while at the federal level, problem-solving becomes a quagmire of politics, bureaucracy, red tape, and corruption. Can you imagine trying to solve problems on a worldwide level, dealing with a government run by jealous and envious foreigners who despise our traditions and covet our wealth?

Our Founding Fathers designed a government to protect our individual liberties and provide a framework for personal advancement. Life under the New World Order has been described in agonizing detail in two of the best-selling books of our century: Aldous Huxley's *Brave New World* and George Orwell's *1984*. Both books describe what life is like when government has all the power and the people have no freedom or liberty. Huxley describes how an all-powerful centralized government uses drugs and brainwashing to keep an apathetic population docile and subservient. Life is like an ant colony, and every aspect of one's career is mandated by the State. The family unit has disappeared and even reproduction is rigidly controlled by the State.

Prophetic Warnings

It was in 1949 that George Orwell published *Nineteen Eighty-Four*, his great novel warning of a totalitarian future. So powerful was its impact that we now speak of the use by dictators of highly advanced technology as being "Orwellian." Orwell's story of a Commu-Nazi superstate introduced such terms as "Big Brother," "newspeak," and "doublethink." But George Orwell did much more than enrich our vocabularies; he wrote a prophetic warning about a nightmare world which has, each year since, become more of a reality. In

Orwell's story, Big Brother of the Socialist Superstate watched you. Orwell speculated that in the society of the future, television would watch you instead of *vice versa*. This could come about, but in the meantime, the job is being done by the computer, a technological development which Orwell didn't foresee.

Former Congressman Cornelius Gallagher checked with the General Accounting Office and found that the bureaucrats had let *seventy thousand* grants and contracts from the Department of Health, Education and Welfare, and another ten thousand from the Manpower Administration, for "behavior research." There have always been ambitious intellectuals who craved control, but until very recently, they have not had the money and the opportunity to grab the levers of power and implement their plans. At the time Orwell authored *Nineteen Eighty Four*, behavioral science was in its comparative infancy. Perry London writes in his book, *Behavioral Control*:

> As 1984 draws near, it appears that George Orwell's fears for Western democracy may have been too pessimistic, or at least premature, but it is also clear that his concepts of technology by which tyranny could impress its will upon men's minds were much too modest. By that time, the means at hand will be more sophisticated and efficient than Orwell ever dreamed, and they will be in at least modest use, as they have already begun to be, not by the will of tyrants but by the invitation of all of us, for we have been schooled to readiness for all these things and will demand their benign use regardless of their potential risk. The capacity for control will continuously grow, evolving from benevolence.

London makes it clear that such relatively primitive methods of behavior control as those used by the Nazis and the Soviets are already outdated by the modern technology and behavioral research available to "American" planners. Our boys have developed means to make the people *beg* for tyranny.

The Mind Manipulators

When Rudyard Kipling wrote of "little tin gods on wheels," he had in mind just such creatures as Dr. B. F. Skinner, chairman of the Psychology Department at Harvard University, who is the virtual god of these sophisticated people controllers. Dr. Skinner is not some obscure Dr. Frankenstein working in his basement with a hunch-back named Igor. *Time* magazine calls B. F. Skinner "the most influential of living American psychologists." In a recent Johns Hopkins University poll, psychology faculties and graduate students around the nation named Skinner as the most respected social scientist in the world.

Operating on a $283,000 grant from the federal government's National Institute of Mental Health, Professor Skinner has published a frightening book entitled *Beyond Freedom and Dignity.* Yes, that's right—you paid for it. *Time* magazine of September 20, 1971, drives home the point of Skinner's book as follows:

> Its message is one that is familiar to followers of Skinner, but startling to the uninitiated: we can no longer afford freedom, and so it must be replaced with control over man, his conduct and his culture. This thesis, proposed not by a writer of science fiction but by a man of science, raises the specter of a 1984 Orwellian society that might really come to pass. . . .

Like the "Insiders" behind Orwell's INGSOC, Skinner believes our society can no long afford liberty. *Time* reports:

> "My book," says Skinner, "is an effort to demonstrate how things go bad when you make

a fetish out of individual freedom and dignity. If you insist that individual rights are the 'summum bonum,' then the whole structure of society falls down." In fact, Skinner believes that Western culture may die and be replaced, perhaps, with the more disciplined culture of the Soviet Union or [Communist] China. . . .

Professor Skinner, the idol of America's behavioral scientists, is preparing a society along lines described by Orwell in *Nineteen Eighty-Four* as those of Eurasia and Eastasia. In *Walden Two,* an earlier book, Skinner has his alter ego declare:

> I've had only one idea in my life — a true *idee fixe*. To put it as bluntly as possible — the idea of having my own way. "Control" expresses it — the control of human behavior. In my early experimental days, it was a frenzied, selfish desire to dominate. I remember the rage I used to feel when a certain prediction went awry. I could have shouted at the subjects of my experiments, "Behave, damn you! Behave as you ought!"

Skinner is the virtual prototype of what has been called "the humanitarian with a lash." Like Big Brother, he believes that man has no free will, and since he has no free will, it is better for "the clever ones" to plan and run his life rather than leave it to the vagaries of the market place. And Dr. Skinner does not hesitate openly to advocate Human Behavior Modification by "mind management." Even the pursuit of happiness is to be abolished. He states: "It is not difficult to demonstrate a connection between the unlimited right of the individual to pursue happiness and the catastrophes threatened by unchecked breeding." Hitler said it in a slightly different way — he said it in German.

Yet here is Professor B. F. Skinner of Harvard — the

most influential living American psychologist — being subsidized with more than a quarter of a million dollars in tax money to promote a society where you will be a docile humanoid and every facet of your life will be planned and controlled by "the clever ones."

Skinner proposes a system of rewards and punishments to produce behavior desired by Big Brother's social engineers. He would produce a nation of Pavlovian dogs conditioned to salivate on a signal provided by Big Brother. And these people are not content with controlling your behavior by controlling your environment; the Skinnerites are also after your body. A whole battery of new mind-altering drugs has been developed to control your behavior. There are drugs to give you amnesia, drugs to make you passive, drugs to control your sex impulses, and on and on and on. Big Brother already is dispensing drugs to "hyperactive" children in the public schools. Next there will be the forced drugging of "criminal types" and then of "potential criminal types." And last will come the drugging of reactionaries said to be potentially guilty of what in Orwell's newspeak was called "thoughtcrime."

The "clever ones" even want to get their chisels *inside* your brain. "In the past the mind belonged to the philosopher. Today it belongs to the neurophysiologist," says Dr. José M. R. Delgado, a brain researcher at Yale. Claiming that startling advances in electronics, along with increased knowledge of the workings of the human brain, have made possible "significant changes" in a man's behavior, Delgado cites the need now to "establish which kinds of behavior to modify." He offers as possible means of behavior control:

1. Implanting electrodes deep in the brain of mental patients and preventing or provoking certain kinds of behavior by stimulating brain centers with tiny electrical charges.

2. Implanting tiny tubes in the brain and releasing into them drugs which change the activity of brain centers and hence behavior.

3. Having a direct line of communication from a brain to a computer and back to the brain without having information pass through the sense organs.

Dr. Delgado explains the complicated procedures involved, and then notes: "It is possible to control behavior secretly because there are no visible wires or electrodes. Day-and-night supervision is possible without even touching the individual."

How delightfully direct this all is! These people are so confident that they tell us openly how they plan to control us.

Who Will Watch The Watchers?

But one aspect "the clever ones" don't like to discuss is who shall control the controllers. The would-be controllers tell us not to worry—that we can trust the watchers to watch each other. The wolves will watch the wolves to make sure no chickens are devoured. The Skinners of Harvard will decide what is "socially desirable" behavior for the Delgados of Yale. Aldous Huxley, who like Orwell was haunted by just such a nightmare of the future, has asked:

> Who will mount guard over our guardians—who will engineer the engineers? The answer is a bland denial that they need any supervision. . . . Ph.D.s in sociology will never be corrupted by power. Like Sir Galahad's, their strength is as the strength of ten because their heart is pure; and their heart is pure because they are scientists and have taken six thousand hours of social studies.

The truth is that these social planners are just as corruptible and hungry for power as anyone else. And we must bear in mind that the totalitarian planners of what Orwell described as the Outer Party are financed, and therefore ultimately controlled, by the "Insiders" of the

Inner Party who have motives of their own. The game, of course, is the New World Order. And control of your life is the target.

A dying George Orwell wrote *Nineteen Eighty-Four* as a warning to us. His message is that once political and scientific power are centralized, we will have no chance of escaping tyranny.

The Secret IRS Plan To Watch You

Mr. Paul Des Fosses worked for the Internal Revenue Service for almost twenty years. He has in his possession a document from the IRS called "The Strategic Plan for the Next Five Years." What it calls for, among other things, is a profile on every taxpayer, a permanent record in the hands of the IRS of every financial transaction made. According to the Five Year Strategic Plan, every Internal Revenue agent will have at his fingertips a computer terminal with which he can call up all of the information on every taxpayer. This will include such things as voter registration rolls, property tax records, automobile registration and drivers' license records, Federal Reserve records, Federal credit union records, administration records, Farmers' Home Loan, FHA, and on down the list.

The plan calls for the preparation of these "profiles" as quickly as possible and will contain information from all government agencies, investigatory records, state tax files, and even records on the state and county levels. Private credit bureau records will also be included in these personal information files.

Mr. Des Fosses reminds us that, "This is an agency that has unlimited power and it is also an agency that is very anxious to use that power to control people. I feel that the purpose of this profile is to provide the IRS with absolute control over every individual. The IRS has gone from strictly a tax-collection agency and tax-enforcement agency to become, in essence, a national secret police force!"

This plan went into effect on October 1, 1985, and as much as this seems to be an illegal scheme under the Privacy Act of 1974, there was no objection or opposition to this tyrannical scheme by the Reagan-Bush Administration.

On the subject of computers, *Daily News Digest* for October 30, 1985 informs us that 35 out of 142 domestic federal agencies use or plan to use electronic surveillance methods to spy upon Americans; 36 agencies, not counting those in foreign intelligence, maintain 86 computerized record systems, keeping 288 million files on 114 million Americans. Big Brother is, indeed, watching you!

The Motive Behind The Deed

Every crime must have a motive. What is the motive behind the New World Order? Why have the world's richest and most powerful men spent billions of dollars to promote such an alien concept? These are obviously not men who systematically toss big money away on a whim. There is a motive and method in their "madness." It is the natural disposition of these men to seek power, and no degree of power appears to .quench their thirst for more of it.

International Communist leaders are in agreement, but they want to be in command of the operation and in charge of the New World Order. What is at stake is control of the world's natural resources, the money system, manufacturing, trade, energy and transportation—in other words, the ultimate monopoly of monopolies. Socialism, in practice, is not a program to redistribute the wealth but to *concentrate* it, while buying off the proletariat and the under class with subsidies and welfare grants. Socialism's practice is the opposite of its theory; it is the royal road to monopolistic wealth and power for the super-rich. This, then, is the motivation for the crime known as the New World Order. The New World Order means control—and control is the name of the game. If you control the apex of a socialist World Government, you control the world.

What would be the ingredients of a New World Order? Among the building blocks that would comprise this monstrous edifice, there would be:

- A world tax system,
- A world court,
- A world army,
- A world central bank with a common currency,
- A world welfare state,
- Compulsory worldwide economic planning,
- Abolition of private firearms,
- Mandatory population control, and
- Control of education.

It is obvious that once the United States becomes part of the New World Order, it would not be allowed to secede; the New World Order is forever. While the New World Order is sold as the route to permanent peace, in reality it is probably a guarantee of war; when the American people realize that they are being enslaved, they will strike back in righteous anger, no matter what the odds.

As we shall show in subsequent chapters of this book, the nuclei for many of the elements necessary to create the New World Order are already in place.

The inevitability of this "New World Order" line of propaganda is merely a newer model of the old "better red than dead" sales pitch a generation ago. We are told in various ways and in words selected to fit the particular occasion that this New World Order is a sign of progress, an evolutionary inevitability, and that we shouldn't resist it but should submit supinely and even seek to enjoy it.

This propaganda line is preached by the Socialists, promoted by the Regionalists, and bankrolled by the Monopoly Capitalists. When the Communists and other

Socialist species preach this doctrine, they call it dialectical materialism and say it is historically inevitable. When the doctrine is promoted by the Regionalists, New Federalists and other kinds of Centralists, they praise it as progress toward utopian peace and justice through World Law. When the Monopoly Capitalists finance the movements preaching and promoting the New World Order, they see it as a way of gaining control of all natural and human resources, of monopolizing production and distribution and controlling the world market in their particular field — or fields — of operation. Power, Pelf, and Prestige comprise their Holistic Trinity.

Forgetting Past Lessons

Distinction must be made between political internationalism and economic internationalism. The first involves this vision of global interdependence among political institutions (UN, IMF, World Bank, etc.), international cooperation between governments and central banks, on up to full World Government or one-world socialism. The latter is simply free trade among individuals and private firms who happen to live in different geographical areas of the world. After serving as this country's first President, George Washington observed in his Farewell Address: "The great rule of conduct for us in regard to foreign nations is in extending our commercial relations, but to have with them as little political connection as possible." That is, unhampered economic trade with people of other nations, but avoid political entanglements.

This policy was the very heart of American foreign policy for our first hundred years as a Nation. When war broke out in Europe in the wake of the French Revolution, both France and England tried to involve us. But Washington proclaimed the neutrality of the U.S., and the Congress supported him. During the Napoleonic Wars we remained neutral and therefore remained independent. Even when we went to war against England in 1812, it was done independently of other warring powers. President Madison, asking Congress for a Declaration of War, added this stipulation: "Avoiding all connections which might entangle it in the contest or views of other powers." Despite wars and rumors of wars, as a Nation, we remained resolutely independent in our relations with other Nations until after the turn of the 20th century.

National Independence means the independence of the U.S. Government from domination, control, or political influence of foreign governments. This kind of national independence began to fade when we became involved in world wars to make *the world safe* from this or that. By the end of the shooting phase of World War II, we were made to believe that it was our "manifest destiny" to replace the British Empire as the world leader among all nations on this side of the "Iron Curtain." Ours was no longer a national role; it became a global role. We became "Uncle Sugar" to the world. Our dollar became the currency of world trade. U.S. strategic forces of bombers, rockets and submarines provided an "atomic umbrella" for the great zone that stretched from Norway to the border of Mainland China. U.S. ground troops and tactical air force units spread across the globe, defending nations (as with South Korea) and fighting subversion (as with Vietnam). The United States looked upon itself as the world's policeman. Presidents, beginning with Kennedy, began to deliver, not State of the Union addresses, but State of the World messages.

Then came the change in strategy and tactics. With the failure of the UN as an embryo World Government, especially after the Bay of Pigs fiasco and the Vietnam involvement, we were told by the Elitists that we couldn't "go it alone" as world rulers; interdependence was necessary and instead of a "One World Government" we would have a "World Community." So, the advice and the warnings of Washington, Jefferson, Madison,

Adams, Monroe, and the other great Americans who spoke of and fought for national independence were shelved and forgotten.

Here is how Donald McAlvany, newsletter writer and lecturer, put it in the June 1980 issue of his *Gold and Monetary Report*:

> The history of the twentieth century can best be understood by coming to the realization that for the first time in the course of human events, *the whole world has come under the influence of a single idea.* This idea, which goes by many names and under many guises, always ends up in some form of collectivism, which crushes the lives and aspirations of individuals in its utopian quest for heaven on earth. It has been called Communism, Nazism, Fascism and Socialism. Whatever the differences of these ideas, their similarities are overwhelming. Cut from precisely the same cloth are the "milder" versions of this same philosophy: "Fabianism" in England, the "welfare state" in the United States and the "middle way" in Sweden. . . .
>
> Unfortunately, the U.S. is also in the grip of the idea of collectivism. Whatever the merits or demerits of any or all of the government interventions . . . one assumption underlies and motivates them all: namely, that individuals and voluntary associations of men cannot be trusted to provide for themselves and others by pursuing their own self-interest. They must be directed and controlled in their activities by an interest that is *outside of* and *above* them as individuals. Under the sway of this idea, government has asserted its power into virtually every area of American life. Twenty-five years of collectivist education in the high schools and universities of America have conditioned a gen-

eration of Americans to believe that the government can manage and solve all of their problems, needs and wants from the cradle to the grave. In addition, a burgeoning government bureaucracy, eager to apply "crisis management" to the problems of the environment, of energy, of the consumer, of the economy, and of human suffering (problems which in many cases that government has created), takes new freedoms from the people with every day that passes.

Yes, the Megabankers and their bought-and-paid-for intellectual mouthpieces have been making plans for us. In subsequent chapters, we will let them reveal those plans to us in their own words. The name of the game is the New World Order.

Chapter Two

The Merger Maniacs

"Half the publications and broadcasts issued by the United Nations are anti-American. A report by the General Accounting Office analyzed 90 UN media programs between 1983 and 1985 on apartheid, disarmament, 'new world order' and Palestine. Only one supported U.S. interests; the rest were neutral or negative, derived from Soviet bloc and third world spokesmen and UN resolutions and conferences."
— *Washington Times*
April 18, 1986

This chapter provides an overview of the establishment forces and organizations who are working for a New World Order. We'll look at this network, which is informally headed by David Rockefeller, and its goals, structure, component organizations, and some of its key members.

While we live in what has been called the most fascinating era in history, it might also be said to be the most frightening and confusing. The mass media daily drown us in threats of atomic extinction or ecological disaster.

But the captains of misinformation also say they are building an ark to rescue us from the flood. It is called World Government. Most of these political internationalists, however, tactfully avoid using the term World

Government because it frightens the geese; instead, they use code phrases such as "new international order" or "New World Order." Ersatz Noahs of the Establishment repeat that slogan over and over. Once your cranial antennae become sensitive to the phrase, you notice that it is used constantly by the financial, political and academic elite.

When one considers the variety of potential synonyms for World Government, it does seem curious that so many of America's elitists use the same euphemism. Perhaps it is not coincidence. One is tempted to conclude that something more than mere happenstance is involved when it is discovered that many of these people belong to the same club, lodge, fraternal order, or whatever you wish to call it — the Council on Foreign Relations.

This organization, the name of which is usually abbreviated as CFR, consists of approximately 2,400 titans of business, banking, government, the academy and the world of foundations. The CFR is the core of what is generally referred to as "The Establishment" in this country.

In 1985, according to the CFR's Annual Report, of the total membership, 897 were residents in New York, 139 in Boston, 571 in Washington and the remaining 769 scattered elsewhere across the United States and overseas. Broadly categorized, the membership profile is as follows:

Profession	Number of Members
Business executives (including banking)	649
Academic scholars and administrators	497
U.S. Government officials	262
Non-profit institution administrators	366
Journalists, correspondents and communications executives	250
Lawyers	241
Other	111
TOTAL	2376

Basic to understanding the Establishment is the fact that for some wealthy individuals, the quest for power is an insatiable mania. Global monopoly and world government have been the special dream of some twisted souls throughout history. Ghengis Khan attempted to rule a world kingdom with absolute authority. Alexander the Great, some of the Caesars, Napoleon—all dreamed of world conquest. In recent times, Hitler set out to dominate the world in total fashion; the Communists are today working toward that goal. And the elitist Establishment in the U.S. seeks what it calls a "New World Order"—a euphemism for a one world socialist government.

The Quest For Ultimate Power

The question that is racing through the minds of most readers at this point undoubtedly is why the Rockefellers, considered the world's foremost capitalists, have spent hundreds of millions of dollars financing their alleged enemies, the socialists and Communists.

One would assume that, since the Rockefellers are thought of as capitalists, they would have used their fortune to foster the philosophy of individual liberty. But, just the opposite is true. We have been unable to find a single project in the history of the Rockefeller foundations which promotes free enterprise. Indeed, except in the fields of health and science (and some of these grants are highly questionable) almost all of the Rockefeller grants have been used directly or indirectly to promote economic and social collectivism.

Reasonable men ask what could motivate the Rockefellers to finance collectivist efforts which seem so totally at odds with their own interests. They forget that John D. Rockefeller was a Machiavellian who boasted that he hated competition. (He was heard to say, "Competition is a sin.") Whenever he could, Rockefeller used the government to promote his own interests and to hinder his competitors.

Monopoly capitalism is impossible unless you have a government with the power to strangle would-be competitors. Would-be monopolists, therefore, want an all-powerful, centralized government, because they can more easily control it at its apex and, through its interventions, secure rigged markets and monopoly privileges they could not obtain by competing in a free-market economy.

Would-be monopolists such as the Rockefellers promote socialism, because socialism is the most interventionist, centralized system of government. Socialism is the ultimate monopolistic system. No competition is allowed. After all, what could be more monopolisitc than socialism — a system in which the government owns and controls the major means of production (the various industries), while the monopolistic clique behind the scenes owns or controls the Socialist State? The Socialist State serves them as a legal holding company with which they merge their competitors under their control. And all of this is done in the name of "the People," of course! If it were done openly for "selfish" motives, this power grab would be roundly denounced. But since it is sold as a means of "serving mankind," the whole scam attains legitimacy in the eyes of the lumpen intelligentsia and altruistic "do-gooders."

The easiest way to control or eliminate competitors is not to best them in the marketplace, but to use the power of government to *exclude* them from the marketplace. If you wish to control commerce, banking, transportation and natural resources on a national level, you must control the federal government. If you and your clique wish to establish worldwide monopolies, you must control a World Government.

The motive, then, is simply the achievement of power and control of its Siamese twin, wealth. If one understands this, then the seeming paradox of the super-rich advocating socialism and world government no longer seems a paradox. It becomes obvious that it is the only means for achieving their goal of ultimate monopoly.

The reality of socialism is that it is not a movement to divide the wealth, as its super-rich promoters would have us believe, but a movement to consolidate and control wealth. It is not a movement to crush monopoly, as its less sophisticated adherents mistakenly believe, but a movement to establish and maintain monopoly. If you control the apex, the power pinnacle of a World Government, you have the ultimate monopoly.

There is no contradiction between socialism and monopolism. The former is the road to securing the latter. They are both opposed to free-market competition and individual diversity.

Two Sides Of The Same Coin

World Government is promoted from both the top and the bottom of the conspiratorial apparatus. In his book, *The Bolshevik and World Peace*, published in 1918 when he was Commissar of War in the first Russian Communist government, Leon Trotsky declared that "the task of the proletariat is to create a far more powerful fatherland, with a greater power of resistance — the republican United States of Europe, as the foundation of the United States of the world." He argued that "the only way in which the proletariat can meet the imperialistic perplexity of capitalism is by opposing to it as a practical program of the day the Socialist organization of world economy."

Revolutions require vast amounts of money and superb organization. The "downtrodden masses" can provide none of the former and usually little of the latter. The super-rich of international finance can, and have, provided both. Gustave le Bon truly observed that revolutions always come from above, noting: "The people make riots but never revolutions." In *The Surrender of An Empire*, the brilliant English historian Nesta Webster observed:

Had the Bolsheviks been, as they are frequently represented, a mere gang of revolutionaries out to destroy property, first in Russia and then in every other country, they would naturally have found themselves up against organized resistance by the owners of property all over the world, and the Moscow blaze would have been rapidly extinguished. It was only owing to the powerful influences behind them that this minority party was able to seize the reins of power and, having seized them, to retain their hold of them up to the present day.

The New World Order banksters of finance capitalism are in on the game. Some of them say so openly. James Warburg is not only a member of the CFR, but a scion of the international banking family which was principally responsible for the creation of the Federal Reserve System that controls our money, and which also financed Lenin and Trotsky from its New York and Frankfurt operations. On February 17, 1950, he told a Committee of the U.S. Senate: "We shall have world government whether or not you like it — by conquest or consent."

For the world's Rockefellers, government can be used to run interference for business operations and to secure special privileges and advantages over competition. The Rockefellers have been working for six decades to control the U.S. Government so they can replace *private* enterprise with *privileged* enterprise — and they have enjoyed considerable success.

Even so, the bulk of the Rockefeller wealth is located outside the United States. The family has assets and does business in some 125 different countries, including the USSR and Communist China. This family, you see, long ago recognized the need to manipulate U.S. foreign policy to enhance their international assets. They have also long recognized that a world government would simplify their problems even more. Between the mega-capitalists who lusted for control of world markets, and idealistic dreamers who expected somehow to solve the thorny problems that have always plagued mankind, there developed a symbiotic relationship. The result was a cooperative push toward world government. Both helped promote a New World Order under central political control, each for their own reasons.

The Heart Of The Establishment

As previously noted, the keystone of the Establishment is an organization called the Council on Foreign Relations (CFR). It was created in 1921 by J. P. Morgan and other international bankers who felt there was a growing need for world government. The CFR was founded for the specific purpose of conditioning Americans to accept world government as a desirable solution to the problems of the world.

The Council on Foreign Relations is headquartered at the quietly elegant Harold Pratt House in New York City. The membership list of approximately 2,400 comprises a veritable "Who's Who" of big business, high finance, the media and top university figures. Until his recent retirement for age, mandated by CFR bylaws, the chairman of the board has been David Rockefeller. However, few would deny that David Rockefeller is still the moving power behind the CFR, just as he is the moving power behind the Chase Manhattan Bank, from which he is "retired" for the same reason.

From the CFR ranks have come the key personnel, especially in the area of foreign policy, for the Roosevelt, Truman, Eisenhower, Kennedy, Johnson, Nixon, Ford, Carter and Reagan Administrations. Indeed, the CFR serves as a virtual employment agency for the federal government, *regardless* of which party is in power. You might say it functions sort of like a secretarial pool— Secretary of State, Secretary of Defense, Secretary of Commerce, Secretary of the Treasury. . . .

It is, in fact, difficult to name a U.S. Secretary of State in the last four decades who was not selected from CFR ranks. In an article in the *New York Times* magazine back in 1972, Anthony Lukas explained how the system works: ". . . everyone knows how fraternity brothers can help other brothers climb the ladder of life. If you want to make foreign policy, there's no better fraternity to belong to than the Council. . . ."

Fourteen years earlier, in an article for *Harper's* appropriately entitled "School for Statesmen," liberal columnist and CFR member Joseph Kraft explained that the Council "has been the seat of . . . basic government decisions, has set the context for many more, and has repeatedly served as a recruiting ground for ranking officials." Note, however, that until recent outside exposure forced its hand, CFR members were, on the whole, remarkably taciturn about their club.

The extent of CFR influence in our government was confirmed by John Franklin Campbell in *New York* magazine in 1972, after public exposure had begun to spread: "Practically every lawyer, banker, professor, general, journalist and bureaucrat who has had any influence on the foreign policy of the last six Presidents—from Franklin Roosevelt to Richard Nixon—has spent some time in the Harold Pratt House. . . . If you can walk—or be carried—into the Pratt House, it usually means that you are a partner in an investment bank or law firm—with occasional 'trouble-shooting' assignments in government. You believe in foreign aid, NATO and a bipartisan foreign policy. You've been pretty much running things in this country for the last 25 years and you know it."

Anthony Lukas said much the same thing in the *New York Times*:

For the last three decades, American foreign policy has remained largely in the hands of men—the overwhelming majority of them Council members—whose world perspective was formed in World War II and in the economic reconstructions and military security programs that followed. . . . The Council was their way of staying in touch with the levels of power. . . .

Such admissions from the very Establishment *New York Times* seemed nothing short of revolutionary for November 21, 1971. For, despite the fact that members of the CFR have had a virtual lock on the major communications media in our country, almost nothing had appeared about the group until such writers as Dan Smoot, Mary Davidson and myself began exposing its cardinal role. Commenting on this penchant for virtual secrecy, *Times*man Lukas admits:

> One of the most remarkable aspects of this remarkable organization, whose 1500 members include most figures who have significantly influenced American foreign policy in the last 30 years, is how little is known about it outside a narrow circle of East Coast insiders. So far as I could determine, no graduate student has written a Ph.D. thesis on it. Most newspaper references are brief notations that some notable has spoken there (omitting what he said, for all Council proceedings are off the record.)

When an organization contains as many powerful individuals as does the CFR, and yet receives almost no publicity, one must conclude that it has made secrecy its business. Increased public exposures from this writer, and others since then, have made the CFR more well-known, but while the CFR has come out of its closet, it has done so very quietly and without compromising its vows of secrecy.

Fact vs. Fiction

Since the Council on Foreign Relations has received increasing exposure by such research journalists as yours truly and others, some conventional skeptics have tried to either explain away or dismiss the crucial role played by the CFR in world and national affairs. It is therefore important that we deal with certain of the clichés which attempt to whitewash the CFR and its sinister designs.

Cliché Number One: *"The Council on Foreign Relations is not, as its critics charge, a secret organization."*

It is true that one can write to the Council at 58 East 68th Street, New York City 10021 and request a copy of its Annual Report, which includes a list of current members. You can also read the books, monographs and magazines published by the CFR to confirm its commitment to political internationalism and World Government. Of course, the average person never takes the time and effort to go to the library and search out and actually read this sort of turgid prose and double-talking gobbledegoop. But it can be done.

However, you cannot find out who sets CFR policy directions or anything at all about its internal operations. While *general* meetings are open to all *members*, Anthony Lukas reports in the *New York Times* magazine that, "Invitations to attend seminar meetings are more restricted," adding that, "the Council's talks and seminars are strictly off the record. An indiscretion can be grounds for termination or suspension of membership. . . ."

When an organization with as many influential members as the CFR is almost unknown, it is clear that that organization has made secrecy a cardinal virtue. Why? Why the absolute secrecy if the CFR has nothing to hide? The only answer ever given by CFR apologists is that many of these briefings are presented by key government officials. But, why would government officials disclose otherwise secret information to members of the Council on Foreign Relations? The CFR apologists can't have it both ways.

Finally, it is known that there are secret memberships in the CFR—those who, for political or other reasons, prefer that their membership not be reflected by their names appearing on the official membership list. How many secret CFR members are there? We don't know. We do know, however, that the Reece Congressional Committee to investigate the tax-exempt foundations discovered that there were a number of secret members of the Council at the time, including left-wing industrialist Cyrus Eaton and the late Senator J. William Fulbright.

Cliché Number Two: *"The CFR is made up of progressive-minded men who mean well."*

Anyone who has made even the most cursory study of secret societies know that they are organized as circles within circles within circles. It would be a serious mistake to assume that all, or even most, of the members of the Council on Foreign Relations are hard-core "insiders." Yet, as most of us know from experience, most organizations are run by a small handful or clique of active leaders, while most regular members take a more passive, dues-paying role.

Membership in the CFR is by invitation only. Many undoubtedly join for social or business purposes and are not in the least aware of how and why they are being used. Only the most ruthlessly ambitious and amoral are brought into the Inner Circle. Besides, even if we believe that CFR members are sincere and "mean well," it does not follow that the CFR and its influence are necessarily salutary. The road to socialism is paved with "good intentions." A look at the disastrous foreign-policy record of the past forty years should give any honest person an indication that something is wrong with what the CFR has been doing.

Cliché Number Three: *"The CFR is a prestigious, high-brow organization composed of many of America's most famous, wealthy and powerful men."*

This is hardly a defense. Our whole point is that the hierarchy comes from the respectable world of the upper-crust Establishment. We are not talking about neighborhood hoodlums or lower-level systems of organized crime like the Cosa Nostra or Mafia. The fact that these men are powerful enough or wealthy enough to buy respect in the mass media and in academia doesn't change the nature of their plans and schemes. The fact that their activities and interests are global rather than on a smaller scale only means that the stakes are even bigger than those in the numbers rackets or drug smuggling.

Cliché Number Four: *"The CFR is merely a research and study group and does not promote any particular policies."*

The idea that the CFR is policy neutral and takes no policy stands is absurd. The CFR and its special-interest groups conduct "studies" on various aspects and crisis areas in foreign affairs. These studies are always implicitly biased toward the creation of a New World Order as the alleged solution to the particular problem in focus. It must not be assumed that these studies" look at all sides or viewpoints of an issue. All of the Council's "studies" and materials implicitly or explicitly promote political internationalism and variants on the theme of World Government under various labels and euphemisms, most notably the phrase "New World Order." No consideration is given to individualist-free market alternatives. Pro-freedom, anti-Communist points of view are routinely ignored.

When the CFR members enter government policy making positions, these "studies" serve as agenda items for implementation. In short, when one wipes away the camouflage of policy "neutrality" and scholarly detachment, one sees that the CFR is an extremely powerful, vested-interest, lobbying group fronting for big financial and corporate-socialist interests.

Cliché Number Five: *"The CFR is a voluntary organization and has no way to force its members to follow any particular course."*

This is true as far as it goes. But only those who are willing to "go along" get the important opportunities for advancement and promotion. Remember that in secret societies, being in the general membership means being on the outer-most circles. General membership can be looked upon as sort of a trial period in which they find out who will go along with the program and who will resist. Those who are willing to go along tend to get the government appointments, federal contracts, foundation grants and the other perks that the New World Order Establishment can hand out. Those who won't play ball serve as camouflage for the inner circles. Members of the inner circles get invited to the special, private meetings with the real movers and shakers of the world. Discipline does not have to be formal to be real.

Cliché Number Six: *"Members of the CFR are not all of the same mind, but represent a diversity of viewpoints."*

Since the CFR has over 2300 members, it would be ridiculous to contend that they all think alike or agree on all subjects. In the past ten years, since the CFR has received some exposure and come under attack, it has added some "conservative" members to its roster to give it a flavor of ideological diversity; but this is mostly window-dressing.

Don't fall for the smokescreen that the CFR is a diverse organization because John Clodhopper, an "outspoken conservative," has been asked to join. John may rationalize that by joining, he can bring a touch of patriotic sanity to the Merger Maniacs, or get a peek at the machinations of the New World Order builders from the inside. He is just kidding himself; he's just being used as a red herring. It is the inner core of the CFR that makes policy decisions.

The Fix Is In At The Top

Another fascinating fact about the Council is that while some of its key members were brought into the organization because of their expertise, power, or position, many have achieved fame, wealth or power *because* of their membership. Lukas reminds us:

> When Henry Stimson—the group's quintessential member—went to Washington in 1940 as Secretary of War, he took with him John McCloy, who was to become Assistant Secretary in charge of personnel. McCloy has recalled: "Whenever we needed a man we thumbed through the roll of Council members and put through a call to New York." And over the years, the men McCloy called, in turn called other Council members. . . . Of the first 82 names on a list prepared to help President Kennedy staff his State Department, 63 were Council members. . . .

George Wallace made famous the slogan that there is not a dime's worth of difference between the Democrat and Republican parties at the policy-making level. The reason is that the Council on Foreign Relations, as Joseph Kraft put it, "plays a special part in helping to bridge the gap between the two parties, affording unofficially a measure of continuity when the guard changes in Washington."

But the guard never really changes. Every four years, Americans have the privilege of choosing between CFR candidates. In 1952 and 1956, Adlai Stevenson (CFR) challenged Dwight Eisenhower (CFR). In 1960, it was Richard Nixon (CFR) vs. John Kennedy (CFR). In

1964, the conservative wing of the G.O.P. stunned the Establishment by nominating its candidate over Nelson Rockefeller (CFR). At which point the Establishment proceeded to blacken Barry Goldwater as a dangerous radical who would abolish Social Security, drop atom bombs on Hanoi and in general act the part of a reincarnated Adolf Hitler. Goldwater went down in smashing defeat.

Having disposed of the challenge to the Establishment in 1964, the CFR was firmly back in the saddle in 1968. That year the CFR's Richard Nixon was pitted against Hubert Humphrey (CFR). The 1972 "contest" featured Richard Nixon against George McGovern (CFR). In 1980, Ronald Reagan, not a member of the Council on Foreign Relations, proved so popular with the American people that the Establishment was forced to punt. It maneuvered one of its own in as Vice President and then proceeded to surround Reagan with over 100 CFR members.

When Republicans are in power, the Democratic types in government go back to Ivy League Colleges, foundations and think tanks. When the Democrats are in power, the CFR Republicans go back to their banks, brokerage houses and multinational corporations. It's a giant game of musical chairs in which Establishment Team A interchanges with Establishment Team B—and *vice versa*. While real political and ideological differences exist between the two parties at the grass-roots level, there really isn't a dime's worth of difference at the top.

A New Road To World Order

The CFR strategy for conditioning Americans to accept a world government was made clear in the April, 1974 issue of *Foreign Affairs*, the deadly dull house organ of the Council on Foreign Relations. In an article entitled "The Hard Road to World Order," Richard Gardner writes openly that "if instant world government, [UN] Charter review and a greatly strengthened

International Court are not acceptable to the people, what hope for progress is there? . . . In short, the 'house of world order' will have to be built from the bottom up rather than from the top down. . . . Specifically, an end run around national sovereignty, *eroding it piece by piece*, will accomplish much more than the old-fashioned frontal assault."

Dr. Gardner was talking about *abolishing our American sovereignty*, as well as that of other nations. Do you want to be a citizen in a government that boasts the Ayatollah Khomeini, Muammar Qaddafi, and Comrade Mikhail Gorbachev among its leaders? Richard Gardner apparently does.

The Gardner article proposes the following ten areas for piecemeal erosion of national sovereignty:

- "reform of the international monetary system . . . through revitalization of the International Monetary Fund, which would have unprecedented powers to create new international reserves and to influence national decisions on . . . monetary and fiscal policies.

- "rewrite the ground rules for conduct of international trade. . . . These will subject countries to an unprecedented degree of international surveillance.

- "a steady increase in the resources of the multinational development and technical assistance agencies. This should enhance the authority of the World Bank . . . over the economic policies of rich and poor nations.

- "continued strengthening of the new global and regional agencies charged with protecting the world's environment.

- "international action on the population problem . . . a majority of nations are . . . to have explicit population policies, many of them designed to achieve zero population growth by a specific target date.

- "a World Food Conference has been scheduled to deal with . . . food supplies for the world's rapidly growing population. [Stalin, you will recall, used food control in the Ukraine to starve people into submission, and that's precisely what's going on today in Communist Ethiopia.]

- "there should eventually emerge a new international regime governing the world's oceans.

- "new rules and institutions will almost certainly be created to regulate emerging communications technologies.

- "to limit conventional weapons. It seems inevitable that the UN and perhaps regional bodies will be given new responsibilities for the administration of . . . arms control and disarmament measures, including verification and enforcement.

- "increasing resort to UN forces to contain local conflicts . . . [and] international peacekeeping arrangements to patrol borders, supervise elections, and verify compliance with non-intervention norms."

Framing A New Constitution

Because the U.S. Constitution presents a healthy barrier to this scheme, the Establishment has been pushing efforts to alter the Constitution so that the United States can be merged into a global political stew. Consider the following admission by a top leader in this effort:

> Let us face reality. The framers (of the U.S. Constitution) have simply been too shrewd for us. They have outwitted us. They designed separated institutions that cannot be unified by mechanical linkages, frail bridges, tinkering. If we are to "turn the founders upside down"—to put together what they put asunder—we must directly confront the constitutional structure they erected.

That statement was made by James MacGregor Burns, a director of the Committee on the Constitutional System and co-chairman of Project 87. Both of these groups are using the occasion of the bicentennial of the U.S. Constitution in 1987 to "reassess" our American form of government as framed by our Founding Fathers to secure our freedoms. Of the 41 members of the board of directors of the Committee on the Constitutional System, no less than fifteen are also members of the Council on Foreign Relations.

This was not the first such attack on our Constitution. Consider the following excerpts from a document entitled "The Declaration of INTERdependence," written by Henry Steele Commager (CFR and a scholar often called "the dean of American history") and published in October, 1975 under the auspices of the Philadelphia branch of the World Affairs Council, another Establishment group propagandizing for world government:

> When in the course of history the threat of extinction confronts mankind, it is necessary for the people of the United States to declare their interdependence with the people of all nations and to embrace those principles and build those institutions which will enable mankind to survive and civilization to flourish.
>
> Two centuries ago our forefathers brought forth a new nation; now we must join with others to bring forth a New World Order . . . To establish a New World Order of compassion, peace, justice and security, it is essential that mankind free itself from the limitations of national prejudice, and acknowledge . . . that all people are part of one global community, dependent on one body of resources, bound together by the ties of a common humanity. . . .

Happily for us, this document was soundly denounced by patriots in Congress and it never really got off the ground. For that matter, the United Nations has also

THE MERGER MANIACS 35

proven to be a dismal failure as a vehicle for establishing a world government. So now the planners are attempting to effect world consolidation in a piecemeal fashion, using Dr. Gardner's "end run" scheme. Once enough nations are merged into regional groupings, then the regions can be merged into a one world system.

Enter The Trilateral Commission

To help achieve this "end run" around national sovereignty, an international version of the Council on Foreign Relations came into being. The Trilateral Commission was organized July 23-24, 1972, at the Tarrytown, New York, estate of David Rockefeller. All eight American representatives to the founding meeting were members of the Council on Foreign Relations. The Commission declares that its purpose is to bring together representatives from North America, Western Europe and Japan to "improve the chances of a smooth and peaceful evolution of the global system."

Aaron Latham, writing in *New York* magazine for December 13, 1976, says the Trilateral Commission "began as a jingle in David Rockefeller's bank of ideas. Then David Rockefeller went to a meeting of the Bilderberg Group [the movers and shakers from Western Europe and America who meet secretly once a year under armed guard] — an organization set up by Prince Bernhard of the Netherlands, later a suspect in the Lockheed payoffs scandal. . . . The Chase Manhattan Bank chairman trotted out his [Trilateral] idea once more for old times' sake. The Bilderberg members loved it. Soon thereafter, the Trilateral Commission was conceived. . . ."

The Trilateral Commission is much smaller and more selective than the CFR. It doesn't have any "token conservatives" — only New World Order wheelhorses. Virtually the entire American and European hierarchy of the Bilderbergers and the Trilaterals belongs to the Council on Foreign Relations. Twenty-eight percent of the 97 U.S. Trilateralists are multi-national corporate executives or international bankers.

Actually, the idea for the Trilateral Commission had been discussed in detail by Jimmy Carter's National Security Council head Zbigniew Brzezinski (CFR) in his book *Between Two Ages*. There, Mr. Brzezinski explained that the movement toward a "world community" (his euphemism for World Government), "will in all probability require two broad and overlapping phases. The first of these would involve the forging of community links among the United States, Western Europe and Japan, as well as with other more advanced countries (for example, Australia, Israel, Mexico). The second phase would include the extension of these links to more advanced Communist nations."

Dr. Brzezinski then went on to reveal why this indirect road to world government was now required:

> . . . a [world community] cannot be achieved by fusing existing states into one larger entity. . . . It makes much more sense to attempt to associate existing states through a variety of indirect ties and already developing limitations on national sovereignty.

Richard Gardner said much the same thing in *Foreign Affairs*:

> Few people retain much confidence in the more ambitious strategies for world order that had a wide backing a generation ago — "world federalism," "charter review" and "world peace" through world law. The hope for the foreseeable future lies, not in building up a few ambitious central institutions of universal membership and general jurisdiction, as was envisaged at the end of the last war, but rather in the much more decentralized, disorderly and pragmatic process of inventing or adapting institutions of limited jurisdiction and selected membership to deal with specific problems on a

case-by-case basis, as the necessity for cooperation is perceived by the relevant nations.

The plan now is to bring about world government on
a regional basis, piece by piece, starting with the indus-
trially advanced nations and working backward.

In July, 1977, *Atlantic Monthly* published an article by
Jeremiah Novak entitled "The Trilateral Connection." The
purpose was to attempt to control damage after the CFR
and Trilaterals had finally begun to receive unfavorable
notice in the conservative press. Mr. Novak acknowledged:

> For the third time in this century, a group of
> American scholars, businessmen and govern-
> ment officials is planning to fashion a New
> World Order. Discouraged by UN inadequacies,
> disheartened by chaos in the Bretton Woods in-
> stitutions (the Establishment's International
> Monetary Fund and their World Bank), and
> worried about the United States' waning
> strength, these men are looking to a "commu-
> nity of developed nations" to coordinate inter-
> national political and economic affairs.

Here is as open an admission of the real purpose of
the Trilateral trap as the Establishment is ever likely to
make. Novak even goes on to dispel the liberal-
promoted myth that the New World Order is merely a
product of idealism:

> The Trilateralists' emphasis on international
> economics is not entirely disinterested, for the oil
> crisis forced many developing nations, with
> doubtful repayment abilities, to borrow exces-
> sively. All told, private multinational banks, par-
> ticularly Rockefeller's Chase Manhattan, have
> loaned nearly $52 billion to developing coun-
> tries. An overhauled IMF would provide another
> source of credit for these nations, and would
> take the big private banks off the hook. This pro-
> posal is a cornerstone of the Trilateral plan. . . .

A television special made in 1980, called "The World of David Rockefeller," confirmed David Rockefeller's role as kingpin in all this. This revealing broadcast, aired over PBS on "Bill Moyers' Journal," reinforced Walter Cronkite's comment that the "Rockefellers are the epitome of the nation's permanent Establishment: governments change, economies fluctuate, foreign alliances shift — the Rockefellers prevail."

Moyers, who accompanied David Rockefeller on a trip to eight foreign cities in seven days, gushed that Rockefeller "represents something measured beyond money. He represents power. . . . Rockefeller's own personal fortune is enormous, but his base is the Chase Manhattan Bank with assets over $65 billion [now $85 billion]. Rockefeller owns more of its stock than anyone else. And the bank in turn controls large blocks of stock in dozens of companies here and abroad. Yet the source of this power is something more. Rockefeller sits at the hub of a vast network of financiers, industrialists and politicians whose reach encircles the globe."

In another telling comment, Moyers said, "Some people think that banks today are larger and more important than countries because they operate across geographical and political boundaries, and that they've become a new force in the world." Indeed, "Private citizen David Rockefeller is accorded privileges of a head of state." He even crosses national boundaries without going through customs or showing his passport.

But David has not yet been successful in bringing about a world government. And that is why the Establishment must retain its grip on the U.S. Government whether it is Republican George Bush sitting in the Oval Office or a Democrat skyrocketed to fame like Jimmy Carter was in 1976.

Immensely powerful though it is, the Establishment is neither infallible nor unstoppable. Public awareness of its designs is its most dangerous enemy, so show this book to your friends.

Chapter Three

Multiple Roads to the New World Order

"The United Nations represents a potential threat of very great magnitude. The United Nations is not responsible for Soviet behavior, but the United Nations creates for them, and their allies and supporters, a marvelously useful forum in which to project themselves as reasonable people. . . . This makes it much more difficult for the United States to confront that challenge with boldness because many people in the United States, as well as the rest of the world, begin to accept the Soviets for what they are not."

—Charles Lichtenstein,
Former U.S. Ambassador
to the United Nations

The Merger Maniacs don't put all their eggs in any one basket. They simultaneously promote multiple roads to their goal of the New World Order. In this chapter we shall take you down these various roads. Let us begin with the one that is least likely today, the United Nations.

In order to understand the UN and the threat it poses to American liberty, one must go back to its dusty antecedents and examine the plan and the planners.

A world government under a Parliament of Man has been an ideal of dreamers and schemers since ancient times. The dreamers envision perpetual world peace: a utopia in which the lion will sup with the lamb instead of dining on its carcass. The schemer bedazzles the dreamer with visions of permanently eliminating war, pestilence, famine and want. He plays the "idealists" as Heifetz plays the violin. The schemer has other, less laudable goals.

Among the most important of such schemers have been powerful international financiers and cartelists. Their goal was described by Montagu Norman, former head of the Bank of England, who said they seek to assure that "the Hegemony of World Finance should reign supreme over everyone, everywhere, as one whole supernational control mechanism." This hegemony, or domination, can only be established through a world government controlled from behind the scenes by the New World Order advocates involved in international finance.

The leading representatives in America of this worldwide clique were the firms of J. P. Morgan & Company and Kuhn, Loeb & Company. Members of these international banking concerns were primarily responsible for creating the Federal Reserve System in 1913, which gave them hegemony over America's banking system and, thereby, essential control over our economy.

The League Of Nations

Next, these same men, largely through their control over key newspapers and through "Colonel" Edward Mandell House, their front man who was the Henry Kissinger of the Wilson Administration, worked mightily to push America into World War I. From the ashes of the "war to end all wars," the Merger Maniacs of international finance hoped to create a world government, the League of Nations, which would serve as a conduit for extending their hegemony over all world commerce and finance.

At the same time that the cartelists of international finance were attempting to create a League of Nations, they were also sponsoring and financing the Communist Revolution in Russia. The Bolsheviks were bankrolled by a consortium of bankers, many of them cousins, from Wall Street, London and Frankfurt. While J. P. Morgan & Company and the Rockefeller interests participated, the chief American sponsor was Jacob Schiff, a senior partner of Kuhn, Loeb & Company and one of the original movers behind the creation of the privately owned and controlled Federal Reserve System. As the *New York Journal-American* reported on February 3, 1949: "Today it is estimated, even by Jacob's grandson, John Schiff, a prominent member of New York society, that the old man sank about $20 million for the final triumph of Bolshevism in Russia."

Why did the New World Order promoters of international finance support a movement whose ostensible purpose is to assure their own destruction? The answer is that they needed a geographical base for their revolutionary operations. Soviet Communism would serve as the sword while the Fabian movement promoted Socialism in the West by use of the pen. Here were two arms of the same movement, with the violent arm distracting attention from the ultimately more dangerous non-violent arm.

Following the Armistice of November 11, 1918, Woodrow Wilson journeyed to Paris, accompanied by House, Thomas Lamont (a partner of J. P. Morgan & Company), and Paul Warburg (a partner of Kuhn, Loeb & Company). While Wilson and House bargained in Paris, disillusion was rapidly setting in back on Main Street. As the Peace Conference dragged on, it became more and more obvious to the Americans that the War had not been a moral crusade at all, but had resulted from the machinations of venal politicians whose specialty was secret treaties hidden behind secret treaties — all for the benefit of the monopolists of international finance. The American people quickly became skeptical about any involvement with such intriguers in a League of Nations. Facing a furious electorate, the Senate dared not ratify the treaty and the U.S. did not join the League; without America, the League of Nations was like a cotton plantation without cotton.

But the Peace Conference was far from a total disaster for the conspirators. The Versailles Treaty, which betrayed the terms upon which Germany had agreed to an armistice, was so written as to guarantee that within two decades, the world would once again face general warfare.

Preparing For The Next Time

The New World Order gang, anticipating a second chance, were determined to learn from their mistakes. They quickly established organizations in the major Western countries to propagandize for internationalism and idealize the concept of One World government. The instrument they created to promote these goals in the United States is called the Council on Foreign Relations. The man most responsible for its creation was the ubiquitous "Colonel" Edward Mandell House. Joining House in founding the CFR were such international financiers as Schiff, Lamont, Warburg, Kuhn, Rockefeller and Baruch—the very men who had been so anxious to collar the United States into the League of Nations.

Having failed to bring the United States into the League of Nations, the political internationalists pressured Americans into joining the United Nations. The theme was that World War II could have been prevented had it not been for the "isolationism" of the American people and the U.S. Senate which had rejected membership in the League of Nations. We were given another chance—an opportunity to redeem ourselves—by joining with the United Nations, which represented the second try at World Order.

The United Nations was formed in the wake of a torrent of idealism and the euphoria of victory and peace following World War II. The United States and its allies would join with our "Noble Ally," Soviet Russia, led by "Uncle Joe" Stalin, to jointly steer the world to peace and brotherhood. After having defeated the common enemy of Nazi Germany, the spirit of East-West cooperation was high and the world seemed on the verge of an era of perpetual peace. "Our last, best hope for peace" was the slogan drummed into the public.

"A Record of Twenty-Five Years," published privately by the Council on Foreign Relations in 1947, reveals how it achieved a hammerlock on American foreign policy, leading to the creation of the UN:

> [In 1939] Hamilton Fish Armstrong, editor of *Foreign Affairs*, and Walter H. Mallory, Executive Director of the Council, paid a visit to the Department of State to offer such aid on the part of the Council as might be useful and appropriate in view of the war. . . .

As a result of this meeting, the State Department authorized the CFR to "form groups of experts to proceed with research under four general heads: Security and Armaments Problems, Economic and Financial Problems, Political Problems and Territorial Problems. . . ." Then, according to the CFR, "the Rockefeller Foundation was approached for a grant of funds to put the plan into operation." However, by February of 1941, the State Department took over the whole operation, absorbing the CFR's top operators into post-War planning activities. Remember, this was ten months *before* Pearl Harbor.

Architects Of The UN

During World War II, it was increasingly taken for granted that as soon as the fighting was ended, a new international organization would be formed, and that it would be called the United Nations. (During the war, the Allies were even referred to as the "United Nations.")

Planning for creation of that organization was taken over by members of the CFR — lock, stock and barrel of borscht.

The man termed "the architect of the United Nations Charter" by *Time* magazine in its issue for May 18, 1953, was Russian-born Leo Pasvolsky (CFR), Chief of the Division of Special Research in the State Department. Born of Communist parents, Pasvolsky was raised a radical and infiltrated into our government in 1934. He rapidly rose to the key position from which he worked to effect the transfer of U.S. sovereignty to the United Nations.

Working side by side with Pasvolsky in formulating the UN Charter was Alger Hiss, who was at the same time a member of the Communists' Harold Ware cell in Washington, a Soviet espionage agent, and a member of the Council on Foreign Relations. Hiss played key roles at Yalta and Dumbarton Oaks, where agreements were worked out with the Soviets on the content of the UN Charter. According to lengthy testimony before the Senate Internal Security Subcommittee, it was Alger Hiss who sat at F.D.R.'s side as his top specialist on international organization.

In 1950, the State Department issued an official report entitled *Postwar Foreign Policy Preparation, 1939-1945*, which named the men who did the planning and shaped the policies that led to the creation of the new World Organization. That list and similar official records revealed these men to have been (in addition to Alger Hiss), Harry Dexter White, Virginius Frank Coe, Dean Acheson, Noel Field, Laurence Duggan, Henry Julian Wadleigh, John Carter Vincent, David Weintraub, Nathan Gregory Silvermaster, Harold Glasser, Victor Perlo, Irving Kaplan, Solomon Adler, Abraham George Silverman, William Ullman and William Taylor.

The State Department could hardly have anticipated what a disastrous confession this would prove to be. For since then, with the single exception of Dean Acheson

(CFR), who had himself been hired by Joseph Stalin to serve as Soviet Russia's legal counsel in the United States, *every one of those seventeen men has been identified in sworn testimony as a Communist agent*. It is hardly startling that such men were willing to make every concession to the Soviets at Dumbarton Oaks, Yalta and at the official founding of the United Nations in San Francisco.

The UN Charter was thus a product of both major arms of the International Communist Conspiracy. Our delegation to the San Francisco Conference in April of 1945 was headed by Secretary of State Edward R. Stettinius Jr., a member of the CFR and a former partner in the international banking firm of J. P. Morgan & Company. Serving as Secretary-General of the conference was Alger Hiss, both a member of the CFR and a Communist.

At the conclusion of the San Francisco conference, it was Alger Hiss who was entrusted with taking the Charter to Washington. On page 23 of *Life* magazine for July 16, 1945, was a "picture of the week" showing Hiss arriving in Washington with a large package. The caption read:

> At the conclusion of the San Francisco Conference, the Charter of the United Nations was bundled off to a waiting plane and gingerly placed in a 75-pound safe equipped with a small parachute. Attached to the safe was a stern inscription: "Finder—do not open! Notify the Department of State, Washington, D.C." Chief custodian was Conference Secretary-General Alger Hiss, shown here with the Charter at the end of the cross-country trip. . . .

Only five days of testimony about the Charter were heard in Washington before a vote was taken in the Senate. A few Senators raised their voices against this permanent, entangling alliance, but their voices were a whisper in the wilderness. So universal was the managed acclaim for the United Nations that when the Charter was ratified on July 28, 1945, virtually without debate, few had even bothered to read the thing. The vote was 89-2; the two Senators who voted against the UN had read the Charter.

The UN And Disarmament

The issue of the UN being a road to world government is not a new charge. Its agencies are so blatant in their aims of political internationalism that many pro-UN partisans do not bother to deny the obvious. The *Saturday Review* ran an editorial in its March 23, 1953 issue concerning the one-world propaganda of UNESCO, one of the UN's specialized agencies. It candidly stated:

> If UNESCO is attacked on the grounds that it is helping to prepare the world's people for world government, then it is an error to burst forth with apologetic statements and denials. Let us face it: the job of UNESCO is to help create and promote the elements of world citizenship. When faced with such a "charge," let us by all means affirm it from the housetops.

The ultimate move to strengthen the UN is to give it a monoploy on military power. Up until that time, the United States can still get out of the UN, regardless how anyone may interpret the Charter. The solution dreamed up by the one-worlders is to disarm the United States in favor of a UN army.

On June 23, 1961, John J. McCloy, Special Advisor to the President on Disarmament, sent to the White House the draft of a bill to create a U.S. Disarmament Agency. Mr. McCloy was at the time Chairman of the Board of the Council on Foreign Relations. In his letter of transmittal to President Kennedy, he revealed that the fundamental purpose of the Disarmament Agency would be to bring about world government.

In September 1961, Congress passed the Arms Control and Disarmament Act, conferring on the director of the new Disarmament Agency broad authority, under the general supervision of the President and the Secretary of State, to do just about anything the director might believe to be in the interest of "peace."

Many Congressmen supported creation of this Disarmament Agency because they were afraid of being accused of opposing peace. Not all, however, withered under "Liberal" pressure. Congressman John Ashbrook of Ohio referred to it as "The Surrender Agency," and declared: "The testimony is replete with evidence which indicates this Agency may well be the back door for the one-worlders to accomplish their goal. . . ." The late Congressman James Utt commented that it was an "almost word-for-word duplication of a disarmament proposal advanced by Khrushchev in 1959."

This formal disarmament proposal was later published in a nineteen-page report entitled *Freedom From War: The United States Program For General And Complete Disarmament In A Peaceful World*. Also known as "State Department Publication 7277," it called for transferring control of U.S. nuclear weapons to the United Nations, restricting the American military to the role of an internal police force, and establishing an all-powerful UN Army—sort of like what we saw in the TV movie, "Amerika."

This disarmament plan further provides: "The parties to the Treaty would progressively strengthen the United Nations Peace Force . . . until it had sufficient armed forces and armaments so that no state could challenge it." Remember, this is the *U.S.* proposal!

The Disarmament Agency's Dr. Lincoln P. Bloomfield (CFR) has written:

> Short of a major catastrophe, the difficulties in obtaining widespread public approval and explicit Senate ratification of a genuine world government are obvious. . . . Without disarm-

ament, such a system [of world government] is probably unobtainable. . . . If it [world government] came about as a series of unnerving trips to or over the brink, it could come about at any time.

Thus the threat of the Soviets dropping nuclear bombs on us is built up so that we can be blackmailed into accepting world government through national disarmament in favor of a UN "peace" force. The New World Order promoters have no intention of destroying that which they intend to own and control. If there truly were a military threat from an independent Russia, the crowd at the CFR would be leading the parade for American independence and arms *superiority*; they would not be promoting disarmament.

Adopting Patient Gradualism

The original plan of the New World Order cabal for the disarmament of the United States, and the transfer of our weaponry to the United Nations, called for its completion in 1972. But American Conservatives gave the plan such exposure in the early Sixties that the timetable had to be altered. Conservatives ordered and distributed to their alarmed friends so many copies of State Department Publication 7277 that the Department let it go out of print. An article in the Communist *World Marxist Review* emphasized the need for patience, advising the comrades: "Communists do not adhere to the 'all or nothing' principle. Anything that brings disarmament nearer is a step forward. . . ." It was back to Fabian "patient gradualism."

And so, disarmament talks have been going on with the Soviets for 25 years. During that time we have negotiated with them the Nuclear Test-Ban Treaty (with no inspection, of course), the Outer Space Treaty, the Non-Proliferation Treaty, and the Seabed Treaty. All of these were steps toward SALT—Strategic Arms Limitations

Talks. And SALT is another step toward complete disarmament and world government.

The objective laid down by the State Department back in 1961 has not changed. In 1968, a Disarmament Agency publication called *Arms Control and National Security* explained what has been happening:

> Since 1959, the agreed ultimate goal of the negotiations has been general and complete disarmament, i.e., the total elimination of all armed forces and armaments except those needed to maintain internal order within states and to furnish the United Nations with peace forces. U.S. and Soviet plans for general and complete disarmament were proposed in 1962 and they are still "on the table."

Under the Charter of the UN, any United Nations "peace" force would be under the command of the Under Secretary-General for Political and Security Council Affairs. This is the person who has control of all UN military affairs—including any nuclear weapons we furnish to the UN.

The following is a list persons who have held that post since it was created in 1946:

1946-49	Arkady Sobolev (USSR)
1949-53	Konstantin Zinchenko (USSR)
1953-54	Ilya Tchernychev (USSR)
1954-57	Dragoslav Protitch (Yugoslavia)
1958-60	Anatoly Dobrynin (USSR)
1960-62	George Arkadev (USSR)
1962-63	E. D. Kisilev (USSR)
1963-65	V. P. Suslov (USSR)
1965-68	Alexi E. Nesterenko (USSR)
1968-73	Leonid N. Kutakov (USSR)
1973-78	Arkady N. Shevchenko (USSR)
1978-82	Mikhail D. Sytenko (USSR)
1982-	Viacheslav Ustinov (USSR)

Except for one two-year period, when the post of Under Secretary-General for Political and Security Council Affairs was held by a *Yugoslav* Communist, it has always been held by a *Soviet* Communist. There seems to be a trend here!

Trygve Lie, Secretary-General of the UN from 1946 to 1953, admitted in his book, *In the Cause of Peace*, that this is not coincidence. There was a secret agreement between the U.S. and the USSR to give this key position to someone from the Soviet Union. Despite the fact that the agreement was only for five years, no U.S. President has been so rude as to suggest that the post be given to anyone other than a Communist.

This means that the drumbeaters for a New World Order and those who want the UN strengthened to the point of becoming a World Government powerful enough militarily to quell any international discord, are promoting a situation in which the military arm of such a global government would be under the control of a Soviet general. Perhaps they think this is less embarrassing than merely surrendering directly to the Kremlin. This would solve the PR problem of keeping patriotic Americans from rebelling, as the whole thing would be sold to the people by the media as a great peace plan rather than a de facto surrender.

Our "Friends" In The UN

Of the some 130-plus members of the United Nations, approximately 100 are virulently anti-American and strongly anti-free enterprise in ideology. These are the national voting blocs which control the General Assembly. With this in mind, it becomes understandable why the UN condemned the United States for having 14 U.S. Coast Guardsmen stationed in the U.S. Virgin Islands—while permitting terrorist Yassir Arafat to address the UN about peace while he had a gun hanging out of his belt.

According to information issued by the U.S. State

Department, the United States gets very little support on key votes from several large voting blocs in the General Assembly. In 1984, the latest year for which figures are available, African nations voted with the U.S. only 12.8 percent of the time; Asian and Pacific nations, 14.9 percent of the time; Arab nations, only 10 percent; Mexico, our neighbor to the South, supported the U.S. in its voting pattern less than 10 percent of the time; India, 6.5 percent; and Red China, 11.1 percent.

As a means for bringing peace, the United Nations has proved to be a hypocritical charade, with the world's foremost proponent of war, subversion, propaganda and world conquest as its charter member. Most Americans have probably forgotten that it was the Soviet Union which insisted that the headquarters for the UN be located in the United States. Moreover, it should not be surprising that the entire site for the United Nations headquarters was donated by the Rockefellers, and Chase Manhattan Bank serves as the official bank of the UN.

In short, the UN has been successful as a front for and a tool of America-hating socialists and Communists who have used the UN and its agencies to further their own international goals. This has been so blatant that the United Nations has increasingly lost credibility in recent years in the eyes of American public opinion. As we mentioned in the previous chapter and as we shall elaborate on later in this chapter, the New World Order gang has prepared new routes to their common goal of world statism rather than putting all their hopes on the increasingly discredited United Nations as the core of a future World Super-State. Because the UN has become the House of Hate for the United States, its effectiveness as a potential for World Government has greatly diminished.

Even though the New World Order elitists have partially abandoned the United Nations as the nucleus for a future World Government and have taken a piecemeal, regional approach to global order, it would be a mistake to assume that the UN no longer poses a threat to American interests and security. How big a threat is the United Nations to our national security? When asked that question by Los Angeles radio talk show host Alan Stang, former U.S. Ambassador to the United Nations Charles Lichtenstein proferred these observations:

> The United Nations represents a potential threat of very great magnitude, in my judgment. The United Nations is not responsible for Soviet behavior, but the United Nations creates for them, and their allies and supporters, a marvelously useful forum in which to project themselves as reasonable people, even as they conduct aggression and warfare in many parts of the world. That is a risk; that is a danger, because it is an opportunity for them to exercise what all of us now refer to as deliberate disinformation—the distortion of reality. And this makes it much more difficult for the United States to confront that challenge with boldness, because many people in the United States, as well as the rest of the world, begin to accept the Soviets for what they are not.

The World Federalist Association

Despite the obvious PR problems with the United Nations, every globalist-internationalist group promotes the concept of "strengthening the UN." Some groups are more blatant than others in their call for what amounts to a world bureaucratic dictatorship. Among the most extreme is the World Federalists (formerly the United World Federalists) headed by Norman Cousins (CFR).

The organization was formed in 1947 by Cousins and another CFR luminary, James P. Warburg (of the family so prominent in international banking and which helped set up the Federal Reserve System in this country). There are and have been numerous other CFR stalwarts in the leadership of the World Federalists. Cousins is still honorary president.

The primary objective of the World Federalist Association is to expand the United Nations into a full-fledged world government through the jurisdiction of the World Court, the establishment of an international "peace force" under UN control and a world income tax. The WFA believes that the Soviets, second only to China as the world's greatest mass murderers, are genuinely concerned about any talk of the United States trying to defend itself from a Soviet nuclear holocaust.

Recently, the World Federalist Association hosted a "Peace Committee" delegation from the Soviet Union. According to the January, 1986 issue of *World Federalist*, the news magazine of the World Federalist Association, this meeting, held with the Soviet agents in Washington from October 17-24, 1985, was to reciprocate for the invitation from the Soviet Peace Committee which had led to a visit by three WFA representatives to Moscow in November, 1984.

On December 4, 1985 the Human Rights and International Organizations subcommittee of the House Foreign Affairs Committee held a joint hearing on the UN. At that hearing, World Federalist spokesmen testified in favor of House Joint Resolution 417. John Logue, a Vice-President of World Federalist Association, was one who testified. Among his remarks, reproduced in *World Federalist*, were the following gems:

Peace people — and all people — must see that if we really want to stop the arms race we must have effective world political institutions. We must stop pretending that a UN with a veto in its Security Council can keep the peace. We must stop pretending that the world community will give real power and real funding to a General Assembly that makes decisions by a one-nation, one-vote system. Yes, peace people must stop patronizing the people of the world. It is time to tell the world's people not what they want to hear, but what they ought to hear. What they ought to hear is that if we really want to stop the arms race, if we really want to have peace and promote justice, we must reform, restructure and strengthen the United Nations and give it the power and authority and funds to keep the peace and to promote justice, The Security Council veto must go. One-nation, one-vote must go. The United Nations must have taxing power or some other dependable source of revenue. It must have a large peacekeeping force. It must be able to supervise the dismantling and destruction of nuclear and another major weapons systems. In appropriate area, particularly in the area of peace and security, it must be able to make and enforce law on the individual.

Can you believe what you're reading?

A United Nations with the power to tax and a powerful standing military force at its disposal would be a powerful tool of America's enemies, the socialists and Communists who now control the General Assembly.

The World Federalist Association is just one among dozens of New World Order Merger Maniac organizations promoting the essential specifications and elements of a world super-state — goals shared by the entire fraternity of would-be world planners and architects of the New World Order.

There have been UN Peacekeeping Forces in the past, of course; one recalls how the UN "peacekeeping" troops helped Communist Patrice Lumumba take over the Congo and brutally slaughter innocent men, women and children in hospitals in the province of Katanga back in the early 1960s. The World Federalists want a standing UN Peacekeeping Force — a thin euphemism for a permanent world army having global military authority.

MULTIPLE ROADS TO THE NEW WORLD ORDER

America, after being stripped of its capacity to defend herself, would be at the mercy of whatever clique happened to be in control of the World Federation and its well-trained, heavily-armed international army of mercenaries and draftees. And the ruling class of such a world government would, undoubtedly, be a Communist junta or socialist clique since most nations in the world today are either socialist or Communist. *This* is the "idealistic" goal to which American independence and standard of living are to be sacrificed in the name of the global good!

Of course, these resolutions will not pass Congress in the near future, but using the Fabian approach of *patient gradualism,* the Merger Maniacs will bring them up again and again and, eventually, they could pass — like the so-called Genocide Treaty finally passed in February, 1986, after years of rejection.

Another Road To World Order

As previously noted, the One Worlders had planned the United Nations as their primary vehicle for gaining global government. They hoped to gain a genuine World Government by revision of the United Nations Charter to give it sufficient power. Impatient with the UN path to a world government, others seek another route. We allow the World Federalists to explain it in their own words:

> Some advocates of world order think that global government would have the best chance of realization if a world constitutional convention, independent of the UN, could be held. They propose convening such a convention at the invitation of a group of national governments and they mention India, Japan, Canada, Norway, Sweden, Denmark, West Germany and Mexico as nations most likely to be willing to initiate such a move. Any constitution adopted

would go into effect only after nations comprising a representative cross-section and a preponderance of population and power had ratified it.

Another strategy has been the manipulation of U.S. foreign policy for internationalist ends. It has been said that America's foreign policy is the most *foreign* policy in the world. This is because the policies are generally not in America's national self-interest, but promote the "greater good" of "world order," convergence, interdependence or some other catch-phrase used by the cadre in the State Department and their associates in the Council on Foreign Relations.

The CFR has been the key institution in working for One World Government through its control of American foreign policy since at least World War II. The goal was stated quite clearly over a quarter-century ago. Study No. 7, entitled "Basic Aims of U.S. Foreign Policy," published by the Council on Foreign Relations on November 25, 1959, contained an unabashed call for world government:

> The U.S. must strive to build a new international order which must be responsive to world aspirations for peace and for social and economic change. . . . To accomplish this the U.S. must search for an international order in which the freedom of nations is recognized as interdependent and in which many policies are jointly undertaken by free-world states with differing political, economic and social systems, and including states labeling themselves as "socialist." [Used in this context, for "socialist" read "Communist."]

The CFR planners have been even more specific in some of their writings. For example, CFR member

Harlan Cleveland (who, when working in the U.S. State Department during the Kennedy-Johnson years, tried to bring Alger Hiss back into government) has offered an extensive list of ways to work toward a New World Order. Writing in his *Agenda for the Planetary Bargain* (published as one document among many in a report titled *United Nations*, and released in 1976 by the Senate Committee on Foreign Relations), Cleveland called for the following:

1. Create a World Food Bank.
2. Provide for international control of all sources and supplies.
3. Internationalize commodity markets.
4. Establish international control over the wealth of the oceans and deep seabeds.
5. Provide for international control of the "weather at human command."
6. Rewrite the rules of trade and investment.
7. Create a world currency.
8. Create a world police to "keep the peace when it is threatened and restore the peace when it is broken."
9. Provide special programs to teach the benefits of the New World Order to each of six "categories of American institutions," namely: business, corporations, labor unions, non-profit enterprises, communications media, educational systems and government agencies.

Cleveland is former Ambassador to NATO, former Assistant Secretary of State, a Rhodes Scholar, a long-time member of the Council on Foreign Relations, and director of the Aspen Institute on Humanistic Studies, Program in International Affairs, a leftist think-tank located in Princeton, New Jersey. He makes clear what he is aiming for in that government report. We quote:

> I hope that in the hearing, and whatever report is made by the Committee, you will make a distinction between the future of the United Nations and the future of world order.

There is a long agenda of creative effort just ahead, a complex agenda of international action which some of us have been calling "The Planetary Bargain." . . . Taking it all together, this agenda amounts to a *third try at world order* — the League of Nations having died and the United Nations being unable in its present condition to cope. [Emphasis added].

In more recent years, a special program was launched by the CFR called the "1980s Project" to study the best paths to gaining success at the third try at world order. Assembled for the "1980s Project" were Henry Kissinger, Cyrus Vance, Theodore Hesburgh, Paul Volcker, Miriam Camp, Richard Ullman and other CFR-TC dignitaries. They released a 25-volume series of books enumerating plans for the 1980s.

Later, Harold Brown, Defense Secretary in Carter's Cabinet, addressed a Trilateral Commission conclave in Washington, D.C., pointing out that new leadership and new plans were required "for transition to the world of the year 2000." As a result, Robert O. Anderson of Atlantic Richfield Oil, Aspen Institute, CFR, etc., took the lead in forming a "Committee on the Year 2000," which is designed to provide that new leadership and new plans. Assisting him will be Russell Train, Walter Cronkite, Marian Heiskell of the *New York Times*, Elliot Richardson, Cyrus Vance, and others of the CFR.

New Avenues To A New Order

The Old Boy Network of the New World Order is currently deliberating new ways to sell its scheme to an unsuspecting public. A special committee, chaired by Peter G. Peterson, former Secretary of Commerce and Wall Street investment banker who succeeded David Rockefeller as CFR chairman in October, 1985, has been studying the PR strategy. The Council plans to be more visible and transmit its message more directly to the

American people, rather than confining its influence to the "Liberal" Eastern seaboard. Television broadcasts are among the tactics under consideration for the CFR to expand into Middle America.

Never putting all their money on one horse, the New World Order gang realizes that many regard the UN as a hopeless jungle of many nations rather than a likely nucleus for a true World Government. Besides, it has come to be such a well-known center for Communist espionage and far-left activism that it has lost much of its credibility with the American people who no longer support it as enthusiastically as they once did. Hence, other paths to New World Order are being cleared.

To reiterate, there are three broad roads toward the New World Order. One path is the one we have been describing, that of incrementally increasing the power of the United Nations and its allied institutions until they become, *de facto*, a world government. And certainly the United Nations has played an increasing role in the world since World War II, even though it may have lost its potential for becoming, itself, a World State.

The second road to New World Order involves "regionalism" and "piecemeal functionalism," in which the planet is divided into many regional governments or federal unions to be more conveniently administered by global bureaucrats. The Trilateral Commission is an attempt at this route for achieving a world government. The idea is to weld various nations together into larger regions, and later on, to merge the regions together into one planetary World Government.

Another variation of the piecemeal functionalism route to the New World Order is "economic summitry." Economic summits are actually international political meetings, held annually since 1976, among world planners to agree on the best way to control the world economy. This is an integral part-and-parcel of the "piecemeal functionalism" strategy.

The growing world debt crisis is the usual justification for economic summits, as well as conferences to reform the international monetary mess by pushing for a world currency. The idea is to make the nations and peoples of the world as "interdependent" as is possible so that they are mutually vulnerable to whatever monetary or financial crisis is slated to hit. Then, the leaders proclaim new international institutions or world government as the only viable solution which all nations *must* accept in order to solve problems which all of them have a vested interest in solving because of their interdependence.

This path to World Order relies on increasing the grasp, reach and power of UN subsidiaries and other one-world entities, such as the International Monetary Fund, the World Bank, GATT (General Agreement on Tariffs and Trade), and G-5 countries.

As Don Bell so cogently observed in his *Don Bell Reports*:

> While dealing with the USSR . . . , it occurred to the One World Planners that their old idea of creating a World Government through a reconstructed United Nations, or through any other single centralized authority, was not going to work. So, they scrapped their previous plans, changed the name from World Government to New World Order, and created a series of international agencies. These agencies could hold summit meetings and order could be handed down to the nation-states for execution. "Piecemeal functionalism" was the name adopted for this kind of world government, and to help with the transition from control by independent nation-states to control by international summits, the Trilateral Commission was formed. As a result, we have a New World Order actually in operation, though it is disguised, so few people know what has happened to our government.

Those favoring the New World Order and all it implies for the extinction of what is left of human freedom and dignity may sometimes disagree among themselves and debate over which path is the best to their common goal of One World Government. More often than not, however, they agree to follow all of them more or less simultaneously. Any such debate between One Worlders is like a debate between the Smith Brothers over cough drops. Whichever road takes us to world totalitarianism, the losers will be human freedom, progress and dignity.

In summary, then, there are three roads to the New World Order. The first is by directly strengthening the UN. The second is by indirectly using the UN subsidiaries. The third route is Trilateral regionalism.

The most important point to remember is that Establishment elitists have designed *all three roads* to lead us to the same destination—world government which they control.

Chapter Four

Three Arms of the New World Order

"One of the most powerful propaganda slogans propounded by Leninism and perfected by the French Communist Party was: 'pas d'enemis a gauche'—there are no enemies on the left."

—Arnold Beichman
Hoover Institute

The megabankers of Europe, Great Britain, and the United States are a world power in finance and politics. They are involved in creating booming prosperity and financial bust. They send armies marching, set governmental policies, and manipulate large portions of government budgets. Although it can be argued that they may be the primary movers and shakers in the world, they are not the only power base.

The movement towards centralized control of world politics and finance—the New World Order—has at least three arms. These arms sometimes cooperate and sometimes compete with one another. The three arms are: the megabankers, the Fabian socialists, and the Soviets. There are numerous examples of individuals or institutions which have a foot in more than one camp; some even manage to have a foot in all three.

All three groups work through various organizations and fronts. The megabankers of the United States are organized into the group known as the Council on Foreign Relations and its spawn, the Trilateral Commission. Both of these groups are, to a large degree, the instrumentalities of David Rockefeller and the Chase Manhattan-Exxon nexus. The British Empire is represented by the Royal Institute of International Affairs, an organization which spawned the New York-based Council on Foreign Relations. Continental big money is organized around the so-called Bilderberger group, which tends to be dominated by Rothschild interests, just as the CFR/Trilaterals are dominated by Rockefeller interests.

There is, however, a great deal of interlocking between all three of these groups. They all believe in the divine right of money to rule the world. Their power comes from a combination of Big Money plus Political Power. Big money without Political Power is simply wealth. There are many men who are wealthy but are not necessarily powerful. Bunker Hunt is wealthy (or at least he used to be, before the Insiders decided to make an object lesson of him); David Rockefeller is not only wealthy, he is *powerful*.

The Fabian Socialist Movement

The second power group in the world is the democratic or Fabian socialists. This is a movement of intellectuals. The Fabian Socialist movement had its roots in England around the turn of the century. It was begun by academicians such as George Bernard Shaw and others who were in fact communists (that is, they wanted to remake the world along the lines of the *Communist Manifesto*), but who either were repulsed by bloody revolution, as in Russia, or who simply believed that they, being such refined geniuses, could accomplish the same ends more subtly and less violently. The Fabian Society had as its symbol the turtle, because it believed that socialism could be established through the ballot box, by using patient gradualism. But let us not forget that another symbol of the Fabian Society was the wolf in sheep's clothing. There has never been any doubt about the Fabians' ultimate goal.

The Fabian Society operated under the thesis that if you first put your adherents in the key professorial positions of the most prestigious colleges, these professors would turn out students who would then infiltrate into other teaching positions, the clergy, the government bureaucracy, and the mass media. Slowly, over a period of time, they could persuade the public to vote for democratic socialism under some other label. The Fabian movement was dynamically successful in England and eventually turned the Sceptered Isle into a socialist country through the Fabian-inspired Labour Party.

While the megabankers relied on their control of central banks to be their lever for guiding the economy, the Fabians established Keynesian economics to use government for the same purposes. John Maynard Keynes, an English Fabian Socialist, was one of those key individuals who had a foot in both camps. While his theories of deficit spending to stimulate the economy first captured the academy in Great Britain and the United States, he was also financed and supported by the megabankers.

Following World War I, the Fabian Socialist movement was exported to the United States, beginning largely in the economics department of Harvard University, which in turn spawned teachers at other major colleges across the country. The philosophy also became inculcated in the public education system through the Columbia University School of Education and its leader, avowed socialist John Dewey.

Fabians long ago realized that in the wake of the bloody Bolshevik Revolution, the word "socialism" would be anathema to most Americans. Therefore, they disguised their program as "liberalism" and called themselves "liberals." It was the policies that were important, not the label. A red or pink rose by any other name. . . . Norman Thomas, six-time candidate for U.S. President on the Socialist Party ticket, once said: "The American people will never knowingly adopt Socialism. But, under the name of Liberalism, they will adopt every fragment of the Socialist program, until America will one day be a Socialist nation—without knowing how it happened." And you know something? We did!

For decades, Fabian Socialist liberalism had a virtual hammerlock on American intellectuals. Only in the past two decades has there been a conservative/individualist renaissance which, although still in its infancy, has had a major impact on intellectual thinking in this country. Although the academy and the mass media are still overwhelmingly liberal, at least now there are some strong pro-free-enterprise individualist counterparts. The failure of Keynesian economics, which has led to inflation and endless deficits, has given rise to a large segment of economists who now extol the virtues of the Free Market.

Academics have, however, a very strong tendency to hate the Free Market, which allocates money and other rewards according to performance and not strictly upon intellectual attainments. A college professor with a genius I.Q. resents the fact that a salesman or entrepreneur with an I.Q. thirty points lower makes five times as much money. Many academicians pride themselves as being in the tradition of Plato's philosopher/kings; they believe that monetary rewards should be allocated based upon intellectual accomplishments, not the vagueries of the marketplace. Because the marketplace has failed to reward them appropriately, they want to restructure society to reflect their values. This ethos of envy predominates not only the Halls of Poison Ivy, but the editorial pages of many newspapers, the TV newscasters, and even the pulpits of many churches.

The Socialist Internationale

Closely tied to the Fabians is Willy Brandt's Socialist Internationale, the ostensibly non-Communist, Democratic Marxists of Europe. A British analyst wrote: "There is danger to the world because of the French elections. Our concern is that . . . renewed hope, strength and vitality will accrue to the European Community — meaning the European Socialist State. Working diligently in Brussels, Luxembourg and Strasbourg, the EEC will be regulating, legislating and organizing to erase the sovereignty of France and other members of the Socialist Internationale, heretofore centered in Europe — but spreading globally and fast. Many missed the 'key words' used by Mitterand in his acceptance speech and by his chief aide, Monsieur Rocard. . . . The words (coined at the recent Congress of the Socialist Internationale), are *'militant socialism.'* Each thanked their supporters for their *militant socialist assistance.*"

Commentator Hilaire du Berrier referred to Germany's Willy Brandt as "President in the borderless empire of the Socialist International." Brandt as head of the Socialist International spent three days in early July in Moscow, conferring officially with Breshnev and other Communist leaders, making undisclosed deals which could mean the destruction of adequate NATO defenses in Western Europe, and the uniting of the two Germany's on Russia's terms.

Soviet Communism

The third world force is Soviet Communism. It relies on a combination of military power, terroristic revolution, and subversion to expand its influence. Ironically, Soviet power was financed and nurtured by its alleged mortal enemy, Finance Capitalism, which organized it, nurtured it, and sustained it through the past sixty years. Communism, however, has probably become the Frankenstein Monster which now has an independent basis from its creator. It is a third force which, over the long haul, may wind up destroying its creator.

Much of this book will deal with the history behind the establishment and proliferation of Communism by both Finance Capitalism and the Fabian Socialist movement. Finance capital supported Communism because a dynamic Russia, with a Free Market and its tremendous natural resources, could have been a world competitor. It also supported Communism as part of balance-of-power strategies which provided a rationale for building mega-government in the non-Communist world. These strategies eventually served as both the rationale and the lever for the establishment of the New World Order.

The Fabian Socialists feel a kindred affinity for Communism because both are socialist. Democratic socialists tend to look upon Communists as sort of the Peck's Bad Boy of Marxism. There is a psychological bond — a fraternal brotherhood — between the Fabians and their Communist cousins. *There are no enemies to the Left.*

Arnold Beichman of the prestigious Hoover Institute writes:

> One of the most powerful propaganda slogans propounded by Leninism and perfected by the French Communist Party was: *"pas d'enemis a gauche,"* there are no enemies on the left. In other words, whatever terrible crimes were committed by the Communists anywhere and at any time, there must be no criticism from the non-Communist left lest such criticism (a.k.a. "red-baiting") aid the "capitalist" enemy. The "no-enemies-on-the-left" slogan, one which has paralyzed the moral sense of the liberal-left since the Bolshevik Revolution almost 70 years ago, has a corollary — "no legitimacy on the right"; that is, only Marxist governments in the Third World have legitimacy — all others are by the liberal-left definition illegitimate. For the

liberal-left, intervention in Marxist countries is illegitimate, while intervention against right-wing governments is legitimate.

Beichman then goes on to explain something that may have puzzled you about the apparent hypocrisy of much of our media:

> The fact that there may be proportionately fewer violations of human rights in the Philippines, Chile, Paraguay, and South Africa than there are, say, in the Soviet Union, is to the liberal-left irrelevant to the question of legitimacy of right-wing governments. The liberal-left will tell you that if you want to make a pest of yourself about human rights in the USSR, at least do it quietly, without offending Mikhail Gorbachev. Human rights violations in right-wing countries, however, necessitate demonstrations, marches, invasions of embassies, petitions, and the need to offend the right-wing rulers. Emigration from right-wing countries is free and easy, but not from the USSR. Religious toleration is practiced to a far greater degree in right-wing countries than in the USSR. . . . "No legitimacy on the right" is a slogan which pervades and even saturates democratic culture today. The ultimate target for a strategy of conquest which embodies the no-legitimacy-on-the-right syndrome is, of course, the United States. . . .

After World War II, many Communists in the Western world found it necessary to disguise themselves as "liberals" and "go legitimate." The Cold War made it advantageous for many Soviet sympathizers to become respectable liberals. This is another example of having a foot in both camps.

The Target Of All Three

The ultimate victim of all three of these power groups is the Middle Class American. He is the one who pays the freight in taxes and whose freedom is at stake. In most cases, Mr. Middle America is not even aware of the threat. He is vaguely aware of the Soviet colossus, but conceives of it as something overseas from which the military and the Federal Government will protect him. He is only vaguely aware of the megabankers of finance capitalism and does not understand how they impact on his life. Probably fewer than one out of every one hundred has even heard of the Fabian Socialist movement and makes absolutely no connection between it and liberalism.

True, he may see liberalism as a threat to his pocket-book through taxation, or perhaps through the under-mining of his culture and mores because of its hostility to traditional American and family values. But in most cases, Middle America has no concept that there are powerful forces trying to destroy his liberty. He or she is not by nature a Machiavellian and has no desire to re-order the world. The Middle American, if aware of it at all, considers the New World Order a silly slogan of fuzzy-minded ivory tower intellectuals. He simply wants to have a decent standard of living, be able to send his children to college and enjoy a comfortable retirement.

The typical Middle American has enough problems just running his own life. He's not worried about trying to run everybody else's. He is a farmer or an accountant or runs a hardware store or works for a corporation. The time he is not spending at his job, he wants to relax in front of the television set, drink a beer, watch a ball game or take off and go camping for the weekend. He may get vaguely interested in elections every two or four years, but the rest of the time, he simply tunes out what is going on in the political world.

All three of the power-seeking blocks have a strong vested interest in convincing the members of the Middle

Class that they are in no danger. While the three arms of the New World Order compete with each other to get the upper hand, they cooperate in spiking stories which might wake up a somnambulant Middle Class and work on keeping our attention focused elsewhere. The conspirators realize, even if most Americans do not, that it is an aware and aroused Middle Class which poses the greatest threat to their New World Order schemes.

The megabankers believe that in the end, their money will make the difference. The Communists believe that in the end, it is their brute power that will guarantee their triumph. The intellectuals of Fabian-democratic socialism believe it is their brains which will reward them with the top spots. Most of them live in their own little dream world and are not even aware that they are simply cannon fodder for the other two wings of the socialist revolution. So, the job of the three power blocks is to keep the Middle Class entertained and corrupted by welfare state handouts. Very few people will bite the hand that feeds them. So, subsidies are provided for the bourgeoisie and handouts for the underclass on the theory that no one shoots Santa Claus.

But, how can the Establishment handle the increasingly rising tide of angry Middle Class Americans who form the basis for the anti-Communist movement, the New Right, the Liberty Federation (formerly known as the Moral Majority), and the Libertarian movements? They use a number of tactics. One is to allow the opposition to let off steam, but then block any chance of their programs ever being instituted by the government. The greatest example of this has been the six years of the Reagan Administration.

The Reagan Revolution was the product of revolts by the anti-Communists, New Right, Moral Majority, and libertarians against fifty years of increased centralization through big-D and small-d democratic liberalism. The Establishment let the public have Ronald Reagan and then surrounded him with advisors who let Ronnie keep everyone enthused with magnificent speeches while little was actually accomplished. Federal spending continued to mushroom, deficits exploded, and Communism expanded. But all the while, the rhetoric led the public to believe that just the opposite was happening. Anyone who pointed out that the Emperor was naked as a jaybird was denounced as a paranoid or a fanatic, out of touch with the realities of the pragmatic political world. The immense charisma and charm of Ronald Reagan kept all but the most hard-core hypnotized through both administrations. Apathy reigned in the conservative movement. All is well, God is in Heaven, and Ronnie is in the White House.

For the Middle Class, it was back to watching television and enjoying the good life. Meanwhile, the New World Order marched on!

Chapter Five

New World Order from Nixon-Ford to Carter to Reagan

"It was on the advice of Governor Rockefeller, who described Mr. Kissinger as 'the smartest guy available,' that Mr. Nixon chose him for his top adviser on foreign policy."
— *U.S. News & World Report*
November 1, 1971

There was no Nixon-Ford Administration in foreign policy. There was, instead, a Kissinger Administration. It was Henry Kissinger who made policy both for President Nixon and President Ford; they were virtual figureheads. Almost no decision by these men was ever made without first consulting Dr. Kissinger.

When President Nixon finally told the man he had appointed as Vice President of his decision to resign, the first thing Gerald Ford did was telephone Secretary of State Henry Kissinger.

It was August 1974, and all the king's horses and all the king's men couldn't put Richard Nixon together again. Watergate had already cut deeply, toppling presidential advisers, counselors, election campaign chiefs, an attorney general—and now a President.

The only member of the inner circle untouched by it

all was the pudgy Secretary of State, a man whose less-than-spectacular visage had already graced the covers of more magazines than any other presidential adviser in history. The king of flight-bag diplomats who was continually jetting off to "resolve'" another world crisis, had come to be known variously as "Henry the K," "Superman," "Super Kraut" and other, even more flowery, descriptions.

This was the man—and the myth—to whom the appointed Vice President turned *first* after it was apparent that Richard Nixon, enmeshed in a web of tapes and coverups, was being forced from office by a scandal whose origins had been murkey and whose political outcome was devastating.

Ford prevailed on the whiz-kid super-diplomat to stay on. It was about as tough a sale as peddling a snow cone to a thirsty Arab. *Time* says Ford simply told Henry, "I need you." *Jawohl*, replied Henry. Later, in his first public utterance as President-successor, Ford announced that all was well with the Republic because Kissinger had consented to remain on the job.

The Kissinger Record

The whole scenario seemed strangely out of place for a supposedly conservative, Midwestern Republican. After all, Vice President Ford and President Nixon had both been presented to their party—and to the nation—as "conservative, pro-business" candidates and office holders. Yet, in 1968, Nixon's first major appointment was to place Henry Kissinger in the key post of Adviser for National Security Affairs. But, as presidential adviser, and later as Secretary of State for the outgoing President, Henry Kissinger had:

• Been the primary architect of the "opening" to Communist China, while working secretly behind the scenes to oust the Republic of China from the United Nations, which Free China had helped found.

• Emerged as spokesman for appeasement of and "rapprochement" with the Soviet Union, and promoted policies which guaranteed the Soviet Union a strategic military superiority over the U.S.

• Arranged for supplying the latest American technology and know-how to the Soviet bloc, while waiving $11 billion owed the United States by the Soviet government.

• Provided the USSR with American wheat on incredibly favorable credit terms, while bread prices skyrocketed at home.

• Designed the Vietnam "peace" accords with the North Vietnamese Communists (for which he shared a Nobel "Peace" Prize), agreements which guaranteed the Communists victory in Vietnam in the *first* war ever lost by this country. (We didn't win in Korea, but we didn't lose either; that one was a draw.)

• Handled the intermittent Middle East war so ably that, according to his friend, Soviet Ambassador Anatoly Dobrynin, Kissinger had represented *both* the Soviets and the United States in the negotiations there.

• Alienated such long-time American allies as Turkey and Greece, thus weakening NATO and allowing the Soviet Union to dominate the entire Mediterranean.

• Urged a policy of "reconciliation" with Communist Cuba, a Soviet satellite successfully planted in the Western Hemisphere which subsequently sent "volunteers" to stage a Communist coup in Angola and in Nicaraugua.

• Attempted, despite massive Congressional and public opposition, to surrender American sovereignty over the Panama Canal, and endorsed the claims of a Moscow-lining Panamanian dictator to the vital waterway.

• Supported a boycott of anti-Communist Rhodesia as "a threat to world peace," with the result that the U.S. became dependent on the Soviet Union for chrome ore.

He was the man who said "power is the ultimate aphrodisiac," and who was quoted in *New York Times* magazine as joking, "The illegal we do immediately. The unconstitutional takes a little longer."

A former Kissinger staff member described him this way: "He's got spies in every department. He's running the Ministry of Fear. All of his phones are tapped and he keeps long dossiers." Another Kissinger ex-staffer added: "In my book Hank Kissinger is a suspicious, fearful misanthrope surrounded by people who are compelled to maintain a low profile to keep their jobs. I'd sooner dig ditches than work for him again."

And there have been even more sinister assessments of the Kissinger psyche. Phyllis Schlafly and Rear Admiral Chester Ward (USN-Ret.) produced an exhaustive study of Kissinger deeds, misdeeds, and mentality. Their 800-page analysis, *Kissinger on the Couch*, concludes that Kissinger is obsessed with both megalomania and defeatism. They contend this is a man so driven by a lust for power that he would lie to anyone, including the President, to achieve a goal.

Friends In High Places

How did a German immigrant, who once said his highest ambition was to become an accountant, zoom from academic obscurity to the most powerful position in the White House—all within five years?

At first blush, the phenomenon seems as inexplicable as Richard Nixon leaving the tape recorder on.

Can we really believe that President Nixon plucked Henry Kissinger out of the academic ozone, as *Time* reported, just on the basis of having met him at a cocktail party, and remembering reading an earlier Kissinger book?

Is it reasonable to believe that Nixon, a super partisan, would give the position of what amounted to "assistant President in charge of foreign policy" to a Harvard Professor who never claimed to be a Republican? Are we to believe that Nixon was so enraptured by the genius of this man who can hardly speak English that he gave him one of the most important appointments in his administration?

Well, hardly. Nothing about the Kissinger roller-coaster career makes an iota of sense — not his surprising selection by Nixon as security adviser, not his deliberate acquisition of more power than any similar White House official had ever enjoyed before, not his appointment as Secretary of State, not his survival of the Watergate sweep which eliminated all other Nixon advisers, not his preeminent position in the Ford Administration — unless we ask who placed Henry Kissinger on his Yellow Brick Road in the first place. Henry was not provided with magic glass slippers by the Witch of the East. He had something better.

Once you strip away all of the puffery, press-agentry and Madison Avenue hokum which have been erected around the *persona* of Henry Kissinger, one unmistakable fact emerges: Henry Kissinger is now and, for all of his political life has been, an agent of the mightiest combine of power, finance and influence in American politics: the House of Rockefeller.

Said *U.S. News & World Report* on November 1, 1971: "It was on the advice of Governor Rockefeller, who described Mr. Kissinger as 'the smartest guy available,' that Mr. Nixon chose him for his top adviser on foreign policy."

The *Deseret News* had already quoted a Rockefeller aide as saying: "Rocky set up the job for Henry because he . . . thought it might [!] give (Rockefeller) some voice in U.S. foreign policy."

Henry A. Kissinger also headed the twenty-five man National Security Council charged with forming U.S. defense policies. He helped President Nixon bring "new leadership" to America by picking twenty-three hold-overs from the Kennedy-Johnson Adminstrations for that Council — a little fact almost totally ignored by the media. Columnist Anthony Harrigan, who did comment, noted: "The Kissinger selections would fit in nicely with a Hubert Humphrey or Edward Kennedy administration."

It was Kissinger who engineered America's phased pull-out from Southeast Asia after many years of deliberate no-win strategy involving heavy casualties and highly costly spending on arms and supplies. The consequences of U.S. withdrawal without military victory should be clear to all by now. It led to the predicted bloodbath by Communist butchers, not only in Vietnam, but also in Cambodia where the "killing fields" ran red with the blood of millions.

He sounded the trumpet of retreat instead of victory in Vietnam. Columnist Jules Witcover wrote on June 24, 1969 of a private briefing dinner with Kissinger and eight of the nation's highest-ranking columnists and news commentators. He says Kissinger "suggested strongly that the Nixon Administration is not unalterably opposed to an eventual Communist takeover in Saigon so long as the Administration isn't blamed for it."

As America's Bicentennial year began, Secretary of State Henry Kissinger could (and undoubtedly did) take pride in the fact that, almost single-handedly, he had sewn together a new foreign policy for America. Secret deal by secret deal, *détente* had become a reality.

Clearly, under the cover of *détente*, erected by Henry Kissinger, the Soviet military made tremendous gains at the time the U.S. defense capabilities were being scaled back, or at least not expanding to meet the Communist threat. Kissinger's policies made all of this possible. Kissinger, one of David Rockefeller's chief foreign-policy planners at Chase Manhattan, epitomizes the New World Order mentality.

But this, believe it or not, was not to be the nadir of U.S. foreign policy. For the Carter-Brzezinski Administration was yet to come.

A New Kissinger Clone

In foreign policy, at least, there was no Jimmy Carter Administration any more than there was a Nixon-Ford Administration. It was a Brzezinski administration. In place of Henry Kissinger, there was Zbig, the man who co-founded the Trilateral Commission along with David Rockefeller and who coached the aspiring presidential candidate on foreign policy matters and who subsequently became National Security Advisor under President Carter, the same role as had been played by Kissinger in the previous administration.

The top nineteen positions in the Carter Cabinet, in fact, were held by individuals who had been members of David Rockefeller's Trilateral Commission. This raised suspicions among some—even among some "Liberals." Consider the following by Christopher Lydon from the July 1977 issue of *Atlantic Monthly* magazine:

> I observe here the ban on conspiracy theories in mainstream American journalism and political discussion. So unfashionable are conspiracy theories that if indeed a photograph had been preserved from 1973 or 1974 of the several American members and aides of David Rockefeller's Trilateral Commission—such men as Richard Holbrooke, now an assistant secretary of state; Warren Christopher, the undersecretary of state; their immediate superior, Cyrus Vance (who had been, among other things, chairman of the trustees of the Rockefeller Foundation); Treasury Secretary Michael Blumenthal; Defense Secretary Harold Brown; National Security Council Director Brzezinski and the NSC's analyst of Soviet intentions, Samuel P. Huntington; also then senator, now Vice President, Walter F. Mondale; and a formerly obscure but promising Georgia governor, now President, Jimmy Carter—if, as I say fan-

cifully, some indisputable record had been preserved from three or four years ago of these men signing blood oaths to remember and honor their fellowship if and when one of them came to power, most editors, commentators and indeed politicians would have clucked disparagingly that only nuts think power works that way in America. Maybe they are right.

"On Foreign Policy," the *Atlantic Monthly* article, observed, "What intimations Carter gave suggested the Rockefeller brothers' liberal imperialism, born again." Well, of course, we knew there was *something* "born again" about Jimmy Carter!

Carter soared into the limelight so quickly because he had more than a little help from his friends in the Eastern "Liberal" Establishment — especially top mandarin, David Rockefeller. Even as Governor of Georgia, Carter was already planning ahead and began cultivating closer ties to the Rockefeller Establishment. The most important of these ties to Rockefeller was Carter's charter membership in the Trilateral Commission.

Laurence Stern of the *Washington Post* told this story in the May 8, 1976 issue:

> Until 1973, Carter's credentials in foreign policy matters were limited, except for the overseas trade missions he had organized to see Georgia products abroad. Late in the Fall of 1973, he was invited to dine in London with David Rockefeller of the Chase Manhattan Bank during one of his trade promotion visits. Rockefeller, with the help of Brzezenski, was then establishing the Trilateral Commission, which has become a prestigious forum that has included in its membership the leading businessmen, political leaders and foreign policy intellectuals of North America, Western Europe

and Japan. "David Rockefeller and Zbig (Brzezinski) felt he would be the ideal person to join the Trilateral Commission," related Carter's long-standing supporter, Dr. Peter Bourne of Washington. . . . When Rockefeller, Brzezinski and other recruiters were looking for a southerner to round out the ranks of the commission in 1973 they were also considering Florida Governor Reuben Askew; but they settled on Carter. . . .

Ruthless and cunning politician that he was, Jimmy Carter knew who the real power brokers are and knew what connections to make. Lydon observes the following of Carter's early membership in the Trilateral Commission:

Presumably the much greater value of Trilateral membership was the private reassurance it conveyed that David Rockefeller had deemed him a promising student and had gotten his education underway. The Trilateral Commission's executive director, Zbigniew Brzezinski, became quite literally Jimmy Carter's tutor, and now, of course, directs the White House foreign policy staff, as Henry Kissinger did in the first Nixon term. Perhaps all David Rockefeller hoped for in assembling the American delegation, a Trilateral colleague mused the other day, was to be sure he included the prospective secretary of state in the era following Nixon's. How could he have guessed that his Trilateralists would staff all major policy posts in the new government—including, as if by a miracle, the vice presidency and the presidency?

How indeed?
Yes, Presidents come and go, but whether the Chief

Executive is a Republican or a Democrat, the Rockefeller Establishment maintains its control over the government — especially in the realm of foreign policy (which for reasons of space limitations, is the only area we will discuss in this chapter).

The Creation Of A President

Carter was soon promoted by Establishment publications for the nation's Top Spot. *Time* magazine featured articles which sounded like political ads for Jimmy Carter and carried pictures of the Prince of Peanuts which made him resemble John F. Kennedy, the martyred myth of "Liberal" Democrats who longed for a return of Camelot.

The Georgia Democrat outlined what his foreign policy goals would be as President when he addressed the Chicago Council on Foreign Relations in early April of 1976. His overall aim, announced Carter, was to fashion a "just and peaceful world order." Evidently having learned his Trilateral lessons well from Brzezinski, Carter explained how this goal could be attained, in the following excerpts from his address to the Chicago CFR:

> We must replace balance of power politics with world order politics. The new challenge to American foreign policy is to take the lead in joining the other nations of the world to build a just and stable international order. . . .

Sounding as if he had just read a pamphlet from the World Federalist Association, Carter repeated all the usual "Liberal" myths given as reasons for going to a world government and why there must be world central control over food, energy, population and the environment.

For a presidential candidate, ever mindful of the possibility of public reaction, this is pretty explicit material. When one knows something about the New World Order game plan, his statements stand out like a sore thumb.

Surrounded By Insiders

Among the Trilateralists who found themselves in leading roles in the Jimmy Carter Administration were the following:

Lucy Wilson Benson — Under Secretary of State for Security Assistance

W. Michael Blumenthal — Secretary of the Treasury

Robert R. Bowie — Deputy Director of Intelligence for National Estimates

Zbigniew Brzezinski — Assistant to the President for National Security Affairs

Warren Christopher — Deputy Secretary of State

Richard N. Cooper — Under Secretary of State for Economic Affairs

Richard N. Gardner — Ambassador to Italy

Richard Holbrooke — Assistant Secretary of State for East Asian and Pacific Affairs

Walter F. Mondale — Vice President of the United States

Elliot L. Richardson — Ambassador at Large with Responsibility for UN Law of the Sea Conference

Anthony M. Solomon — Under Secretary of the Treasury for Monetary Affairs

Cyrus R. Vance — Secretary of State

Paul C. Warnke — Director, Arms Control and Disarmament Agency; Chief Disarmament Negotiator

Andrew Young — Ambassador to the UN

For a man who promised us an administration of "outsiders," that is quite a list of Insiders, isn't?

Retreats And Defeats Under Carter

Space limitations do not permit us to deal with all the foreign-policy disasters that took place during the Carter years. But we can touch on a few of the most notable.

Consider Carter's choice of left-wing extremist, Andrew Young, for the post of Ambassador to the United Nations. Young's lack of discretion threatened to let "the cat out of the bag" and alienate the American people from Carter's Trilateral policies of piecemeal surrender. Carter defended the appointment by declaring that Young was the finest public servant that he, Carter, had ever known.

In an interview with *Le Matin* of Paris, Young said "there are hundreds, perhaps thousands, of political prisoners in the United States." Commenting on the trials of Soviet dissenters, he said the situation should not be dramatized, that similar things have happened in the United States and that "It also strikes at the conscience of the entire world when we (the United States) do things like that."

One Carter betrayal which many Americans may still remember was the formal giveaway of our canal in Panama. In fact, it was actually a "payaway" as the American taxpayers were forced to pay billions to help the Marxist government of Panama pay some of the interest on the debts it owes to the big money-center banks in New York.

The Panama Canal treaties were largely negotiated by Sol Linowitz (CFR-TC) who was an official of Marine Midland Bank, one of the banks to which Panama's government owed large amounts of money. This conflict of interest was, of course, covered up in the media and the treaties were forced through the Senate by Vice President Mondale and other Trilateral policy makers.

Despite the fact that the United States had paid billions of dollars to build the Canal and to maintain legal sovereignty over it, a tremendous propaganda campaign during the 1970s told Americans that new treaties were urgently needed to transfer ownership and control over our Canal to the Government of Panama.

Also, we cannot understand what is going on now in

Central America without recalling that it was the Trilateralist Carter Administration which pulled the rug out from under the anti-Communist Somoza government in Nicaragua and sent hundreds of millions of Yankee dollars to support the Marxist-Leninist regime of the Sandinistas.

It was the United States Government which will have put the USSR into Central America. And when the Communists gain control of the Panama Canal, the United States will be under even greater threat to its national security. The Communist terrorism and violence now going on in Central America can largely be laid at the doorstep of the policies pursued by the Trilateral administration of Brzezinski, Carter, Mondale and their Big Banking representatives like Sol Linowitz.

We should also note the remarkable role played by President Carter, Henry Kissinger and David Rockefeller in the tragic drama over the fall of the Shah of Iran and the subsequent rise to power of the Ayatollah Khomeini and the hostage-taking by anti-American terrorists.

The More It All Changes . . .

What about the Reagan Administration? Is its foreign policy directed along the lines of the New World Order plans of the Council on Foreign Relations and the Trilateral Commission? To attempt to answer that question as honestly as we can, let us take a look at the personnel of the Reagan Administration to discern if there has really been a fresh team of policy makers or the same old CFR-Trilateral network which had dominated the previous administrations.

As one can see from the following chart which lists some of the Cabinet and sub-Cabinet posts, the Reagan Administration has many officials from the same New World Order clubs that have run America's foreign policy since World War II and which have been responsible for one disastrous set-back after another for American interests, as one nation after another is turned over to the Communists.

In the original Cabinet appointees, we find the following CFR and Trilateral members:

Malcolm Baldrige — Commerce Secretary

George Bush — Vice President of the United States

William J. Casey — C.I.A. Director

Alexander Haig — Secretary of State

Donald Regan — Treasury Secretary

Caspar Weinberger — Defense Secretary

CFR members among the sub-Cabinet included:

Elliott Abrams — Assistant Secretary for International Organizations

William E. Brock III — Special Trade Representative

Arthur Burns — Member of the Economic Policy Advisory Board

Frank Carlucci — Deputy Secretary of Defense

Richard Darman — Deputy Assistant to the President for Public Liaison

Robert Hormats — Assistant Secretary of State for Economic Affairs

B. R. Inman — Deputy Director of the CIA

Ernest Lefever — Director of Human Rights, State Department

James Lynn — Member of the Economic Policy Advisory Board

Paul McCracken — Member of the Economic Policy Advisory Board

Myer Rashish — Under Secretary of State for Economic Affairs

George Shultz — Head of the Economic Policy Advisory Board

William Simon — Member of the Economic Policy Advisory Board

Walter J. Stoessel Jr. — Under Secretary of State for Political Affairs

Charles Walker — Member of the Economic Policy Advisory Board

Murray Weidenbaum — Chairman, Council of Economic Advisors

Walter Wriston — Member of the Economic Policy Advisory Board

The President has appointed literally scores of other CFR members to important positions in his Administration. Remembering that George Bush is a former director of the CFR, some are wondering if Ronald Reagan is presiding over a Bush Administration!

Of course, there have been many changes since these first appointments were made. Haig is out at State, only to be replaced by Shultz. Baker and Regan switch jobs, and finally Regan is replaced by Howard Baker. Carlucci has moved from State to the National Security Council. But despite all the changes, the CFR/TC is still in control!

In some areas of foreign policy, things *are* better under Ronald Reagan. The rescue of American students on the tiny island of Grenada halted Soviet and Cuban plans to use that island as another base for Communist revolution. Among the captured documents were secret papers showing that Maurice Bishop was a hard-core Marxist in bed with the USSR. There was a secret weapons treaty between Grenada and Moscow as well. Desperate as they have been for an American victory, it gave Americans a renewed sense of pride and patriotism. Of course, there was very little risk in our Grenada operation.

As we go to press, the President has still not been successful in getting Congress to appropriate funds for the courageous freedom fighters who are battling to liberate Nicaragua from a Communist regime. But at least Ronald Reagan has tried.

Aid To The Enemy Continues

The Reagan Administration has been a serious disappointment on the issue of trade with the Communist bloc. While chopping at some of the tentacles, he feeds the head of the octopus. On June 27, 1984, President Reagan extended for another ten years the U.S.-USSR Agreement on Economic, Industrial and Technical Cooperation. The goal is to grant the Soviet Union trade status as a Most Favored Nation, with more taxpayer-subsidized loans to underwrite the risks of our corporations dealing with the Reds.

Pursuant to this goal, U.S. Commerce Secretary Malcolm Baldrige visited Moscow to attend meetings of the U.S.-USSR Joint Commercial Commission. Status as an M.F.N. has already been granted to the brutal Communist regimes of Romania, Hungary and Red China. (This does not mean free trade in the sense of international exchanges between individuals or private firms, but rather through Export-Import Bank credits and other taxpayer-subsidized loans.)

There has been considerable support from Establishment corporations for "normalizing trade relations" between the U.S. and the Soviet Union. At its meeting in New York, the Trade and Economic Council passed a resolution urging expanded trade between U.S. firms and the Soviet Government. At least 230 American corporations are members of this Council and favor that effort.

Secretary of State George Shultz is offering the usual diplomatic double-talk, saying that the Reagan Administration's policy is to "proceed with a sense of realism" and to "undertake a genuinely constructive dialogue and try to work out concrete solutions" for widening trade with the USSR. In an article entitled "New Realities And New Ways of Thinking" in the Spring 1985 issue of *Foreign Affairs*, theoretical journal of the secretive Council on Foreign Relations, former CFR director Shultz states that US policy will be to continue negotiating and improving relations with the USSR despite "inevitable outrages" by the Soviets. He claims to see Mikhail Gorbachev as a "fresh opportunity" to "explore more constructive possibilities" through a "less confrontational approach."

This is the same George P. Shultz who signed the trade accords which gave to the Soviet Union the giant Kama River truck factory, built by American firms in a deal financed by Chase Manhattan Bank. That one produced the trucks and engines that the Reds used in their invasion of Afghanistan! Indeed, on Shultz's watch, Soviet-occupied Afghanistan still has status as a Most Favored Nation trading partner of the U.S. while the puppet Reds slaughter the freedom fighters there.

While President Reagan has correctly characterized the Soviet Union as an "evil empire," his Administration backs pro-Soviet dictatorships around the world. When will we learn that you can't fight Communism by supporting the Communists?

The Administration has continued to cover up Soviet violations of both the Helsinki Accords and SALT I, but has agreed to abide by SALT II even though that treaty was blasted by Reagan during the campaign and was never ratified by the U.S. Senate.

Even worse, the legal and illegal flow of Western technology to the East Bloc continues. Does Romania need an American-subsidized nuclear plant? Done. Does Hungary need an American-subsidized chemical plant? Done. Does Moscow need the means to copy American microchip technology for its missiles? Done.

Meanwhile, in Latin America, our State Department still supports Leftwing dictatorships while continuing moves toward normalization of relations with the Communist Government of Cuba. In the Middle East, Reagan moved heaven and earth to save the Communist-led PLO when it was surrounded in Beirut. The responsibility, like it or not, is Reagan's.

There have been some instances in which Reagan foreign policy has proven a major setback for the

Merger Maniacs of the New World Order. Yes, they got through the infamous Genocide Convention, a treaty which potentially goes a long way toward subverting American sovereignty and the private freedom of American citizens; on the other hand, the One Worlders have not been successful in such legislation as the Law of the Sea Treaty. Also, we should remember that the Reagan Administration has withdrawn U.S. support for UNESCO, the United Nations Educational, Scientific and Cultural Organization — long a Communist spy nest as well as thoroughly dominated by socialist internationalists who hate America.

What Happened To "Our" Victory?

Has Ronald Reagan been seduced by the Eastern "Liberal" Establishment, or were his fine Conservative speeches never anything more than play acting for the only paying audience left to an over-the-hill matinee idol? Observers of the ongoing Reagan melodrama have been speculating about these questions since well before he assumed office. For example, in an intriguing article published in the August 1980 issue of *Playboy*, Robert Scheer described the distrust which "Insiders" of the Establishment apparently held for Ronald Reagan during his bid for the Presidency:

> Reagan's sloppiness has caused him to be viewed with suspicion by the elite Northern wing of the Republican Party, probably less for what he did as governor than because they doubt his stability or fear that he may actually believe in some of his proposals for dismantling the Federal Government, which, after all, does serve the interests of the big corporations. His proposal to return us to the gold standard must have been viewed as primitive by the economists at Chase Manhattan. Nor can the managers of multinational corporations, who have

done quite well in a complex and changing world, be terribly sanguine about his sledge-hammer nostrums for the world's problems. These gentlemen are internationalists par excellence — world statesmen more interested in cutting deals with the Russians than in holy crusades against them.

The Rockepubs shunned Reagan for the same reason the American Right was attracted to him: his speeches against Big Government and betrayal of U.S. interests abroad. Scheer goes on to recount a story of pre-election attempts by Rockefeller partisans to head Reagan off at the pass or to surround him with their kind of people. Consider the following:

> Prior to the New Hampshire primary, David Rockefeller convened a secret meeting of like-minded Republicans aimed at developing a strategy for stopping Reagan by supporting Bush and, failing that, getting Gerald Ford into the race. Reagan heard about the meeting and was, according to one aide, "really hurt." This aide reports that Reagan turned to him and demanded, "What have they got against me? I support oil, I support big business — why don't they trust me?" The aide suggested charitably that maybe it was because he was once an actor and that he attended too few important lunches in the East. In any event, when Reagan scored his resounding triumph in New Hampshire in February, the overture to the East began to work. New York establishment lawyer Bill Casey, who became campaign director the day of the New Hampshire victory, began building bridges and promising that a more moderate Reagan would emerge after the Republican convention.

Could Ronald Reagan have been so naive as not to have any idea how power games are played by the Rockefellers and the Eastern Establishment? If so, did someone lay it all out for him? How else can you explain Reagan's sudden selection of William Casey, an aging Wall Street attorney and comparative political neophyte, to be his new campaign manager? Casey, after all, was a member of the Council on Foreign Relations. As head of the Exim Bank, he had been a major force in all those profitable technology "sales" to the Soviets. He was, well, reliable.

But it apparently took William Casey and his friends a while to get things under control. A few weeks later, during the Florida Republican primary, candidate Reagan was asked if he would allow any members of the Trilateral Commission into his Cabinet if elected. He gave the following reply to that question in a campaign briefing on March 17, 1980:

> Let me just say that I believe what prompts your question is that the present Administration, beginning with the President and Vice President, . . . has something in the neighborhood of 19 of its top appointees all from a single group. Now, I don't believe that the Trilateral Commission is a conspiratorial group, but I do think its interests are devoted to international banking, multinational corporations and so forth. I don't think that any administration of the US Government should have the top 19 positions filled by people from any one group or organization representing one viewpoint. No, I would go in a different direction.

By summer, however, Reagan had already brought in a team of advisors, headed by William Casey, from the Council on Foreign Relations and the Trilateral Commission. The fix was in!

A Heartbeat From The Oval Office

The one decision of significance left to be made was who would be his running mate. Conservatives were demanding a Vice Presidential candidate who shared their philosophy, well aware that age might make Mr. Reagan a one-term President. "Liberals" calling themselves "moderates" wanted one of their own to "balance the ticket" and save face for their primary losses. There were several potential Vice Presidential candidates acceptable to most Conservatives and grass-roots Republicans. Only two of the prominently mentioned candidates for the Number Two spot were absolute anathema to Conservatives: Senator Howard Baker and George Bush. Both were perceived as divisive "Liberals" and (more importantly) both were "former" CFR members and longtime associates in the Rockefeller wing of the GOP.

Ronald Reagan had repeatedly and publicly promised that he would pick a running mate who would share his publicly expressed Conservative views. Two weeks prior to the Motown Convention, in personal conversations with Joseph Coors and Senator Paul Laxalt, Reagan had promised that under no circumstances would the Vice Presidential post go to George Bush. Moreover, the primary campaigns between Reagan and Bush had become increasingly vitriolic after New Hampshire; some predicted that a Reagan-Bush ticket would become an embarrassment for the GOP because the Democrats would run videotapes of Bush calling Reagan "trigger happy" and characterizing his tax-cut proposal as "voodoo economics."

After ducking a bizarre deal pushed by William Casey and Henry Kissinger to try to bring Gerald Ford onto the ticket as a "Co-President," Reagan suddenly decided on George Bush. Staunch Reagan supporters were aghast and chagrined. Senator Paul Laxalt, one of Mr. Reagan's most important supporters over the years and a key man in his campaign, tried desperately to reach Reagan by phone—but it was too late. The GOP standard bearer had already been hustled out of his hotel room to make the formal announcement.

At the Thursday morning press conference in which Reagan, Bush and their wives made their debut together, your reporter tried desperately to be recognized to ask about Mr. Bush's Trilateral connection. The question we wanted to ask Governor Reagan was: "If, as you implied in New Hampshire and Florida, George Bush's membership in the Trilateral Commission disqualified him from the Presidency, why does it not disqualify him from the Vice Presidency?" Swamped by a throng of reporters, we did not get a chance to ask our question. And the rest of the press seemed much more interested in such heavy inquiries as: "Governor, how do you think Nancy will get along with Mrs. Bush?"

The Bush selection was a disaster for the Republican Right. For decades, Conservatives within the GOP have been fighting to rid the Party of its Rockefeller Left and country-club hacks. With Reagan's stunning victory over Bush, it seemed the Republican Party was at last rid of Rockefeller control. Reagan could have kept his promise and seen to it that his potential successor was a Conservative. He did not. By selecting George Bush as his running-mate, Ronald Wilson Reagan not only put the Eastern "Liberal" Establishment back in the game, but David Rockefeller's boy is now heir apparent to succeed Reagan as President. A battle won on Tuesday was lost on Wednesday and now must be fought all over again.

Reagan supporters were knocked for a loop when it was announced that James Baker (CFR), former campaign manager for George Bush, would hold the critical post of White House chief of staff. Baker, described by many as a "Texas-style Elliot Richardson," is a member of the "Limousine Liberal" side of the Republican Party who showed no regard whatever for the principles of less government and more individual responsibility.

Why would Reagan bring in his political opponents

to run things after winning the election? Who was using whom? Did Mr. Reagan deliberately allow his Administration to be captured by Eastern Establishment clones and career bureaucrats? Was he always just an actor willing to be a figurehead in order to cop the great role? Or has he simply been surrounded and isolated by non-ideological and Establishment advisors happy to let him make speeches while they run the show?

The truth is, despite Ronald Reagan's many years in the political limelight, including an eight-year stint as governor of our most populous state, there is much that we still do not know about him. Where does the actor stop and the "real Reagan" begin? How much does he really know about how the Establishment New World Order Big Boys manipulate U.S. foreign and domestic policies from behind the scenes?

In any case, no matter his intentions, or how sound his inclinations, the major policy decisions of a President can be no better than the advice and information he has upon which to base his decisions.

Chapter Six

Building the Soviet Military-Industrial Complex

"Within weeks, many of you will be looking across just hundreds of feet of water at some of the most modern technology ever invented in America. Unfortunately, it is on Soviet ships."
— Secretary of the Navy John Lehman,
To Annapolis graduating class,
May 25, 1983

The greatest scandal of the twentieth century has been the systematic construction of the Soviet military-industrial complex with Western technology, know-how and capital, primarily from America. Compared to this, the much ballyhooed Watergate tempest was the equivalent of stealing a chicken from a henhouse. The fact that the Soviet military-industrial complex carries the label, "Made in the U.S.A." has been documented to a fare-thee-well by such scholarly works as Joseph Finder's *Red Carpet*, Charles Levinsen's *Vodka-Cola* and four authoritative books by Professor Antony Sutton, our nation's foremost expert on Western technological transfers to the Communist bloc and the military implications of this outside assistance.

In 1971, the Hoover Institution at Stanford University released Sutton's massive three-volume, *tour-de-force* entitled *Western Technology and Soviet Economic Development*. A product of ten years of meticulous research of government files, company records, engineer reports and previously unavailable data, Sutton's *Western Technology* still stands as the most thorough analysis ever published of strategic transfers from the West to the Communist bloc. This encyclopedic study proved beyond a shadow of a doubt that the Soviet Union is a technological parasite of the Western economies, with the United States acting as its chief host. As incredible as it may at first seem to most people, Sutton's voluminous evidence provides empirical proof that 90 to 95 percent of Soviet technology has been provided by or taken from the semi-capitalist West!

Subsequently, Sutton focused on the military consequences of the infusions of American technology to the Soviets in a very readable sequel to the three-volume academic compendium he did while at Hoover. This 1973 book was entitled *National Suicide: Military Aid to the Soviet Union*, the blockbuster which blew the cover off of the biggest, dirtiest secret in America. While the U.S. Government spends hundreds of billions of tax dollars on national defense each year, supposedly to protect us primarily from the Soviet military threat, it turns out that government officials and certain elements of the business community in the United States have been working together discreetly to provide the Communists with the kinds of trade goods and technology they need to build up and maintain their ominous military establishment!

There has, of course, been much Establishment resistance to Professor Sutton for making these revelations. Although several titles are listed in the card catalogue, all of the Sutton books have been removed from the shelves of the Library of Congress by persons unknown. And when in 1972, Antony Sutton testified about American military aid to the Soviet Union at the

Republican National Convention in Miami, his testimony was restricted to a closed hearing of the Platform Committee and was given an icy reception at the insistence of representatives of the Nixon-Kissinger White House. A press conference which had been scheduled for Professor Sutton was quickly cancelled. Apparently, he had stepped on too many sensitive toes. When he returned from Miami to the Hoover Institution, Sutton was called on the carpet and ordered to make no more public statements concerning the implications of U.S. transfers of technology to Communist regimes. Antony Sutton is no longer a Fellow at the Hoover Institution.

In 1986, Antony Sutton released a new bombshell of a book entitled *The Best Enemy Money Can Buy*, which updates his earlier *National Suicide*. In this chapter, with the author's permission, we will synopsize some of the highlights of that extremely important work.

A Scandal The Press Ignores

Taken together, Sutton's Hoover study and his two sequels on aiding the Soviet military constitute a shocking commentary on a fundamental weakness of the Soviet socialist system and reveal a serious and equally disturbing weakness in U.S. Government policy in dealing with the Communists. The conclusions are clear: the Soviets, having a socialist and therefore an essentially parasitic system, have been, and largely continue to be, heavily dependent on Western technology, know-how, innovation and credit. They have used, and continue to use, these technological transfusions from the West to erect the most fearsome war machine the world has ever seen. Yet, despite such Soviet attrocities as the brutal invasion of Afghanistan, the shooting down of unarmed commercial airliners, the support of such terrorist kingpins as Libyan dictator Khaddafi, the equipping of Communist guerillas and insurgents in Africa and Central America, and the continual Soviet drive for world domination, the U.S. Government continues to expand this policy of trade and aid.

Antony Sutton's facts and conclusions remain unchallenged and uncontested. They also remain ignored. Where are the investigative reporters? Woodward and Bernstein, where are you now? And where are the rest of the "news hawks" seeking fame and fortune by publicizing this monumental scandal? Where is a crew from "Sixty Minutes" or "20/20"? Could it be that the financial horsepower behind the treason trade is so great that the Establishment media won't touch this subject with the proverbial eleven foot pole? How many times can these journalists simply turn their heads and pretend that they just don't see?

We don't know the full answer to all these questions, but we do know that the scandal of the twentieth century attracts less media ink than some jock sniffing snow or some soap opera floozy running off with somebody's husband.

The deaf mute blindmen — to quote from Lenin — are those multinational businessmen who see no further than the bottom line of the current contract. Unfortunately, these internationalist operators have disproportionate influence in Washington. Fearing the possibility of an outraged public protest directed against the firms involved in this activity, export license information and other documents related to American trade with and technological transfers to the Soviets have been kept officially classified by the U.S. State Department. This has been true since large-scale transfers of Western technology to Soviet Russia began back in the 1920s, and this suppression of data from the public continues to the present day. Is this policy of secrecy regarding specific U.S. companies trading activities with Communist regimes justified for national security reasons? Hardly! Professor Sutton observes:

> Even today, U.S. assistance to the Soviet military-industrial complex and its weapons system cannot be documented from open U.S.

sources alone because export license memoranda are classified data. Unless the technical nature of our shipments to the USSR is known, it is impossible to determine their contribution to the Soviet military complex. The national security argument is not acceptable as a defense for classification because the Soviets know what they are buying. So does the United States government. So do U.S. firms. So do the deaf mute blindmen. The group left out in the cold is the American taxpayer-voter.

Although some government records have become available as a result of congressional pressure and the efforts of such researchers as Antony Sutton, much of Professor Sutton's investigation relied on huge quantities of technical data from private sources and foreign archives. Clearly, Sutton's job would have been much easier had he had ready access to State Department and Commerce Department data such as export license memoranda and other relevant information concerning U.S. trade with the East bloc governments.

Why fear public opinion? Or are certain sectors of our society to be immune from public criticism?

Building The Soviet War Machine
Soviet dependency on our technology, and their use of this technology for military purposes, could have been known to Congress on a continuing basis in the 1950s and 1960s if export license information had been freely available. The problem was suspected, but the compilation of the proof had to wait several decades until the evidence, ironically, became available from Soviet sources. In the meantime, Administration and business spokesmen were able to make absurd statements to Congress without fear of challenge. *In general, only those who had already made up their minds that Soviet trade was desirable had access to license information.*

These were the deaf mute blindmen only able to see their own conception of events and blind to the fact that we had contributed to construction of Soviet military power.

For only one example, in 1968, the Gleason Company of Rochester, New York shipped equipment to the Gorki automobile plant in Russia, a huge facility previously constructed for the Soviets by the Ford Motor Company. The Gleason deal was kept secret in the United States. Discovery of this shipment did not come from the "classified" export licenses, of course, but from foreign press sources. Public knowledge of license application for any equipment for export to Gorki would have resulted in strong protest from concerned Americans and in Congress.

Why? One must remember that the United States was in a war in Vietnam at that time and that the Soviets were supplying the North Vietnamese with the military supplies and armaments to kill American and South Vietnamese soldiers. The Gorki plant produces a wide range of military vehicles and other equipment of military end-use. Many of the trucks used to supply the Communists on the Ho Chi Minh trail were GAZ vehicles from Gorki. Moreover, the rocket launchers used in the Middle East against Israel are mounted on GAZ-69 chassis made at Gorki and which run on Ford-designed engines manufactured at Gorki.

Is it any wonder that both government officials and corporate honchos wanted to keep this treasonous activity hidden from the American public? Yet, this is only the proverbial tip of the iceberg—and the policy of secrecy continues.

Congressional action in the Freedom of Information Act and pledges of speedy declassification of records and documents concerning U.S.-Soviet trade relations have not altered this basic situation. Important records covering the history of the past seventy years are still buried by the bureaucratic planners at the departments of State and Commerce.

This does not mean, however, that specific congressional investigations have not turned up incredible cases of technological transfers which have placed America at definite risk vis-à-vis Soviet military capabilities. One such instance, termed "a life and death matter" by Congress, involved the proposed shipment of ball bearing machines to the USSR. (U.S. Senate, Committee on the Judiciary, *Proposed Shipment of Ball Bearing Machines to the U.S.S.R.,* Washington, 1961)

These were very special ball bearing machines. These machines precision-processed miniature ball bearings used by the U.S. Defense Department for missile guidance systems. These precision bearings came from 72 Bryant Centalign Model B machines, devices manufactured by the Bryant Chucking Grinder Company of Springfield, Vermont.

The Soviets desperately needed the ability to mass-produce these precision ball bearings to increase the accuracy of their inter-continental ballistic missles. The Soviet Union did not have the equipment for such mass-production processing, and neither the USSR nor any European manufacturer could produce such equipment. Bryant Chucking Grinder Company was the only firm producing such equipment. A Commerce Department claim that there were other manufacturers was shown to be inaccurate. In 1961, the Department of Commerce approved export licenses for Bryant Chucking to send thirty-five such special machines to the USSR, which would have given the Soviets a capability of about half that of the U.S. in mass producing these special ball bearings for use in guided missiles.

Bryant Chucking, it should be noted, went ahead with the deal, with the blessings of the Commerce Department and over the objections of the Department of Defense. As representatives from Defense pointed out at the time, at least 85 percent of the kind of bearings manufactured and processed with the help of Bryant's Centalign-B machine were being used in military defense, including such applications as sophisticated missile guidance systems, navigation, fire control, synchro and servo-mechanisms and control systems in aircraft, ships, missiles and space vehicles. The function performed by the Centalign-B machines was a critical link in the mass production of special precision ball bearings, and the Bryant machine was the only piece of equipment in the world for perfoming that task satisfactorily.

Improving Soviet Missile Accuracy

Using advanced technology acquired from the West, the Soviet military-industrial complex began to catch up to the U.S. Even so, by the late 1960s the Soviet missiles were still very inaccurate by American standards. The American public was assured by State Department experts that even though the Communists had missiles with much larger warheads than ours, our missiles were much more accurate and could hit their designated targets. Indeed, according to Avraham Shifrin, a former Defense Ministry official in the USSR who defected to the West, Russian missiles could hardly find the United States, let alone a specific target! The technological roadblock to improved accuracy for Soviet missiles was their still-lagging ability in the area of mass-producing those precision ball bearings.

Not to worry; the guilty madmen in Washington came to the rescue. After all, we wouldn't want the Soviets to fall too far behind, since that would disturb the assumption of "parity" on which our policy of Mutual Assured Destruction was (and still is) based.

In 1972, just before the presidential election, Nicholaas Leyds, general manager of the Bryant Chucking Grinder Company, announced a contract with the Soviets for 164 grinding machines. Anatoli I. Kostousov, Minister of the Machine Tool Industry in the Soviet Union, then said they had waited twelve years for these machines, which included mostly the banned models: "We are using more and more instruments of all kinds and our needs for bearings for these instruments is very great. In all, we need to manufacture five times more bearings than 12 years ago."

Under President Nixon and National Security Adviser Henry Kissinger, license for export of these 164 Centalign-B machines was approved.

By 1974, the Soviets had MIRVed their missiles and were in mass production. Is this important? MIRV capability is the ability to deploy a number of warheads from a single missile—vastly increasing nuclear throw-weight. The Kremlin's third generation missiles of the early 1960s did not have this capability. As admitted by a report from the Department of Defense, ". . . it was not until the fourth generation that the technology became available to the Soviets, allowing greater throw-weight and greatly improved accuracy so that high-yield MIRVs could be carried by operational missiles."

The fourth generation Soviet ICBMs are the SS-17, the SS-18 and the SS-19, which now have the capability to destroy most of our Minutemen missiles with only a portion of their warheads. The accuracy of Soviet missiles has so improved that they can guarantee a high proportion of hits on a target as small as the White House. America is now threatened by a Soviet first-strike ability.

On March 8, 1983, Secretary of Defense Weinberger not only made this massive Soviet increase public, but admitted something not admitted in the early 1970s: the newly achieved accuracy was derived from our U.S. technology.

> We see from the strategic forces that the Soviets have dramatically increased their offensive strategic capabilities. The number, the explosive power and the accuracy of their ICBMs, an accuracy which, as we've said many times, has been largely derived from technology they have taken from us, is far greater than they would need to simply deter the attack. Their

hardening of their silos, their provisions for re-loading some of their larger ICBMs, a reload capability, refire capability which we do not have, and their enhanced strategic defenses, to-gether with all of their writings and their exer-cises and the funds they've spent on civil defense, all of that suggests that they are developing the capability, and believe they are developing the capability which is equally important, of fight-ing a prolonged nuclear war.

Today, the Communists hold a truly awesome threat over the heads of Americans and Europeans. This threat would not exist today if it were not for the actions of President Nixon, National Security Adviser Henry Kiss-inger and the other prominent MADmen who, under the delusions and cover of détente, provided the Reds with the assistance they sorely needed to catch up and surpass the United States in missile warfare. Incredibly, the poli-cies continue under Reagan-Bush. (In fact, the White House has a list of more than 150 Soviet weapon systems which use U.S. technology.)

Putting The Soviets On Wheels

Now let's examine one scandalous example of how the United States has greatly aided Soviet expansionism and especially its invasion of Afghanistan, where the war against Soviet imperialism continues to this day.

Former Congressman Ron Paul of Texas has charged that American tax dollars built the road used by the Red Army in the Soviet invasion of Afghanistan. "Every one is rightly concerned about Russian aggression in Afghanistan," said Congressman Paul. "But we should be especially angry that U.S. government aid helped make it possible. From 1961 to 1965, the U.S. Army Corps of Engineers worked in Afghanistan building 300 miles of double-lane highway through the most inacces-sible mountain territory on earth."

And Paul continues, "The completion of the road, rising as high as 1.5 miles above sea level, complete with fifty bridges and two thousand culverts, was an engineering triumph but a financial and political disaster. Not only did the American people suffer more inflation and taxes because of this foreign welfare—over $100 million in 1980 terms—but the project set up the Afghans for an easy invasion. We were careful to connect our road to the one that the Soviet Army engineers were building. Could anything be more symbolic of our chaotic foreign policy?"

Keep in mind that **any** motor vehicle industry in any country is an important factor in that country's warmaking potential. Numerous military products can be made by adapting automobile plants to produce such items as aerial torpedoes, aircraft cannon, aircraft instruments, aircraft engines, aircraft engine parts, aircraft ignition testers, aircraft propeller subassemblies, aircraft machine guns, propellers, aircraft struts, aircraft servicing and testing equipment, airframes and so on.

We have already mentioned the Gorki plant built by Ford Motor Company. Even though the military output of both the Gorki and ZIL complexes was well-known to American intelligence and therefore to successive administrations, both Democrat and Republican, U.S. aid for construction of *even larger* plants was approved and carried out in the 1960s and 1970s. Antony Sutton writes:

> Under intense political pressure from the deaf-mute blindmen, U.S. politicians, particularly in the Johnson and Nixon administrations under the prodding of Henry Kissinger (a longtime employee of the Rockefeller family), allowed the Togliatti (Volgograd) and Kama River plants to be built. The Volgograd automobile plant, built between 1968 and 1971, has a capacity of 600,000 vehicles per year, three

times more than the Ford-built Gorki plant,
which up to 1968 had been the largest auto plant
in the USSR. Although Volgograd is described
in Western literature as the "Togliatti plant" or
the "Fiat-Soviet auto plant," and does indeed
produce a version of the Fiat-124 sedan, the
core of the technology is American. Three-
quarters of the equipment, including the key
transfer lines and automatics, came from the
United States. It is truly extraordinary that a
plant with known military potential could have
been equipped from the United States in the
middle of the Vietnamese War, a war in which
the North Vietnamese received 80 percent of
their supplies from the Soviet Union.

All key machine tools and transfer lines came from
the United States. While the fixtures and other tooling
was designed by Fiat, over $50 million worth of key spe-
cial equipment came from American suppliers. As incredible as it may seem to some readers, some of this
equipment was listed on the U.S. Export Control and
Co-Com rosters as strategic. But, for the Johnson Administration (and later the Nixon Administration), this
was only a temporary obstacle. The restrictions were ar-
bitrarily abandoned at the behest of such administration
officials as Dean Rusk (Secretary of State) and Walt
Rostow (National Security Adviser). Professor Sutton
lists some of the companies involved in the project:

Leading U.S. machine-tool firms participated in supplying the equipment: TRW, Inc. of
Cleveland supplied steering linkages; U.S. Industries, Inc. supplied "a major portion" of the
presses; Gleason Works of Rochester, New
York (well known as a Gorki supplier) supplied
gear-cutting and heat-treating equipment; New
Britain Machine Company supplied automatic

lathes. Other equipment was supplied by U.S. subsidiary companies in Europe, and some came directly from European firms (for example, Hawker-Siddeley Dynamics of the United Kingdom supplied six industrial robots). In all, approximately 75 percent of the production equipment came from the United States and some 25 percent from Italy and other countries in Europe, including U.S. subsidiary companies.

Despite the clear intention of the Soviets to use vehicles from the Gorki plant for military purposes, the Western press had extolled the virtues of Ford and other firms in developing the Soviet auto industry.

Only a few years later, an even larger truck manufacturing complex was built by U.S. firms for the Soviet Union—the infamous Kama River factory. This mammoth facility still stands by far as the largest truck factory in the entire world. This plant, spread over 36 square miles along the Kama River, has an annual output of 100,000 multi-axle 10-ton trucks, trailers and off-the-road vehicles. It was evident from the outset, given absence of Soviet technology in the automotive industry, that the design, engineering work and key equipment for such a facility would have to come from the United States.

In 1972, under President Nixon and National Security Adviser Henry Kissinger, the pretense of "peaceful trade" was abandoned and the Department of Commerce admitted (*Human Events*, Dec. 1971) that the proposed Kama plant had military potential. Not only that, but according to a department spokesman, the military capability was taken into account when the export licenses were issued for Kama.

Professor Sutton supplied us with a list of American firms which received major contracts to supply production equipment for the gigantic Kama heavy truck plant:

- **Glidden Machine & Tool, Inc.**, North Tonawanda, New York—Milling machines and other machine tools.

- **Gulf and Western Industries, Inc.**, New York, NY —A contract for $20 million of equipment.

- **Holcroft & Co.**, Kovinia, Michigan—Several contracts for heat treatment furnaces for metal parts.

- **Honeywell, Inc.**, Minneapolis, Minnesota—Installation of automated production lines and production control equipment.

- **Landis Manufacturing Co.**, Ferndale, Michigan— Production equipment for crankshafts and other machine tools.

- **National Engineering Company**, Chicago, Illinois —Equipment for the manufacture of casting.

- **Swindell-Dresser Company** (a subsidy of Pullman, Inc.), Pittsburgh, Pennsylvania—Design of a foundry and equipment for the foundry, including heat treatment furnaces and smelting equipment under several contracts ($14 million).

- **Warner & Swazey Co.**, Cleveland, Ohio—Production equipment for crankshafts and other machine tools.

- **Combustion Engineering, Inc.**—Molding machines ($30 million).

- **Ingersoll Milling Machine Co.**—Milling machines.

Professor Sutton pulls no punches in fingering those officials who were and are responsible for this disastrous deal. He writes:

> Who were the government officials responsible for this transfer of known military technology? The concept originally came from National Security Adviser Henry Kissinger, who reportedly sold President Nixon on the idea that giving military technology to the Soviets would

temper their global territorial ambitions. How Henry arrived at this gigantic nonsequitur is not known. Sufficient to state that he aroused considerable concern over his motivations. . . . The U.S.-Soviet trade accords, including Kama and other projects, were signed by George Pratt Shultz, later to become Secretary of State in the Reagan Administration and long known as a proponent of more aid and trade to the Soviets. Shultz is former President of Bechtel Corporation, a multi-national contractor and engineering firm. American taxpayers underwrote Kama financing through the Export-Import Bank. The head of Export-Import Bank at that time was William J. Casey, a former associate of Armand Hammer and now (1986) Director of the Central Intelligence Agency. Financing was arranged by Chase Manhattan Bank, whose then Chairman was David Rockefeller. Chase is the former employer of Paul Volcker, now Chairman of the Federal Reserve Bank. Today, William Casey denies knowledge of the military applications, although this was emphatically pointed out to official Washington fifteen years ago. We cite these names to demonstrate the tight interlocking hold proponents of military aid to the Soviet Union maintain on top policy making government positions. On the other hand, critics of selling U.S. military technology have been ruthlessly silenced and suppressed.

Why weren't George Shultz and William Casey questioned about their roles in this treasonous deal during their confirmation hearings before they joined the Reagan Administration? The answer is blowing in the wind. Avraham Shifrin, former Soviet Defense Ministry official, says that, "The (American) businessmen who built the Soviet Kama River truck plant should be shot as traitors." We second the motion!

Computers And Control Data

While we obviously cannot cover or even mention every case of technological treason discussed in Professor Sutton's most recent book, we would be remiss if we didn't dwell, at least for a moment, on the role played by Control Data Corporation in the area of computer treason.

The development of the integrated circuit or silicon microchip has been the innovation which more than any other has changed and is still changing the kind of culture in which most people in the Western countries live, work and play. It represents a quantum leap in the ongoing industrial revolution and we in the West are in the transition to a culture and economy which will largely revolve around the computer and the electronic chips which go into any modern computer.

The semi-conductor revolution began in northern California's Santa Clara County (nicknamed "Silicon Valley") where semi-conductors were first mass produced in the 1970s. The advanced semi-conductor industry was a difficult challenge to the socialist world because they could not duplicate it. Being by nature parasitic, the Soviets had to depend on California for the semi-conductor technology it employs in its military systems. Every single Soviet weapon system, according to Professor Sutton, uses semi-conductor technology which originated in California and which has been bought, stolen or otherwise acquired from the United States.

We can only touch upon a few of the specific cases and ways the Reds have gained the use of this technology —a technology which is crucial to all modern warfare and without which the Soviets would be so far behind America militarily as to no longer constitute a significant threat. Yet, certain American-based corporations, with the encouragement of the U.S. Government, continue to help the USSR catch up technologically and militarily. Needless to say, this is a MAD policy.

The prime culprit in the United States is the Control Data Corporation, headed up by Chairman William C. Norris. In 1973, Control Data Corp. (CDC) agreed to provide the Soviets a wide range of scientific and engineering information, including construction and design of a large, very fast computer (75 to 100 million instructions per second is fast even by today's standards!) and also detailed manufacturing techniques for semi-conductors and associated technologies.

Highly significant is a comparison of Control Data Corporation's public argument to the media and Congress with this 1973 agreement and its totally one-sided presentation of the national security argument. One can only conclude that some CDC statements are deliberate untruths. Professor Sutton makes this statement by comparing Control Data public statements, particularly those of Chairman William Norris, with internal documents and agreements with the Soviet Union. These documents are confidential, but Sutton has them in his possession.

On December 19, 1973, CDC Chairman, William Norris contradicted the contents of his 1973 technical assistance agreement with the USSR and, in a letter to Congressman Richard T. Hanna, made the statement, "We have offered the Socialist countries only standard commercial computers, and these offerings have been in full compliance with the export control and administrative directives of the Department of Commerce."

In an attempt to defuse the criticism Hanna's congressional committee was hearing against CDC's sale of advanced Cyber computers to the Reds, Norris made the following comments in his letter:

Many persons, including some of the witnesses before your Committee, mistake the offering for sale of old or even current state of the art hardware for transfer of advanced technology. This is not unusual because in many cases it is difficult for those who are not technically well informed to distinguish advanced computer technology.

Sutton refutes Norris' misleading statement with the following comment:

> Norris is comparing apples and oranges. What is "old" or "current" in the United States is far beyond "state of the art" in the Soviet Union. When Norris was offering a million operations per second CYBER computer, the run-of-the-mill Soviet technology was in the order of several thousands of operations per second, and that was on copies of imported equipment. If multinational businessmen like William Norris were honestly mistaken in their information or somewhat shaky in their logic, then perhaps they could be forgiven. After all, to err is human. Unfortunately, evidence proves beyond doubt that at least some of these deaf mute businessmen have deceived both Congress and the American public in an unseemly haste to make a buck.

Sutton's book includes ample evidence to indicate even more doubletalk and deception from CDC and William Norris. Control Data Corporation gave the Soviets sufficient technical information to set up a purchasing and espionage program by letting them know exactly what they needed to have for their military applications. Without these transfers, the Soviet military could not have been computerized and the Red military juggernaut would be much less of a danger to the world in general and America in particular. And we wouldn't have to spend hundreds of billions of hard-earned tax dollars on a military defense budget which purports to protect us from the Soviet menace!

Even the NASA Space Shuttle has been copied! In 1984, U.S. intelligence sources reported that the Soviet Union is building a "carbon copy" of the Space Shuttle. Retired Lt. Colonel Thomas Krebs, former chief of the DIA space systems branch, reported: "We've seen the Soviet orbiter and it's identical to ours." The only difference between the shuttles is reported as an additional set of engines below the fuel tank, thus an increased payload capacity. The Soviets were able to purchase a complete set of Space Shuttle's plans. These were unclassified and made available by NASA to any interested party. The Soviets were an obviously interested party, although it is beyond comprehension why the NASA people would release a technology with obvious military implications. The NASA excuse is that the plans were released to improve coordination with commercial suppliers of equipment.

Working Both Sides Of The Street

Not surprisingly, based on a policy of pragmatism, it is often the case that the same companies doing business with the Communist bloc are also doing business with the U.S. defense establishment — working both sides of the street, so to speak. Sutton observes:

> Financing of the Siberian gas pipeline is an excellent example of the two-faced nature of the deaf mute blindmen. In great part, those who financed this vast expansion in Soviet ability to wage global war at Western taxpayers' expense are also prime military contractors for Western governments. General Electric supplies guidance systems for Polaris and Poseidon missiles and jet engines for U.S. military aircraft, while at the same time supplying equipment for

Soviet military end uses—on credit at preferential terms that could not be obtained by an individual U.S. taxpayer. In brief, because the U.S. government guarantees these Soviet orders, General Electric is in a position to have the U.S. taxpayer subsidize its contracts in the Soviet Union while the same taxpayer is shelling out for the U.S. Defense budget.

As we stated at the outset of this chapter, this whole issue constitutes the greatest scandal of this century, yet the Washington Establishment and the "Liberal" mass media have ignored and covered up this sorry record, a sickening situation which continues today under the Reagan Administration. The people and companies who have been involved have yet to be brought to justice What are we to conclude about our policy of tax-supported "trade" with the Communist enemies of our nation?

The real reason for making the Soviet Union a power equal to or surpassing the power of the United States was to make people fear the possibility of a war and to accept a New World Order, a world government that would eliminate the possibility of a major war, and, incidentally, make all multinational investments safe and all loans secure.

One can rationalize that the corporations involved in building the Soviet military-industrial complex have done so out of greed; but this does not explain the support by the Megabankers and "our" government.

If this information does not make your blood boil, if it does not raise your righteous indignation, then nothing will—and America is doomed. In the immortal words of Howard Beal, you should be mad as hell and not stand for it any longer. This book tells you what you can do about it.

Chapter Seven

Greenbacks for Soviet Reds

"Who knows which political system works? The only thing we care about is how they pay their bills."

— Thomas Thebold
Citibank

Most Americans are under the impression that until the period of *détente* was ushered in by the Nixon-Kissinger administration in the early 1970s, contact between this country and the Soviet Union was minimal. This supposedly led to mutual distrust and misunderstanding, sometimes verging on paranoia. Some "Liberals" even believe that the Cold War was a terrible misreading of Soviet intentions promoted by ultra-rightwing American militarists. Soviet strategy alternates between playing the peace pipes and beating the war drums. Every time the Kremlin launches one of its phony peace campaigns, the gullible "Liberals" get all warm and toasty with visions of the lamb co-existing with the hungry lion.

Every time there is a changing of the guard in the Politburo, you can count on the Establishment media to trumpet the opening of a "new era of understanding" with the new, "enlightened leadership taking over the reins in Moscow." You can count on this with the regularity of the swallows returning to Capistrano. The current "star" treatment being accorded Mikhail Gorbachev is just one more example in a long line of Soviet butchers being promoted as reasonable peace seekers. (Gorbachev has more accurately been characterized as Stalin with a computer.)

Whenever conservatives point out that the professional "Liberals" are parroting pro-Communist tommyrot, the "Liberals" feign horror and shriek "McCarthyism" or "Red baiting." What is that old saying about if the shoe fits?

However, the largely unknown truth is that there has been cooperation between the Commissars and their alleged blood enemies, the Super Capitalists, on an ongoing basis since before the Bolshevik Revolution. It is not an exaggeration to state that the entire Communist movement has always been fueled with Monopoly Capitalist dollars. While the proof is overwhelming and irrefutable, the Establishment opinion makers and members of the academy avoid the subject like Dracula avoiding the sign of the cross.

If the international Money Trust had viewed the Bolshevik Revolution as a threat to their world-wide investments, they would have and could have crushed the serpent in its cradle. Instead, the big guns of the Money Trust invested billions in the nurture and care of the baby Bolshevik dynasty. Common sense and all of their other investment and business practices suggests that they would not put their money where they are not sure of some form of control.

This is a mind-boggling concept, we admit. How the mechanism works — and if indeed it does exist — we don't know. We do know that whatever the international bankers are, they are not stupid; nor are they frivolous.

A hint is contained in a story which we believe to be true but cannot document. In 1967, a fraternity brother of ours at Stanford was working for IBM in New York. On Friday night he put a colleague on the bus to JFK International Airport from the old Eastside terminal. While waiting for the bus, my friend noticed a beautiful young woman whom he described as looking like Elizabeth Taylor in her youth. She was putting a big bear of a man who appeared to be in his late fifties on the bus. After the bus departed, there was a scramble for taxis and my suave friend, Gallahad-type that he is, offered to share his cab with the young woman.

After introducing himself to her, he discovered she spoke English with a very thick Russian accent. She explained that she was a Soviet ballerina and that the man she put on the bus was her new husband. She said they had been staying with David Rockefeller to whose apartment she was returning. She revealed that her husband's job was to run the Orient for the Chase Manhattan Bank in Hong Kong. My friend asked her how she liked living in Hong Kong. She replied that she had never been there. She said her husband communicated with Hong Kong by telephone from Moscow. My friend was stunned. In those pre-détente days, the concept of cooperation between supercapitalist David Rockefeller and the Communists was mind-blowing. In amazement, he asked her what a representative of Chase Manhattan Bank was doing in Moscow. Her reply was, "Who do you think runs Soviet economy?"

As we said, we can't prove this story. Dismiss it as apocryphal if you wish. If you heard it from the guy on the next stool at the soda fountain, you would doubtless categorize it as bull feathers. So let's move on to the enormous body of evidence which is fully documented.

Bankrolling The Bolsheviks

Much information is revealed in a book we've mentioned before in these pages, Antony C. Sutton's monumental *Wall Street and the Bolshevik Revolution*. No one has previously told us such things as the following, primarily based on the U.S. State Department Decimal File:

In the Fall of 1922 [five years after the *coup d'état* which inagurated the Bolshevik revolution], the Soviets formed their first international bank. It was based on a syndicate that involved the former Russian private bankers and some new investment from German, Swedish, American and British bankers. Known as the Ruskombank (Foreign Commercial Bank or the Bank of Foreign Commerce), it was headed by Olof Aschberg; its board consisted of tsarist private bankers, representatives of German, Swedish and American banks, and, of course, representatives of the Soviet Union. . . . In early October 1922, Olof Aschberg met in Berlin with Emil Wittenberg, director of the National bank fur Deutschland, and Scheinmann, head of the Russian State Bank. After discussions concerning German involvement in the Ruskombank, the three bankers went to Stockholm and there met with Max May, vice president of the Guaranty Trust Company. Max May was then designated director of the Foreign Division of the Ruskombank. . . .

We need to know who Max May was. He was vice president in charge of foreign operations for Guaranty Trust of New York. And what was Guaranty Trust? It was "the largest trust company in the United States and controlled by the J. P. Morgan firm." Sutton continues:

Guaranty Trust used Olof Aschberg, the Bolshevik banker, as its intermediary in Russia before and after the revolution. Guaranty was a backer of Ludwig Martens and his Soviet Bureau, the first Soviet representatives in the United States. And in mid-1920, Guaranty was the Soviet fiscal agent in the U.S.; the first shipments of Soviet gold to the United States also traced back to Guaranty Trust.

Antony Sutton's book is replete with citations of action by Morgan *and Rockefeller* interests that could only be viewed as pro-Bolshevik, pro-Communist, and it will be necessary for us here to note further instances of this kind.

William Boyce Thompson (1869-1930) is described in part as follows by *Webster's Biographical Dictionary*: "American mining operator, b. Virginia City, Mont. Accompanied American Red Cross mission to Russia (1917-18); tried to get American aid for Kerenski regime, and after Kerenski's fall, urged recognition of Soviet government." Sutton adds much more. Thompson, a director of the Federal Reserve Bank of New York, personally paid the entire expense of the Red Cross Mission to Russia, and in addition, shortly after his return to the United States, gave the Bolshevik Party one million dollars. Sutton reprints the following from the *Washington Post* of February 2, 1918:

> New York, Feb. 2—William B. Thompson, who was in Petrograd from July until November last [actually until December 1917], has made a personal contribution of $1,000,000 to the Bolsheviki for the purpose of spreading their doctrine in Germany and Austria. . . . Mr. Thompson deprecates American criticism of the Bolsheviki. He believes they have been misrepresented and has made the financial contribution to the cause in the belief that it will be money well spent for the future of Russia as well as for the Allied cause.

It was already evident that Lenin had been sent to Russia by the German General Staff in order that he might seize power from the Kerensky regime and take Russia out of the war against Germany, as he did. Edgar Sisson, who arrived in Russia at the time Thompson left and remained for over three months, reported that

Lenin was actually a German agent, but it is not necessary to accept this in full in order to know that the Germans wanted him in Russia, and saw to it that he got there. Thompson returned from Russia to the United States via London, "where in company with Thomas Lamont of the J. P. Morgan firm, he visited Prime Minister Lloyd George." Sutton reprints passages from once secret papers of the British War Cabinet regarding this visit:

> The Prime Minister reported a conversation he had had with a Mr. Thompson—an American traveller and a man of considerable means—who had just returned from Russia, and who had given a somewhat different impression of affairs in that country from what was generally believed. The gist of his remarks was to the effect that the Revolution had come to stay; [Thompson was right about that, and he and other Wall Street operators were one of the main reasons why it has stayed.] that the Allies had not shown themselves sufficiently sympathetic with the Revolution; and that MM. Trotzki [sic] and Lenin were not in German pay [no, they were in *American* pay, except for Germany's furnishing Lenin's transportation from Switzerland to Sweden, en route to Russia], the latter being a fairly distinguished Professor. . . .

Thompson, no doubt strengthened by the company of Lamont, made such an impression on Lloyd George that the latter persuaded the Cabinet to (in Sutton's words) "go along with Thompson and the Bolsheviks." In consequence Bruce Lockhart, a protégé of Lord Milner's, was sent to Russia "to work informally with the Soviets."

The Unholy Alliance

The American International Corporation was organized by Morgan interests "with major participation by Stillman's National City Bank and the Rockefeller interests." Together with Kuhn, Loeb & Company and Guaranty Trust, A.I.C. rescued the Bolsheviks from terminal disaster fifteen years before the Roosevelt Administration extended formal recognition to the Soviet Union. Sutton points out that the Bolsheviks could not have survived without trade, and that Wall Street had the muscle in America "to obtain the export licenses needed to ship goods to Russia." H. G. Wells writes in *Russia In The Shadows* (George H. Doran Company, 1921) how on a visit to Russia in 1920, he ran into Frank A. Vanderlip (a director of American International Corporation and a key Founding Father of the Federal Reserve System) at the Moscow Guest House. Wells is a bit supercilious about the American capitalist:

> Mr. Vanderlip had been staying here, I gathered, for some weeks, and proposed to stay some weeks more. He was without valet, secretary or interpreter. [An interesting thing to be without—an interpreter. GA] He did mention once or twice that it was strictly financial and commercial and in no sense political. . . . I did not even ask how it could be possible to conduct business or financial operations in a Communist State with anyone but the Government, nor how it was possible to deal with a Government upon strictly nonpolitical lines. These were, I admitted, mysteries beyond my understanding.

In a subsequent conversation, Lenin himself let Wells know what Vanderlip had been selling. "What do you think of this new Republican Imperialism that comes to us from America?" the Bolshevik leader asked the British Socialist. Wells writes:

Lenin proceeded to explain the projects with which one American at least was seeking to dazzle the imagination of Moscow. There was to be economic assistance for Russia and recognition of the Bolshevik Government. . . . But some industrial power had to come in and help Russia, I said. She cannot reconstruct now without such help. . . .

Curious, how little some things change in sixty-six years! Capitalists (some capitalists) still think that with their shrewd know-how they can exploit the Communists. In an attempt to resolve something here, let's first quote Sutton one more time. His own wrap-up section is titled, "The Explanation for the Unholy Alliance." I should like to quote it in full, but will only hit the high spots:

What motive explains this coalition of capitalists and Bolsheviks? . . . the simplest explanation of our evidence is that a syndicate of Wall Street financiers enlarged their monopoly ambitions and broadened horizons on a global scale. The gigantic Russian market was to be converted into a captive market and a technical colony to be exploited by a few high-powered American financiers and the corporations under their control. . . . Were these bankers also secret Bolsheviks? No, of course not. The financiers were without ideology. The financiers were power-motivated and therefore assisted any political vehicle that would give them an entrée to power: Trotsky, Lenin, the tsar, Kolchak, Denikin—all received aid, more or less. . . .

Sutton does not use the term New World Order, but in the following he supplies a pretty good semantic equivalent:

The governments of the world . . . were to be socialized while the ultimate power would remain in the hands of international financiers. . . . This idea was knit with other elements with similar objectives. Lord Milner in England provides the transatlantic example of banking interests, recognizing the virtues and possibilities of Marxism. . . . Woodrow Wilson came under the powerful influence of—and indeed was financially indebted to—this group of internationalists. As Jennings C. Wise has written, "Historians must never forget that Woodrow Wilson . . . made it possible for Leon Trotsky to enter Russia with an American passport."

The Rockefellers And Harrimans

After the Bolshevik Revolution, Standard of New Jersey bought 50 percent of the huge Caucasus oil fields, even though the property had theoretically been nationalized. In 1927, Standard Oil of New York built a refinery in Russia, thereby helping the Bolsheviks put their economy back on its feet. Professor Sutton states: "This was the first United States investment in Russia since the Revolution."

Shortly thereafter, Standard Oil of New York and its subsidiary, Vacuum Oil Company, concluded a deal to market Soviet oil in European countries and it was reported that a loan of $75,000,000 to the Bolsheviks was arranged. (*National Republic,* September 1927.)

We have been unable to find out if Standard Oil was even theoretically expropriated by the Communists. Sutton writes: "Only the Danish telegraph concessions, the Japanese fishing, coal and oil concessions and the Standard Oil lease remained after 1935."

Wherever Standard Oil would go, Chase National Bank was sure to follow. (The Rockefeller's Chase Bank was later merged with the Warburg's Manhattan Bank to form the present Chase Manhattan Bank.) In order to rescue the Bolsheviks, who were supposedly an arch-enemy, the Chase National Bank was instrumental in establishing the American-Russian Chamber of Commerce in 1922. President of the Chamber was Reeve Schley, a vice president of Chase National Bank. According to Professor Sutton:

> In 1925, negotiations between Chase and Prombank extended beyond the finance of raw materials and mapped out a complete program for financing Soviet raw material exports to the U.S. and imports of U.S. cotton and machinery. Chase National Bank and the Equitable Trust Company were leaders in the Soviet credit business.

The Rockefeller's Chase National Bank also was involved in selling Bolshevik bonds in the United States in 1928. Patriotic organizations denounced the Chase as an "international fence." Chase was called "a disgrace to America. . . . They will go to any lengths for a few dollars profits." Congressman Louis McFadden, chairman of the House Banking Committee, maintained in a speech to his fellow Congressmen:

> The Soviet government has been given United States Treasury funds by the Federal Reserve Board and the Federal Reserve Banks acting through the Chase Bank and the Guaranty Trust Company and other banks in New York City. . . . Open up the books of Amtorg, the trading organization of the Soviet government in New York, and of Gostorg, the general office of the Soviet Trade Organization, and of the State Bank of the Union of Soviet Socialist Republics and you will be staggered to see how much American money has been taken from the United States Treasury for the benefit of Russia. Find out what

business has been transacted for the State Bank
of Soviet Russia by its correspondent, the Chase
Bank of New York. . . .

Joining Vanderlip and Rockefeller in bankrolling the
industrialization of the USSR was Averell Harriman.
Harriman's partner was Prescott Bush, father of George
Bush. The Bush family fortune is inextricably tied to
Harriman. This explains why the Bush elements inside
the Reagan Administration lead the campaign for more
government guaranteed loans to the Soviet bloc.

We are indebted to the book by Stephen Birmingham
about "The Great Jewish Families of New York," entitled
Our Crowd for much information about the father of
W. Averell Harriman. In this book is traced the progress
of this ex-office boy and son of a poor Episcopal clergy-
man who made a fortune in railroads with the financial
backing of Jacob Schiff of Kuhn, Loeb & Co., who were
also the financial backers of the Communist takeover of
Russia, commonly known as the Russian Revolution.

As early as 1920, Harriman and Co. granted a loan
to Lenin who had been put in business by his father's
friend, Schiff. In 1928, Harriman and Co. were the chief
organizers of the engineering undertaking that put afoot
Soviet heavy industry. It furnished securities for all the
Soviet purchases in the United states and collected all
the commissions.

In 1924, Harriman worked on another deal when he
heard that the world's largest deposit of manganese ore
was being offered for rent by the Soviet government.
Before the Revolution, the field had supplied half the
world's output of manganese, a vital ingredient in the
manufacture of steel. The Chiatura field was estimated
to contain at least a billion dollars' worth of ore, enough
to supply the world for the next half-century. This was to
be the biggest American venture yet granted in Soviet
Russia. In the book *Present-Day Russia* by Ivy Lee, we
read about the Harriman concession:

The Russians consider that the best illustration of their real concessions policy is to be found in the Harriman case. Mr. W. A. Harriman made a contract with the Russian Government involving the development of manganese ore properties in the Caucasus. Under his contract he was to pay to the Government a certain royalty on each ton exported. He was to build a railroad and of course, he had to employ labor to work on his properties. The concession has been found unworkable, however. The Harriman concession has now been renewed upon terms far more favorable to Mr. Harriman. . . . The Russian Government officials instance the Harriman case as an example of their reasonableness and disposition to meet the concessionaire halfway in taking care of unexpected conditions.

So, we see that W. A. Harriman was cooperating with the Communists even *before* they were officially recognized by the United States as the legal government of Russia.

In the book *The Roosevelt Myth* by John Flynn, our "negotiating" ambassador was referred to as follows: "Harriman told various persons that Stalin was not at all a revolutionary communist but just a Russian nationalist."

Always an advocate of the Soviets, Harriman had also been a member of the first Lend-Lease mission to Moscow in 1942, stating at that time that U.S. policy was "to give and give, with no expectation of return, with no thought of a *quid pro quo*." That policy was responsible for sending some $11 billion in American goods and technology to the Soviet police state.

Harriman's spirit of giving (giving other peoples' money and lives, that is) to the Reds was carried over in full force at the Yalta Conference in 1945, at which he played a key role in the betrayal of all central Europe to

Soviet imperialism. You will recall that World War II was started over the independence and territorial integrity of Poland. Forty million people died and Poland was handed over to the Soviets! What a friend. Thanks, Averell!

Harriman was a little sensitive on this subject. The *Boston Herald Traveler* of March 21, 1971 reports:

> A USIA official recently remarked to former Ambassador Averell Harriman that in doing some research for a book, he had come across a telegram dated February 12, 1944. The wire was sent by Harriman, who was then ambassador to Russia, to President Roosevelt, advising FDR that the Soviets had no desire to introduce Communism to Poland. Harriman, who is nearly 80, reportedly told the official, "If you print anything like that in your book, I'll break your jaw!"

The Soviets' Favorite Capitalist

Since theirs is a parasitic system, the Soviets and their captive nations are constantly in need of ever more funds to feed themselves and maintain their evil empire. They can always count on their "enemies," the Wall Street Super-Capitalists, in the crunch.

In the 1972 public television program, "David Rockefeller's World," Bill Moyers relates the story of a Rockefeller cocktail party in Moscow where Soviet officials lined up in the street outside half an hour early in order to meet and greet Rockefeller — even though a few days earlier, their propaganda media had been denouncing the Rockefellers for financial imperialism in the Third World.

David's Chase Manhattan Bank now operates from Number One Karl Marx Square, the most prestigious address in beautiful downtown Moscow. The Soviets know they have a friend at Chase Manhattan! Joseph Finder, in his fascinating book *Red Carpet*, describes the elation of one Rockefeller loyalist when Chase officially arrived in Moscow:

> "This was a major thing," recalls Joseph V. Reed, Jr., Rockefeller's former aide-de-camp, who is as emphatic as his boss is bland. "Imagine — a Chase Manhattan representative office there — a Rockefeller bank in Moscow! It was fabulous. To have the world's preeminent banker-statesman there, well, this is the big leagues."

Rockefeller was at home in this company. In October, 1970, he had had the President of Rumania, Nicolae Ceausescu, to lunch at the Chase and afterward urged that Rumania be granted most-favored-nation status. As Rumania's leading correspondent bank, he said, Chase was interested in a large investment in that country.

Chase's accord with the USSR opened the floodgates. Finder reports:

> Within ten days after Chase's arrival, the Bank of America, Manufacturers Hanover, Republic National Bank of Dallas and other American and European banks flocked to Moscow to discuss opening facilities there. In June, the First National City Bank (as Citicorp's Citibank was then called) announced it had received permission for an office. . . . Although within a few years most American banks pulled out of Moscow, Chase doggedly remained. Certainly it could make loans to the Soviet Union and the Eastern bloc without a Moscow office, but its beachhead in Russia is symbolic. Rockefeller's policy of extending long-term loans contradicted his 1964 declaration that loans given over a period longer than five years "would amount

to aid, and I don't believe we should give aid to
countries trying to subvert or overthrow friendly
governments." Not only had America changed
its mind, but so had David Rockefeller.

How do the Soviets regard David? Georgi Arbatov
of the Soviet Institute on the U.S.A. stated: "He's a
member of the royal family. Some of our leaders think
David Rockefeller can walk on water."

The word used to describe the Soviet's attitude toward Rockefeller is "adoration." Finder quotes George
Gilder, the author of *Wealth and Poverty*, as observing:
"Ironically, nobody knows how to revere, blandish and
exalt a Rockefeller half so well as the Marxists."

The Vodka-Cola Conspiracy

One of the most important sources of information
on the Wall Street-Moscow alliance is the book *Vodka-
Cola* by Charles Levinson. Mr. Levinson is described by
his publisher as former Deputy Director of the European office of the C.I.O. and Assistant General Secretary of the International Metal Workers Federation. He
now serves in the office of the Secretary General for the
International Federation of Chemical, Energy and General Workers Unions. Obviously, Mr. Levinson is not a
product of the Conservative movement.

Nevertheless, Levinson writes in *Vodka-Cola* of
"quasi-clandestine, conspiratorial dealings between
Eastern politico-economic and Western economic au-
thoritarians," and blasts such familiar elements of powers as the Council on Foreign Relations, the Trilateral
Commission, the Bilderbergers, the Rockefellers and
the Chase Manhattan Bank.

Levinson explains how relations between the corporate socialists of the West and the Communist regimes of
the East favor both a drive toward increasing monopolistic control at the international level and a strengthening of the tyrannical slave states under Communism:

The more public and private credits that are advanced, the more "investments" the multinationals make, the more the powerful interests tie into cooperation deals, the greater the political and economic pressure will be to expand commitment. The Western multinationals are, therefore, likely to use their already predominant strength over the political and economic policies of the nation state in support of the unhindered perpetuation of the Eastern regimes with whom they have an ever-growing financial and economic community of interests. Obviously, with investments in the $50-100 billion range and debts on the same scale, the multinationals and the banks would definitely not be content at the prospect of a change in the Eastern regimes. In economic terms, such change would probably result in the repudiation of all external obligations and debts contracted by the present undemocratic, unelected oppressive regimes. . . . The multinationals and banks, therefore, have a vested, direct, financial interest in the perpetuation of these oppressive regimes and must be among their most solid, and tacit, supporters.

Discussing the Trilateral Commission and its dominance in the Carter Administration, Levinson acknowledges the central role played by the Rockefellers, observing that "the Trilateral Commission is the creature of the ubiquitous David Rockefeller." He looks at Rockefeller as the symbol and hyphen between the Vodka-Cola polarities, as well as the controller of the Rockefeller Foundation, the Rockefeller Brothers Fund, the Council on Foreign Relations and the Bilderberg Society.

Because of his association with banks and the oil companies, Levinson names the other Vodka-Cola organizations with whom Rockefeller has overwhelming influence: the Ford Foundation, the Brookings Institute, MIT, Harvard University, Stanford University, Hudson Institute, Rand Corporation and the Russian Studies Institute. "All the programs of meetings and discussions drawn up by these bodies include growing numbers of Vodka-Colanizers from Eastern Europe," Levinson observes.

Using material developed by G. William Domhoff, Levinson describes the Rockefeller network within the multinational corporations, especially those involved in the Vodka-Cola game. On the basis of this analysis, he concludes, "Fifteen members of Rockefeller and Associates alone hold 118 directorships in 97 different companies. The combined assets of all the companies listed add up to over $640 billion."

One of the most encouraging aspects of *Vodka-Cola* is that labor official Levinson does not shrink from using the word *conspiracy* to describe this macabre drama. Consider the following:

> The Carter Administration has, if conceivable, more corporate presence than any Republican Administration in recent history. From the perspective of the Vodka-Cola strategy, it clearly illustrates the consummate skill of the Overworld power brokers in promoting a Democratic president to replace a Republican president equally convinced and committed to Vodka-Colanization. For those inclined to a power-relations theory of history, generally discarded by establishment intellectuals and media-merchants as conspiracy-minded paranoiacs, the composition of the Carter administration lends elegant and rigorous support to theories of Overworld conspiracies. Even for those who just as dogmatically insist that history is largely a sequence of coincidences and uncontinued accidents acted out by individuals of essential

goodwill and integrity, and who refute all suggestions of extensive collusion and continuance among media merchants, foundation functionaries and quasi-clandestine councils and commissions and power lobbies, Vodka-Cola composition of the Carter Administration is proving embarrassingly difficult to ignore.

American Committee On East-West Accord

Writing in *Human Events* for September 27, 1980, Washington-based journalist Thomas G. Gulick commented at length on the disturbing relationship between certain high-technology firms and the politics of *détente*. Mr. Gulick had interviewed officers of the American Committee on East-West Accord, a group which promotes aid and trade with the Soviet Union and its satellites. Looking over its membership list, Gulick observed:

> ACEWA boasts a number of prominent names. Until his appointment as secretary of commerce — Commerce being the agency which reviews applications for high-technology trade to Russia and other Communist countries — Philip M. Klutznick was a member. Another ACEWA man is Dr. Armand Hammer, chairman of Occidental Petroleum, who has made huge chemical plants in the USSR whose by-products can be used to make explosives and who has done business with the Soviets since the 1920s.

Among ACEWA's founders and officers are Keynesian economist John Kenneth Galbraith; George Kennan, the former US Ambassador to the Soviet Union and key member of the CFR; Donald Kendall, chairman of Pepsico, which sells soft drinks to the USSR and markets its vodka; the Reverend Theodore M. Hesburgh, the member of the CFR who is president of Notre Dame; and, Robert D. Schmidt, executive vice president of Control Data and activist for *détente* and trade with the Russians. A self-appointed "ambassador" for Red trade, Schmidt has made more than forty trips to Russia, and travels there four or five times a year according to Carl Marcy, who is another officer of ACEWA. Marcy, former chief of staff for the Senate Foreign Relations Committee and an assiduous advocate of *détente*, is of course also a member of the Council on Foreign Relations.

Creating A Mountain Of Debt

Most of the industrial goods "sold" to the Reds in recent years have not been paid for in hard currency but financed by loans from the U.S. Government or the major international banking institutions. The provision of Western credit to the Communist regimes has become so serious an issue that even a number of "Liberal" journals are expressing horror.

For example, an excellent article by James M. Whitmire in the June, 1980 issue of *The Washington Monthly* describes the Soviet debt as a weapon threatening the West. It is entitled "Moscow: The Real Secret Weapon," and the cover illustration shows Chairman Leonid Brezhnev holding up a facsimile of an American Express card *à la* the Karl Maldin TV commercial. Leonid is saying, "Don't leave home without it." The expiration date reads: "Never!" Whitmire's article declares:

> This could devastate the West without a shot being fired. Incredibly, it is not only a weapon we are constructing for the Russians — but paying for as well. The weapon? Debt. Quietly, assiduously, Western bankers since the mid-1970s have allowed the Soviet bloc to pile up $60 billion to $80 billion in outstanding debt, according to *The Washington Monthly's*

sources. The magnitude of this debt is such that a Soviet default might spark a financial panic capable of collapsing the capitalist banking system.

The U.S. sells the Reds our advanced technology, and lends them the money to buy it! The money goes to the firms which export the technology or to the farmers who sell the wheat. But from where does the money for those loans come? It is created out of thin air by the federal inflation machine.

Vladimir Ilich Lenin is reputed to have said that "the capitalists will compete with one another to sell us the rope with which we will hang them!" If Lenin said that, he was wrong—we are *giving* it away! Since the loans are being financed either through more taxation or inflation, the American people are being forced to finance their own destruction.

It is clear that as the Soviet military machine grows with the help of Western technology, the Reds will decide they don't have to pay these loans. Concern is growing among Western financial institutions as some of the satellites are having trouble paying even the below-market interest charges on the loans they have already secured.

Poland alone owes the West some $19.6 billion. Months of strikes by Poland's workers have greatly hurt production, and the promises of more food and higher wages for the workers will further drain the already weak economy. To help Poland out, German banks made loans to the Warsaw regime totaling $677 million. Other Western banks, led by the Bank of America, followed by granting a loan of $325 million. Good money after bad is being loaned because the international bankers of the West have an increasing vested interest —as pointed out by Charles Levinson—in seeing that the current Communist regimes continue to remain in power.

As you would expect, the institutions extending the

loans are the New World Order banks of what Levinson calls the Overworld elite. Citicorp is the largest lender to the Reds, followed by Morgan Guaranty Trust, Chase Manhattan and Hanover Trust. Other loans to the Reds have been secured through the Export-Import Bank of the U.S. Government.

The Soviets know they will never be forced to pay. The bankers cannot tow away the Kremlin in case of default. The Communist leaders, therefore, are virtually certain at some point to use the threat of default to obtain concessions from the West. If they simply cancelled their debts, this might precipitate economic collapse. Having a vested interest in continued East-West trade and fearing that curtailing more loans would cause the Reds to announce default, the banks continue to pay for the rope. In fact, says Whitmire, "lending to the Soviet bloc continues at a furious pace, despite the loans' questionable merit from either a political or a financial point of view. Western bankers, caught in an 'undertow syndrome' of sending good money after bad, seem determined to make our position even weaker."

For the Soviets, *détente* has been a golden opportunity to bleed American technology and become a serious military threat to the West. From the standpoint of Western bankers, it has meant the prospect of interest on fat loans and profits on multinational sales. To assure this it has been necessary to help keep the Communist regimes politically safe and economically stable. And, if default comes, the banks expect to fall back on the fact that most of their investments are insured by an agency of the U.S. Government. Which means, *you* will pay the bill.

Before leaving the ranks of working journalists to join the White House staff as Director of Communications, Patrick Buchanan wrote an essay entitled "Let's Freeze the Debt Bomb." Buchanan writes that in 1973, the Warsaw Pact nations, harnessed together in the Kremlin counterfeit of the Common Market called

Comecon, had $9.3 billion in debts outstanding to West-
ern Europe and the United States. By 1983, Pact debt
had risen ninefold to $80 billion. With Yugoslavia added,
Communist Europe owed $100 billion to the govern-
ments and financial institutions of the West. The equal
of half a dozen Marshall Plans had been consumed; and
at the decade's end, half of the Communist regimes were
illiquid, insolvent or bankrupt. Poland, Rumania and
Yugoslavia were rudely demanding a rescheduling of
old loans and new infusions of Western capital, while
threatening a general default that would send the great
banks of West Europe toppling like a line of dominoes.
Buchanan asks:

> How did we arrive at a juncture where the
> United States is presented this apparent Hob-
> son's choice: Either accept the indefinite
> siphoning of your wealth into the looted vaults
> of the communist and socialist world to enable
> them to "service" their debts, or call a halt to in-
> come transfers and risk collapse of the interna-
> tional financial system, the crash of the Big
> Banks, and a repeat of 1933? How did we reach
> a point where President Reagan and the U.S.
> Treasury Secretary are pointedly warned that
> either they allow this indefinite milking of
> America's savings or accept the fate of becom-
> ing Hoover and Mellon to their own genera-
> tion? Have we, truly, no other option?

Buchanan relates Mr. Rockefeller's reasoning for the
credit. "Just because a country is technically called
Communist, doesn't mean that capitalist institutions
such as the Chase Bank can't deal with them on a mutually beneficial basis, and, indeed, we do deal with most
of the so-called Communist countries of the world on a
basis that has turned out well, I think, for both of us."
For ten years, Western governments and banks com-

peted with one another in the generosity of the terms they offered to Moscow; for ten years the Marxist economies were sustained on capitalist credit. The Soviet military buildup, surely the most awesome and perhaps the most decisive in history, may be said to have been financed by Western banks.

The money was lent without regard to ideology. "Who knows which political system works?" is how Thomas Thebold, heir presumptive at Citibank, casually dismissed a reporter's question from the *Wall Street Journal*. "The only thing we care about is how they pay their bills."

Why do super-capitalists back Communism, which is supposed to be "against capitalism"? The answer, of course, is that capitalism is *not* abolished by Communism! All that happens is that capitalism is turned into a state monopoly with a new, very small minority of privileged elite of commissars, managers, and bureaucrats holding down the best positions in the Marxist state.

The privileges of capitalism, and its potentialities for abuse, are simply transferred to new hands. No wonder many rich and influential individuals are Communist handmaidens. Communism is simply a confidence trick where a cabal of unscrupulous men, with a most effective propaganda machine at their disposal, acquire power by pretending to nationalize a nation's wealth for "the workers."

It's a scam—one that has been played successfully against us for over five decades. Now, it's time to say "no!"

Chapter Eight

Disarming for a New World Order

"Peaceful coexistence and the current development of our new weapons' systems are designed to achieve global military supremacy by 1985, by which time the forces of world Socialism will be in a position to dictate their will to the remnants of capitalist power in the West."

— Leonid Brezhnev
April, 1975

It is an incontrovertable fact that at the end of the Second World War, the United States of America had by far the most powerful military capability in the entire world. The Axis powers had been devastatingly crushed. The United States was the only nation which possessed the awesomely destructive atomic bomb. There was no nation in the world—not even Soviet Russia—which had sufficient military capability to pose a serious threat to the security of the United States.

It was not very long before the situation began to change. As the United States began dismantling the war machine it had erected during the war, the Soviets continued feverishly to build up theirs. Soon the Reds acquired The Bomb. Then, after a number of years, the Soviets emerged as a powerful international menace when they began deploying intercontinental ballistic missiles. Still, even in the 1960s—and despite talk of a "missile gap" between America and the Soviets—the United States was clearly superior to the Soviets, both in strategic nuclear weaponry and in terms of conventional forces. The Reds were 'way behind in the arms race.

Today, however, the United States is no longer Number One in military power. We have fallen to second place behind the Soviet Union. Now, the Soviet Union enjoys first-strike capability against the U.S. and maintains an elaborate ABM (anti-ballistic missile) system to block a retaliatory strike by the West. Continuing to add onto what is already the most awesome offensive military power the world has ever seen, the Soviets now have the world's largest air force, a huge tank force, an enormous army, and a world-wide active navy.

Despite this chilling Soviet lead in both strategic and conventional military forces, the Kremlin continues to deploy new weapon systems everyday. While the U.S. Navy filled the missile launch tubes of its Polaris submarines with concrete—in compliance with the SALT I Treaty—the Soviets have modified their nuclear submarines to carry supersonic cruise missiles with an intercontinental range of more that 3000 miles. Yes, the Soviet military threat is all too real.

How bad is America's military preparedness compared to that of the Soviet Union? In a sobering address to the Conservative Political Action Conference in Washington, D.C. more than a year ago, Senator Malcolm Wallop (R.-Wyoming) had this to say about the strategic balance:

Anyone who examines the strategic balance will see that the Soviets today have more ballistic warheads able to cover a higher percentage of U.S. and allied targets than five years ago; that our active defenses against such warheads are still precisely zero; and that passive defenses (redundancy and hardening) have fluttered just above zero. It is just as clear that our ability to threaten Soviet strategic forces or any Soviet forces in the near future on a time-urgent basis will remain strategically insignificant.

So, the bad news is that, as compared to five years ago, the Soviets can strike our most important forces more surely, using a smaller percentage of their arsenal, while we, despite some efforts that are too little and too late, have no prospect either of threatening a disarming first strike or of actually striking the Soviet Union's reserve missile forces in reaction.

Although military balances are difficult to quantify, the Soviet Union has amassed an effective 6-to-1 advantage over the U.S. in nuclear and conventional military capabilities and is extending that lead even as the United States pursues disarmament talks and abides by SALT agreements which have not worked. Retired Admiral Elmo Zumwalt, former Chief of Naval Operations, has observed:

> A Soviet missile attack today would destroy *all* of our ICBMs, 95 percent of our aging B-52s and half of our missile subs—all of those in port. If the Soviets initiate a first strike, they would kill 100 to 160 million Americans. Our retaliation would leave 10-20 million Russians dead—less than the Soviet Union lost in World War II and apparently an acceptable loss to Soviet military planners.

Perhaps the best source of facts and figures on the current military balance between the U.S. and the Soviet Union is an excellent book entitled *Soviet Military Supremacy*, by two brilliant and authoritative authors, Quentin Crommelin, Jr. and David S. Sullivan. We highly recommend that the reader get and read the entire book by sending $5.95 to the Citizens Foundation, 1701 Pennsylvania Ave., N.W., Washington, D.C. 20006 to receive a copy.

The Disarmament Lobby

How have the Communists been able to construct such a formidable military threat to world peace? Their economy is known to be backward, beset by inumerable shortages, lack of coordination, and mind-boggling inefficiencies. How could they possibly outdistance America in the arms race?

All of this has been accomplished by massive technological transfers from the Western nations—especially the United States—to the Soviet bloc. As with any socialist system, the Soviet economy has been unable to advance technologically on its own to any significant extent. Instead, it has parasitically depended for its economic development and military advances on technological aid and U.S.-financed "trade."

How the Soviet military-industrial complex has been built up by Western (primarily American) technology through aid and taxpayer-financed trade was discussed in some length in Chapter Six. Now we want to expose the other half of the equation: our own disarmament.

Pro-disarmament propaganda began in earnest at the very dawn of the nuclear age, when Leftist scientists and academics, standing at the wailing wall of disarmament, began to bemoan their fear that America's superior nuclear capacity would somehow frighten a worried Soviet Union into launching a major war. Their "solution" to this peril began with the Pugwash Conferences —and might conclude with the forced surrender of a disarmed U.S.

In 1955, the Parliamentary Association for World Government issued a call for a series of "Conferences on Science and World Affairs between Russian and American scientists and intellectuals." The first of these was held in 1957 at the home of Russophile Cyrus Eaton in Pugwash, Nova Scotia. Eaton, who began his career as secretary to John D. Rockefeller and was for years a business partner of the Rockefellers in promoting Red trade, earned the Lenin Peace Prize for fronting the deal and financing the first five Conferences. Since then, more than twenty have been held, most of them outside the United States. All have been financed by the tax-exempt Rockefeller-CFR foundations.

On September 23, 1960, three years after the first Pugwash Conference, the Soviets presented a plan for "total and complete disarmament" to the United Nations. It called for a systematic reduction in arms by major powers of the world. The so-called "Soviet plan" immediately became the beneficiary of extremely influential American support, when a group of powerful proponents of disarmament within the CFR endorsed it.

This was no mere happenstance. A secret CFR disarmament program, entitled "Study No. 7," was made public a few months later. Prepared by the Council on Foreign Relations for the Senate Committee on Foreign Relations, "Study No. 7" argued that the United States "must: (1) search for an international order . . . in which many policies are jointly undertaken by . . . states with differing political, economic and social systems, and including states labeling themselves as 'socialist.'" [That is, Communist.] In order to build such a "new international order," the CFR said, we must "maintain and gradually increase the authority of the UN," and "conduct serious negotiations to achieve international agreement on limitation, reduction and control of armaments."

And here is the amazing part: This CFR position paper had preceded the Soviet proposal of September 23, 1960, by nearly a year. Pugwashed or not, the two schemes were almost identical! This Pugwash-CFR conspiracy is one of the most brilliant achievements in psychological warfare since the Trojan Horse. While Americans were being told of the horrors of nuclear war and the supposed advantages of limiting our defenses, the Russians were arming to the teeth.

In September of 1961, the Department of State released Publication 7277, entitled *Freedom From War: The United States Program for General and Complete Disarmament in A Peaceful World.* It was a three-stage program which provided:

> In Stage III progressive controlled disarmament and continuously developing principles and procedures of international law would proceed to a point where no state would have the military power to challenge the progressively strengthened UN Peace Force and all international disputes would be settled according to agreed principles of international conduct . . . The peace-keeping capabilities of the United Nations would be sufficiently strong and the obligations of all states under such arrangements sufficiently far reaching as to assure peace and the just settlement of differences in a disarmed world.

The same month that State Department Publication 7277 was issued, the United States Arms Control and Disarmament Agency was created by Congress. Within forty-eight hours, the new Agency presented its disarmament scheme to the United Nations. Naturally, it was a carbon copy of the CFR-Soviet-Pugwash proposals presented to the UN *by the Communists* the year before. While the newspapers and TV have prattled endlessly about disarmament, nary a word has been said about the other side of the coin: all such proposals call for *arming* the United Nations! This apparently is the best-kept secret since the formula for Coca-Cola.

In October of 1968, the U.S. Disarmament Agency issued a revised proposal, entitled *Arms Control and National Security*, which declared:

Since 1959, the agreed ultimate goal of the negotiations has been general and complete disarmament, i.e., the total elimination of all armed forces and armaments except those needed to maintain internal order within states and to furnish the United Nations with peace forces. . . . While reductions were taking place, a UN peace force would be established and developed, and, by the time the plan was completed, it would be so strong that no nation could challenge it.

Notice that the document said, "Since 1959. . . ." The U.S. Arms Control and Disarmament Agency was not established until September 1961. But it was in 1959 that the CFR "Study No. 7" was prepared and its contents transmitted to the Soviets.

Implementing The Program

How successful have these New World Order disarmers been in implementing their plans? What has happened to our military strength since disarmament was accepted as official U.S. Government policy? The first Secretary of Defense to implement this policy was CFR member Robert S. McNamara, Secretary of Defense from 1961 through 1968. In *The Betrayers*, Phyllis Schlafly and Admiral Chester Ward discuss McNamara's wrecking job. When Robert McNamara left office, they note, he had:

• . . . reduced our nuclear striking force by 50%, while the Soviets had increased theirs by 300%.

• . . . caused the U.S. to lose its lead in nuclear delivery vehicles.

• . . . scrapped ¾ of our multimegaton missiles.

• . . . cut back the originally planned 2,000 Minutemen to 1,000.

• . . . destroyed all our intermediate and medium-range missiles.

- . . . cancelled our 24-megaton bomb.
- . . . scrapped 1,455 of 2,710 bombers left over from the Eisenhower Administration.
- . . . disarmed 600 of the remaining bombers of their strategic nuclear weapons.
- . . . frozen the number of Polaris subs at 41, refusing to build any more missile-firing submarines.
- . . . refused to allow development of any new weapons systems except the TFX (F-111).
- . . . cancelled the Skybolt, Pluto, Dynasoar and Orian missile systems.

In fact, the authors contended, as Defense Secretary Robert McNamara had destroyed more operational U.S. strategic weapons than the Sovlets could have destroyed in a full-scale nuclear attack!

Supporting McNamara's efforts at unilateral disarmament were CFR members John J. McCloy and William C. Foster. McCloy, who preceded David Rockefeller as chairman of the board of both the CFR and the family's bank, Chase Manhattan, was picked by President John F. Kennedy to be chairman of the General Advisory Committee for the Arms Control and Disarmament Agency. Foster was appointed director of the Agency. In 1969, Foster was replaced as director by Gerard C. Smith, another CFR members. Smith's successor in 1973 was Fred Ikle, who (this will probably not surprise you) is also a member of the Council on Foreign Relations. The Disarmament Agency was later headed by Paul Warnke, a member of both the Council on Foreign Relations and the Trilateral Commission.

The operative phases of the disarmament lobby began in earnest when CFR New World Order operatives persuaded President Lyndon Johnson to propose the Strategic Arms Limitation Talks (SALT) in 1966. The SALT talks to negotiate a first disarmament treaty were scheduled for July 1968. They were postponed until

November 1969 because the Soviets were busy with their invasion of Czechoslovakia—only two weeks after Soviet officials signed the Declaration of Bratislava, guaranteeing Czech independence!

We have made such great progress at SALT that when the first meetings were scheduled in 1968, the Soviets had only 850 long-range missiles while the U.S. had 1,054. But following the seventh SALT meeting, when President Nixon signed accords in Moscow on May 26, 1972, the Soviets had 1,618 ICBMs either deployed or under construction while we, in turn, still had 1,054—the same number as in 1968. This is the way the disarmament lobby has negotiated for us. We have frozen production and exported U.S. technology to permit the Kremlin first to catch up and then to surpass us.

SALT II was signed in Vladivostok in November of 1974 by President Ford at the time the Soviet-backed Communists were over-running Southeast Asia and conducting genocide in Cambodia. As with SALT I, SALT II (which has never been ratified by the U.S. Senate) was designed to place limits on American weapons rather than slowing the Soviet military build-up. Among other provisions, the U.S. and USSR were supposed to be limited to 2,400 land and sea-based missiles and long-range bombers through 1985. When he came home from Russia, President Ford crowed, "We put a firm ceiling on the strategic-arms race. What we have done," he stated with a straight face, "is to set firm and equal limits on the strategic forces of each side, thus preventing an arms race . . . Vladivostok is a break-through for peace. . . . Future generations will thank us!" Ford played linebacker too long with no helmet!

The *National Observer* for December 14, 1974, expressed amazement: "With such fanciful descriptions, Mr. Ford, he of the plain word and honest face, is beguiling us—or has been beguiled—and is merely repeating the phrases the beguilers used on him."

The Scheme Continues Under Reagan

The "Spirit of Geneva" in the wake of the Summit between President Reagan and Soviet Party Chief Gorbachev has evoked the same kind of enthusiastic expectations that peace negotiations have stimulated in the past. Secretary of State George Shultz (CFR) told Congress on February 5, 1986 that the current "thaw" in U.S.-Soviet relations "presents a rare moment of opportunity" to achieve nuclear disarmament.

In fact, the Reagan-Gorbachev summit has been promoted and used by the propaganda outlets of the Merger Maniacs to cast the illusion that we are now partners with the Soviets in something called "the peace process"; this is to help obscure the truth that this process is part of the phased negotiation of our eventual surrender into a New World Order.

But at least we are talking, say those who desire "dialogue" with the Communists. What harm can come from merely negotiating arms control? We return to Senator Malcom Wallop who snaps one back to reality with the following observations:

> The reality is that reducing the Soviet threat through arms control alone is beyond reality. The Administration knows this perfectly well. How does it know? Because it has no plans— and is not making any plans—to enforce Soviet compliance with arms control agreements that are "in force" now. Knowing that the Soviet Union is violating and will continue to violate those agreements, the Administration continues to adhere to them "so long as the Soviet Union does likewise." This is beyond reality and living a lie.

But hasn't President Reagan spent more on defense and engaged America in an unprecedented military buildup? This is the impression we are given from the media, isn't it? Are we really safer under the Reagan Administration because of his beefing up of our military defenses? Unfortunately, despite the rhetoric, we have undergone a *build-down*, not a military build-up.

Don McAlvany, editor of *The McAlvany Intelligence Advisory*, explains the grim reality: "Every cent of the Reagan defense buildup announced in March 1981 has been deleted plus an additional $38 billion. Actual defense spending is $156 billion below the Reagan 5-year plan. So much for the media disinformation that U.S. military spending and strength have grown dramatically under Reagan—it is a lie! They have declined and the Soviet gap has grown. Meanwhile, the Reagan Administration and its disarmament negotiators are deceiving the American people into thinking that we have closed or are closing the gap—that we are negotiating from strength. *Not true!*"

It should be understood, moreover, that the price tags of many of the items bought by our defense dollars have gone up well beyond the rate of inflation. We are paying more and buying less compared to just a few years back. So much for the widespread myth of America's giant military buildup!

The So-Called "Peace" Movement

Meanwhile, the "peace movement" is being cranked up again by the Surrender/New World Order crowd. The same kind of hysterical and irrational mentalities were involved in the ill-fated 1986 "Great Peace March." It was to be quite a media event. Columnist Donald Feder had this to say about this motley band of peace-niks in the February 13, 1986 *Washington Times*:

> The transcontinental peace "schlepp" epito-
> mizes the mentality, or lack thereof, of the sur-
> render lobby. They need drama—marching
> mobs, arms waving placards, sit-ins, lie-ins,
> raffles and the rest. . . .

Since they're so enamored of symbolism, perhaps they'll consider a real peace march. Mixner & Co. could start in Berlin, at the infamous Wall where hundreds have lost their lives in bids for freedom. They would proceed to Poland for a chat with Solidarity leaders, who are denied the right to organize and protest in their own land.

Next they'd head for the Soviet Union, to visit the gulags and see what awaits political activists if communism triumphs. They could stop in Afghanistan to meet children with limbs blown off by bombs disguised as toys, compliments of those peace-loving Soviets.

What the so-called "peaceniks" want—or claim they want—is a bilateral freeze on the deployment of nuclear weapons by both the United States and the Soviet Union. They maintain that such a mutual freeze would be "verifiable"—that we could tell if the Communists are cheating (as they have done under past treaties). But a freeze would not be verifiable at all. Even our sophisticated monitoring systems cannot see through the tops of roofs and beneath the earth where the Soviet missiles are poised. Also, the Soviets' missile launchers are reusable, whereas ours are not. This means they can hide missiles, to be used later from the launchers we know about.

The only way that mutual freeze or disarmament could be verifiable (at least theoretically) would be if on-site inspection were permitted by both sides. This the Soviets have consistently refused to allow. The Soviets will never agree to full on-site inspection of their military capability. It is not in their military interest to do so. This means they will never agree to a real verifiable freeze or disarmament strategy. Carl Sagan and other "freezeniks" say that the United States should go ahead and freeze anyway, even if the Soviets do not. He is really advocating a *unilateral* weapons freeze.

Given the very wrong ideology of Communism and the fanatical madmen who believe it, the "nuclear freeze" initiative is analogous to being locked with a madman in a room which is filled with dynamite. He has a shotgun aimed at you and you have a shotgun aimed at him. Sagan would have you throw down your gun as a show of "good faith" and as a means of preventing your opponent from shooting you.

The freezeniks always bemoan the possiblity that, due to the complexities of the technologies involved, something could go wrong in either the Soviet or American missile systems which could trigger an accidental launch leading to a full nuclear strike which, in turn, would lead to a global conflict. It is precisely because of such a possibility that a non-nuclear missile defense system is desperately needed. A ballistic missile defense shield would be the best, most practical way of defusing a nuclear war by intercepting any such accidental or miscalculated misfire of nuclear missiles.

If the disarmament lobby truly wants peace—and what rational person doesn't?—a nuclear weapons freeze clearly would not bring it about. A real Strategic Defense, as advocated by General Daniel O. Graham of High Frontier, is the means—or part of it. It is far better to defend lives than to avenge them or threaten to avenge them. Prevention is always a far better solution than correction after the fact. The space-based anti-missile system does not put weapons into space; it puts *anti-weapons* in space which can in no way harm a hair on the head of any person, Russian or American.

A policy of Peace Through Military Superiority, aimed at actually *defending* America by High Frontier and cruise missiles, must be put into effect as quickly as possible. That approach, coupled with a policy of minding our own business, permitting free trade and sound money (a market gold standard) will do more to bring world peace and prosperity than anything else.

Yet, incredible as it may sound, the Reagan Administration, which is supposed to have been pursuing the Strategic Defense Initiative (SDI) for the last three years, seems to be sabotaging real efforts along these lines by sacrificing practicality to long-term "feasibility studies" which seem never to be implemented.

What We Must Do

As we have shown previously, the Soviet Union, which has never accepted the policy of Mutual Assured Destruction (MAD), has been creating (with Western technology and other aid) the greatest military build-up the world has ever seen. The Soviets have many of their military factories already underground, and they have an elaborate civil defense system with underground shelters in major cities. We have no civil defense worth mentioning. Even if we decided to launch a meager retaliatory missile strike and some of our missiles got through, the Soviets would suffer a much smaller population loss than they could inflict upon the United States.

What could be done to extricate ourselves from being blackmailed into surrender on the installment plan by this horrible situation? Is there a way out at this late date? We believe there is, if we work quickly and the right programs and policies are pursued by the right people. All is not lost, yet. We can do some things to neutralize our current awful vulnerability.

First, we must keep in mind that the real danger is not destruction (as when Soviet missiles target our missile silos and bomber bases rather than civilian populations), but defeat/surrender. The Soviets want our factories and farms, not a pile of cinders. They want to enslave the American people, not incinerate them.

We must abandon MAD and orient our overall policy toward *defense* by going for some form or system of intercepting and neutralizing incoming missiles and nuclear warheads, no matter where they are launched. In other words, we must organize our efforts along a new strategy for national survival. Only by doing this in some form can we counter the growing despair, defeatism and paralysis in our dealings with Communism and terrorism.

While several specific technologies and approaches have been proposed along these lines, let us consider here one with which we are especially impressed. This is a radical plan offered by Lieutenant Colonel Lannon Stafford, formerly with the Strategic Air Command and the National Aeronautics Space Administration, and associate professor of Electrical Engineering Technology at Arizona State University. In an exclusive interview with Professor Stafford, he gave us hope by detailing what could be done if we had the will to do it, and do it soon. He emphasized that the first step is in recognizing the nature and extent of our present strategic vulnerability:

> The Soviet Union represents a strategic threat primarily because of land-based ICBMs, submarine-launched missiles, and an enormous bomber force. They have a huge conventional military force which could be deployed against Western Europe within a matter of hours. In addition, the Soviet Union is deploying the most deadly air defense system in history, as well as the only ballistic missile defense system.
>
> While it is not widely known, the Soviets have demonstrated the capability of tracking a submerged submarine at operating depths from a satellite equipped with synthetic aperture radar. (Synthetic aperture radar, by the way, was invented in this country at the firm I formerly worked for — Goodyear Aerospace. Yet we have never to my knowledge orbited such a system.)
>
> Perhaps the major threat to the West, in spite of the awesome nuclear threat, is the widespread Soviet-sponsored terrorism and subversion, designed to destabilize and overthrow non-Communist governments all over the world.

That is the threat we face. What are we doing about it? Here is how Prof. Stafford summarizes the situation:

> To counteract these threats, we are now spending about $300 billion a year on "defense." About half of this (some $159 billion) goes to support our troops and auxiliary forces in Europe and Southeast Asia (NATO and SEATO). The largest part of our defense spending goes for personnel, and only about 15% of our forces have combat MOS (Military Occupation Speciality) numbers. This means that of all our military personnel, only about one out of six is an actual fighting man. The rest are support people. So most of our spending goes for salaries and personnel — not weapons.
>
> By comparison, we spend only about $10 billion to $20 billion on new strategic weapons — missiles, bombers, subs, ships, etc. That's less than seven percent of our total military budget! And what we buy for all this spending is a MAD policy of Mutual Assured Destruction — which could more properly be called Assured Suicidal Revenge.

There *is* a better way. Here, for starters, is what Prof. Stafford says we should be doing:

> We desperately need a crash program to intercept incoming ballistic missiles and bombers, using off-the-shelf technology. We need a retaliatory strategic force which can punish any aggressor who dares to launch an attack on the United States. We need an effective military force to defend U.S. territory against any invader. We need an effective civil defense for our citizens.
>
> We do *not* need fancy new bombers which

will disappear on their parking ramps under mushroom clouds. We do *not* need fancy new tanks to repel an attack from Canada (unless Washington persists in its trade war with our allies). We do *not* need more missile subs to be knocked out before a war ever starts. We do *not* need huge new aircraft carriers which evaporate in a nuclear blast.

Here's what I recommend. I'd save perhaps $250 billion of that defense budget by cutting out new bombers, carriers, subs, and tanks. I'd chop off most U.S. standing forces and incorporate a sizeable part of that force in an enlarged National Guard, much as Switzerland has done. No more NATO or SEATO commitments; those nations are rich enough to provide their own defense.

For retaliatory forces, I would recommend flocks of ground-launched, intercontinental-range cruise missiles. Such missiles, with their terminal guidance, are inherently accurate. They can hit the desired *floor* of a targeted building. They can be launched upon first warning of any attack, but they can be recalled within an hour or so in the event of a false alarm. Cruise missiles, being simply small unmanned aircraft, can be launched instantly, can carry electronic countermeasures to protect themselves, and can be programmed to detonate their nuclear warheads when actually under attack.

These and other possibilities of things we could do *right now*, or at least very soon, are very encouraging. The idea is to use *technology*, rather than bodies, to provide our defense. I agree completely with Prof. Stafford that a policy of strict defense, coupled with overwhelming retaliation if we are attacked, would do more for peace on this globe than any number of politicians' treaties.

This approach, coupled with a policy of avoiding entangling alliances, permitting free trade with our allies, and going to a free-market gold standard for sound money, would do more to bring peace to the world than anything else I can think of.

Although time is short, it is perhaps not too late to reverse this not-so-gradual process of surrender on the installment plan. The first step is to tell the truth to the American people. Because, as Winston Churchill found just prior to World War II, one must first awaken the people with the truth before they can be motivated to do something about it. And we are in an even more perilous a situation today than England was before the Second World War.

Stand up now or give up later!

Chapter Nine

The Sellout Strategy

"It's very dangerous to be a friend of the United States."
— King Hussein of Jordan

King Hussein once told journalist Arnaud de Borchgrave, "It is very dangerous to be a friend of the United States." Other foreign leaders have echoed this sentiment. This is because the U.S. State Department has had a policy of trashing America's friends and allies with alarming regularity and going back many decades, starting with the sellout of Eastern Europe to Uncle Joe Stalin at Yalta and Potsdam.

Remember what happened to the Shah of Iran? To Anastasio Somoza of Nicaragua? To Fulgencio Battista of Cuba? To Chiang Kai-shek in his battles against Mao? In every case, we pulled the rug out from under an anti-Communist ally — only to see an avowed enemy (usually a Communist) assume power instead.

With his "revolutionary firing squads," Ayatollah Khomeini has exterminated his enemies without any pretense of trial. Mao Tse-tung and Chou En-lai murdered some 60 million of their fellow Chinese citizens, and today's Communist government in mainland China continues such barbarities as forced abortions and government-decreed infanticide.

The Sandinistas in Nicaragua have practiced unspeakable tortures and brutalities upon the Mesquito Indians and others in Nicaragua and are manifestly exporting their Marxist/Leninist "revolution" to surrounding nations in Central America.

Yet, in every case, the issue of "human rights" and "social needs" was trumpted by Western media and government observers as the rationale for failing to come to the aid of the non-Communist or anti-Communist governments which preceded them. This pattern has happened over and over and over during the past several decades. While the non-Communist governments (the so-called "right-wing regimes") were certainly not perfect and in some cases admittedly corrupt, in case after case the Marxist-Leninist regime which emerged after the overthrow or forced resignation of the previous leader was so brutal, so tyrannical, so bloody that it made the previous governments look like model states by comparison.

Still, it seems that our State Department never learns the lesson history teaches so clearly. So our policy of destabilizing our friends and undermining our allies continues to this day.

If this were simply the workings of chance blunders by incompetent bureaucrats, we could at least expect that the mandarins at State would make a few mistakes in our favor once in a while. But such pro-American "mistakes" have been very few, if they have existed at all. When someone makes a thousand mistakes in a row, and *never* seems to learn from these "mistakes," one can almost be certain that *it was planned that way.*

Too Consistent To Ignore

Who has been behind this repeated, planned betrayal of America's interests by betraying its allies? It has been coordinated by the very same group of elitist world-order advocates who have consistently pushed for U.S. submergence into a New World Order! These are the international socialists in our government and at the

United Nations and other internationalist institutions who, in virtually every single case, are members of the Rockefeller-manipulated Council on Foreign Relations, Trilateral Commission and various Establishment off-shoots of these organizations.

If you have followed the happenings in international affairs for the last two or three decades, and you are perceptive enough to realize that the foreign crises in which America has become involved are due to U.S. foreign policy during this period, then the people you should blame are the CFR/Trilateral experts who have been formulating and implementing those policies. They are the ones who have been in control—and no one else.

Consider some of the great tragedies this clique of global manipulators has caused. In 1959, there was the sellout of Cuba by our U.S. State Department to known Communist Fidel Castro. U.S. Ambassador Earl E. T. Smith, who was envoy to Cuba at the time, has revealed that the U.S. State Department ordered him to sell out Batista and to turn over the country to Castro. This cannot be ignored!

In 1961, our government again betrayed the Cuban people at the Bay of Pigs fiasco. No air support was given at the last moment, even though it had been promised to the Cuban freedom fighters. The rug was yanked out from under this attempt by Cuban patriots to take their country back from Communist dictatorship. This cannot be ignored!

In 1963, there was the overthrow and subsequent murder of Vietnam Premier Ngo Diem, a devout Catholic who had never taken a human life. The orders for this sell-out came from Averell Harriman and Roger Hillsman of the U.S. State Department. This cannot be ignored!

There then followed the long, brutal, no-win war in Vietnam, as planned by Robert S. McNamara and company. The "Pentagon Papers" revealed that it was, in fact, McNamara who first demanded to send troops to

Vietnam on the pretext that it was necessary in order to *win*. This, of course, was blatant hypocrisy; at the very same time, McNamara was muzzling the military by having the word "victory" stricken from their speeches.

The heart cries out at the final cost of our Vietnam folly: 55,000 Americans dead, 300,000 wounded, and millions of Vietnamese dead or enslaved. Those, such as Robert McNamara, who got the United States into the Vietnam War and then refused to pursue a policy of victory, have the blood of millions in the "killing fields" of Southeast Asia on their treacherous hands. This cannot be ignored!

In 1973, under Richard Nixon and Henry Kissinger, the U.S. agreed to a phony treaty which left Vietnam in the hands of the Communists. This State Department treachery cannot be ignored!

Finally, in 1975, the final and crushing blow came when the radicals in the U.S. Congress cut off all aid to those still fighting the Communists in Southeast Asia. The result was the tremendous escalation of the bloodbath and the mass exodus of the "boat people" from Southeast Asia as they fled by the millions from the horror of Communism. This cannot be ignored!

This was followed by the sellout of Angola, Mozambique, Iran, Rhodesia, Panama, Nicaragua, El Salvador, the Philippines, Hong Kong and Taiwan. Even under the current Administration, we are apparently doing the same thing. The Reagan Administration has imposed economic sanctions against the Republic of South Africa, put pressures on Israel to let the PLO terrorists leave Lebanon when they could have been wiped out, and provided only too-little-and-too-late assistance to the contras fighting to take back Nicaragua from the Communist Sandinistas. To be sure, the Reagan Administration *did* come to the rescue of the island of Grenada, and this was welcomed by the people there, but this hardly counterbalances the policies of sellout in all those other areas in which U.S. foreign policy has been involved.

This is nothing new. As we have already noted briefly, it goes back at least to World War II (at the time the Council on Foreign Relations was consolidating its hold on the the U.S. State Department) when we delivered Poland, East Germany and the other nations of Eastern Europe to Soviet domination, a tyranny which makes Adolf Hitler seem almost mild by comparison!

Yet, we are told in our history books that World War II was fought in order to preserve the freedom and independence of Poland and other countries in Eastern Europe! It was, after all, Hitler's and Stalin's joint attacks on Poland that marked the beginning of that tragic global conflict. The U.S. left the Poles stranded just as we would later ignore and abandon the East Germans, Hungarians and Czechs who revolted against their Communist masters.

The Pattern Of A Sellout

The pattern of sellout follows a four-phase program; we call it the Four Steps of Subversion:

Step One is VILIFICATION of the anti-Communist leader or government.

No matter how much better the leader, compared to what has gone before in his particular country, he is increasingly contrasted to some alleged ideal social democrat and, of course, falls far short of demands based on such a standard. Charges of corruption were leveled against Somoza, the Shah, Chiang Kai-shek, Marcos and all others who were betrayed by our State Department and news media flunkies.

There was probably a good deal of truth to at least some of these charges. But you almost never hear charges of corruption and "human rights violations" directed against Communist or avowedly Marxist regimes. Why this double standard? Why the cover-up of Communist and Marxist regimes which are hundreds of times worse than the non-Communist governments they overthrew? Because the propagandists are not intellectually honest or objective.

As V. I. Lenin said in a memorandum he sent to his foreign minister in 1921, "To tell the truth is a petit bourgeois habit, whereas for a revolutionary to lie and lie convincingly is not only a sign of intelligence, but an imperative when furthering a revolutionary cause. That is fundamental. Anything that moves that cause forward becomes the truth, and anything that retards a revolutionary cause becomes an untruth."

Step Two is GLORIFICATION of the Communist leader or revolutionary forces seeking to overthrow the existing regime.

Remember that Fidel Castro was called "The George Washington of the Caribbean" by the *New York Times* and his Marxist-Leninist ties and inclinations were covered up. The Sandinistas were said to be bringing democracy to Nicaragua, so we sent them millions in foreign aid to help consolidate their revolution. Mrs. Aquino was presented as the Joan of Arc of the Philippines, and every effort was made to portray her as the true choice of the overwhelming majority of the people, even before the election was held.

While there is little doubt that the Marcos regime was corrupt, one suspects that what has followed is not exactly as pure as undriven snow. In many underdeveloped nations, the problem is that if a government is strong enough to resist being overthrown by its opponents, it often sacrifices certain standards of due process and human rights we take for granted. While if a government should, by chance, genuinely protect the persons and properties of the people and retain a good "human rights" record, it often becomes too weak to maintain itself in power. The left-wing "revolutionaries" are always praised by the Western media as infinitely superior to the old regimes.

Step Three is BEAUTIFICATION of what life will be like under the new Marxist regime.

After the revolutionaries seize power and gain a monopoly over all the communications media in their country, one hears only a symphony of praise for alleged accomplishments by the new Peoples' Republic. The Western press eats this all up and presents this palpable propaganda as serious news.

But the greatest emphasis on the Heaven to come is just before the revolution. People are given a vision of prosperity, peace and brotherhood, a dream which they want to believe. The promises are never fulfilled, of course, and are either forgotten or Western leftists explain the failure away by saying that "the revolution was betrayed." The revolution is always betrayed if you believe in the beautiful dream promised by socialism because, in reality, it always becomes a nightmare.

Step Four is RATIONALIZATION of the results by the Western media and government officials.

After Communism takes over a country, everyone is told that it cannot be reversed, that "you cannot turn back the clock" once Marxists are in power. This is part of the nonsense about Communism being the "inevitable wave of history." (This is referred to as the Brezhnev Doctrine—"Once Communist, Always Communist.") Nothing could be farther from the truth, but the belief by many in this notion, instilled by years of propaganda from Western media as well as Communist sources, helps the Reds maintain control once they have toppled a non-Communist or anti-Communist government.

Our media experts strive to give the impression that "it's too late to anything about it now," or we musn't intervene to liberate a Communist country because "it is too risky to world peace and might cause nuclear war." We simply have to accept the situation and learn to live with the Communist victors. And another country goes down the drain. South Africa, South Korea, Argentina and Central America are next on the Communist hit list as they close in on the ultimate target—the U.S.A.

The CFR's 1980s Project

A crucial part of this sellout strategy has been the use and distortion of the concept of "human rights" by the One Worlders and their dupes as a weapon to undermine and cut off assistance to anti-Communist trading partners of the U.S., while justifying greater trade relations and "building bridges" to Communist regimes. This technique is spelled out in a book entitled *Enhancing Global Human Rights*, published under the auspices of the Council on Foreign Relations and its "1980s Project." The authors are Jorge I. Dominguez, Nigel S. Rodley, Bryce Wood and Richard Falk.

What is the 1980s Project? And how important is it in the Establishment's hierarchy? We quote from the introduction to the book, written by Richard H. Ullman, the Director of the 1980s Project:

> The 1980s Project is at once a series of separate attacks upon a number of urgent and potentially urgent international problems and also a collective effort, involving a substantial number of persons in the United States and abroad, to bring those separate approaches to bear upon one another and to suggest the kinds of choices that might be made among them. The Project involves more than 300 participants. A small central staff and a steering Coordinating Group have worked to define questions and to assess the compatibility of policy prescriptions. Nearly 100 authors, from more than a dozen countries, have been at work on separate studies. Ten working groups of specialists and generalists have been convened to subject the Project's studies to critical scrutiny and to help in the process of identifying interrelationships

among them. The 1980s Project is the largest single research and studies effort the Council on Foreign Relation has undertaken in its 55-year history, comparable in conception only to a major study of the postwar world, the War and Peace Studies, undertaken by the Council during the Second World War.

If it is "the largest single research and studies effort" in the entire history of the CFR, you can believe that it is important!

During 1975 and 1976, the ten Working Groups which launched the 1980s Project met to explore major international issues and to draw up initial plans and proposals of the 1980s Project studies. The following is a list of those who chaired those initial Project Working Groups:

Cyrus R. Vance, Working Group on Nuclear Weapons and Other Weapons of Mass Destruction

Leslie H. Gelb, Working Group on Armed Conflict

Roger Fisher, Working Group on Transnational Violence and Subversion

Rev. Theodore M. Hesburgh, Working Group on Human Rights

Joseph S. Nye, Jr., Working Group on the Political Economy of North-South Relations

Harold Van B. Cleveland, Working Group on Macroeconomic Policies and International Monetary Relations

Lawrence C. McQuade, Working Group on Principles of International Trade

William Diebold, Jr., Working Group on Multinational Enterprises

Eugene B. Skolnikoff, Working Group on the Environment, the Global Commons and Economic Growth

Mariam Camps, Working Group on Industrial Policy

And where did the funding come from for this Project for global convergence? According to the book's introduction:

> The 1980s Project has been made possible by generous grants from the Ford Foundation, the Lilly Endowment, the Andrew W. Mellon Foundation, the Rockefeller Foundation and the German Marshall Fund of the United States.

The entire book seethes with left-wing propaganda. It attacks anti-Communist governments as "human rights" violators. While there is a mild reprimand of the Soviet KGB, the book quickly neutralizes this criticism by equating the KGB with the American F.B.I.!

The most important aspect of this book is its introduction and emphasis of a definition of "human rights" which is totally alien to the American concept of individual rights. For example, the authors push the idea that human rights include "human needs" and that these needs must be met by political redistribution schemes. Listen to it in their own words:

> Broadly speaking, "human needs" include those aspects of existence necessary to secure the basic development of the person: adequate nutrition, housing, medical care and education. Contemporary listings of human rights, such as the Universal Declaration on Human Rights, include these basic needs as human rights alongside the traditional civil and political rights mentioned above. Those who emphasize these basic needs contend that their assurance or deprivation is just as much a subject for and a result of state policy as is the assurance or deprivation of traditional civil and political rights. When, either through negligence or through deliberate acts of policy, governments deny the basic needs

of persons living within the territory they control, they violate their human rights just as surely as they violate the human rights of political opponents whom they muzzle or jail.

Notice this subtle reversing of the meaning of human rights, from the traditional American concept of having a right to be protected in one's person, liberty and property from criminal violation and government meddling, to a new notion that people have "rights" to what they need and that their needs are to be fulfilled by the state. How can that be done? Why, by taking from those who earned wealth and giving to others who haven't.

This new notion of "human rights" to someone else's property is a favorite of socialists, Communists, and naive utopians. Needless to say, it is completely contrary to the concept of individual rights on which this country was founded — to be secure in one's person and property from the threat of assault or theft, whether by a criminal or by government itself.

Note too that the above assumes throughout that it is the function of the government to dispense foodstuffs and other resources to its citizens. This necessarily means a socialist system in which the government owns and controls the economy and everybody in it. Their idea of "human rights" only demands that the disbursement of the goodies be equal to all, rather than favoring some over others.

Ignoring Free Enterprise

The idea of goods and services being provided by a Free Market economy — that is, the system the United States was built upon — rather than by government is totally ignored. This is not an alternative the CFR elitists want to consider. The authors of the book go on to attack the relatively free-market nations as being responsible for the woes of the "Third World" (poor socialist regimes) and call for this agenda:

Not surprisingly, given considerations such as these, recent years have seen increasingly widespread recognition of the difficulty of drawing a distinction between "human rights" and "human needs." Within the West, there is also a growing recognition that to some degree, the misery of the least advantaged states has been exacerbated by actions and policies on the part of the advanced, industrialized, market-economy states, and that the latter have a responsibility to contribute to the alleviation of human needs in poor countries. There is thus a growing recognition of the legitimacy of demands for resource transfers from rich to poor countries and for structural changes in the world economy to assure that such resource transfers occur on a regular and continuing, rather than on an ad hoc, basis. . . . Human needs and human rights have necessarily been a central concern of the 1980s Project. It is a truism, yet one often lost from sight, that human beings are the irreducible minimum at the center of all the phenomena explored by social studies. All the policy measures delineated in the 1980s Project have an ultimate effect upon human beings, even though the human core is often lost from sight amidst abstract phrases like "maintaining nuclear deterrence," "reforming the international monetary system," "implementing global industrial policies," "damping armed conflicts," and the like. All of these actions are taken in the name of welfare—the welfare of national societies or of "global society," but ultimately the welfare of individual human beings.

In other words, not only does this book, reflecting the policy aims of the CFR Establishment, distort and reverse the concept of "human rights" to a nation which legitimizes state theft of private property, and not only do these world planners assiduously leave out free market/private enterprise as a system to consider, but they are clearly advocating a World Welfare State.

What these people are saying is this: If a country is basically Free Enterprise and allows for some differences in levels of wealth (since some people will always earn more than others) then *that* country violates "human rights!" But, if a government of a country is socialist and owns everything and allocates food and other needs according to an egalitarian theory, then no matter how many people are liquidated by that state or how many people die of starvation or disease, *that* country observes and supports "human rights!"

All that these would-be elitists care about is equal distribution of goods and services—even if that means equal distribution of the poverty and misery. This tactic reverses the concept of human rights to mean a Socialist-Communist system as opposed to our American concept of individual rights to life, liberty, property and the pursuit of happiness and our Constitutional guarantees of freedom of speech, press, religion and assembly.

This game of semantic antics with the concept of "human rights" is one of the main reasons one anti-Communist government after another is being toppled. In all the bullfeathers about "human rights violations," one truth must be kept foremost in mind: Without private property, no individual rights are possible. The new, distorted notion of "human rights" promoted by the 1980s Project of the Council on Foreign Relations is a deception intended to have people accept Communist revolutions overthrowing non-Communist governments. But even more important, it is an attack on the concept of private property itself. The goal of Communism is "building socialism" and the goal and essence of socialism is simply, always and everywhere, the destruction of any and all private property rights.

Many people forget, or are unaware, how important Aesopian language and semantic warfare is in the Socialist-Communist strategy. To put over on the American people a notion which changes the concept of "rights" to one synonymous with legalized theft and global plunder is truly a propaganda feat of stupendous importance.

Seizing All Natural Resources

A prime motive behind the planned sellout of one non-Communist government after another is to put strategic natural resources under Communist control, so that the West generally, and America specifically, can no longer obtain these resources from its traditional trading partners such as South Africa. The drive is to foment opposition to trade with anti-Communist countries (again, like South Africa) while at the same time promoting more taxpayer-subsidized and underwritten trade and aid with socialist and Communist regimes.

It is vitally important for the American people to realize that every major problem our country faces around the globe can be traced to the coordinated efforts of these power-mad people. They are intent on forcing the United States into a dependency on Communist regimes for our vital supplies. Once they have acheived that, they can blackmail us (they think) into giving up our freedom and independence to get needed raw materials. That's why you see the frantic efforts on the part of the State Department to turn over as much of the world's resources as they can to Communist revolutions.

The attack on the Republic of South Africa and America's trade relations with that country is not a spontaneous response to apartheid. It is part of the organized disarmament program coordinated by the Surrender Lobby in this country. Robert Dale Wilson, Director of the Office of Stragegic Resources, recently called the attention of Congress to the following facts:

Of particular importance with regard to the issue of South Africa are platinum, chromium, manganese, cobalt and vanadium. All of these minerals are of critical importance, not only to our industrial base, but also to our defense system. Chromium is used to produce stainless, full-alloy, and high-strength, low-alloy steels, high-purity fero-chromium, and electrolytic chromium metals. These materials, in turn, are used in the production of tanks, ships, military hospital equipment, naval nuclear propulsion systems, B-1 landing gear and other industrial equipment.

Manganese is used in the production of fero-manganese which is used to produce steel. Steel is used in a variety of applications including ships, tanks and other military vehicles, buildings and bridges. Platinum is used as a catalyst in electrical and electronic applications, as a chemical catalyst in petroleum distillation and in dental and medical application. . . .

Close substitutes do not exist in a number of applications. For some, substitutes are available, but can only be used with a reduction in product performance or an increase in costs. A disruption in the supply of these minerals would affect the United States' chemical, electronics, power equipment, iron and steel, petroleum refining, transportation and manufacturing industries.

Is it any wonder that the Soviets want to deprive us of the vast mineral wealth of southern Africa?

The American public must be made aware that South Africa is our only real source for these crucial minerals and strategic metals. This is one of the major reasons behind the drive to isolate the U.S. from South Africa. Noted historian and expert on South Africa, Otto Scott, author of *The Other End of the Lifeboat*, puts it this way:

I'm worried because, in all the noise that's being raised about South Africa, I'm not sure the average American realizes that our survival as a nation and a people relies on maintaining good relations and especially trade with South Africa. Without South Africa, we will have to do without a military establishment, without an oil refining industry, without a chemical industry, without being able to make any new planes, tanks or ships, without being able to make any more of our own steel, without being able to maintain our electrical industry, our medical industry, or our transportation industry.

The protests against South Africa and the disinvestment movement is an integral part of the goal of disarming the United States even more than it already has been disarmed. The idea is that we will become dependent on the Soviet Union for crucial minerals or will become so militarily enfeebled by lack of access to those minerals that we can no longer provide any real resistance to our merger with the U.S.S.R. into the New World Order.

As Mr. Scott observes:

What I suggest to you today is that South Africa is the key to not only all Africa south of the Sahara, but to the survival of the United States. To blockade South Africa, to cut off its mineral flow to the West, would cripple Europe and America alike. It would mean the control of the world will fall into the hands that rule the Kremlin. Make no mistake about it; this is a real crisis.

As we have repeatedly pointed out, this and the myriad other crises did not happen by accident; they were planned as part of the program to force America into a New World Order consisting of a socialistic One

World tyranny. This is a sellout of the American people of the first degree!

In principle, we are opposed to U.S. intervention around the world. Those opposed to intervention were once denigrated with the smear term "isolationist." An isolationist was one who subscribed to George Washington's philosophy as laid down in his Farewell Address —while the U.S. should trade with the world, it should not engage in political entanglements with the other nations of the world. For the past forty years, that philosophy has been rejected. The consequence is that we are left with debt, disasters and dilemmas. Now, however, it is the "liberals" who led us into this swamp who are the "new isolationists" when it comes to opposing Communism anywhere in the world.

We repeat — in principle, we too are opposed to intervention. But having helped create and feed the mad dog called Communism, it is morally incumbent upon us to help the peoples free themselves of this tyranny — before it has us all by the throat!

Chapter Ten

Family, School and Church in the New World Order

"Every child in America that enters school at the age of five is mentally ill, because he comes to school with allegiance toward our elected officials, toward our Founding Fathers, toward our institutions, toward the preservation of this form of government . . . the truly well individual is the one that has rejected all those things and is what I would call, the true internationalist of the future."

—Dr. M. T. Pierce
Professor at Harvard

In their efforts to drive the United States into the one world system they plan for us, advocates of the New World Order have targeted the family as their main enemy. The family is recognized as the foundation upon which every great society is based. From Ancient Rome to present-day America, including the countries of China before Mao and Germany before Hitler, the family has been the core of all civilizations. As the building blocks of society, families provide a stabilizing order and identity without which societies of any kind would cease to exist.

The primary objectives of the New World Order which affect the family are: (1) eliminate the traditional family unit as we know it and (2) change the value of the traditional family. As would-be dictators, the architects of the New World Order want the complete and unyielding loyalty of their victims for themselves and cannot tolerate loyalty to God, country or family. These self-appointed rulers realize that their One World Utopia will not exist as long as the limitations of these three strongholds remain.

A child's basic concepts of Judeo-Christian ethics, morality and patriotism are formed primarily by his parents. Because proponents of the New World Order seek to be the major authority in everyone's lives, parental authority must be removed by whatever means are necessary. According to the noted Harvard educator, Dr. M. T. Pierce:

> Every child in America that enters school at the age of five is mentally ill because he comes to school with allegiance toward our elected officials, toward our Founding Fathers, toward our institutions, toward the preservation of this form of government. We have patriotism, nationalism, sovereignty—all that proves that children are sick, because the truly well individual is the one that has rejected all those things and is what I would call, the true internationalist of the future.

In keeping with this theme, fellow humanist Ashley Montague has put it more simply: "The American family structure produces mentally ill children." And what would these elitists do about it? They would use the powers of the very government they seek to destroy to separate children from their parents at birth, protect them from the spiritual influence of the church and the moral precepts of God which are instilled by the families. They would provide for these children what they call "social parenting."

Now that the "problem" of loving, loyal children has been determined by the One World wizards, they seek to cure these "children of the future" of their mental illnesses by subtle methods which are intended to recondition the children for an easier acceptance of their role in the One World system.

Because most children still have an allegiance to their families, despite what has been an all-out drive to erode it, the elitists of the New World Order have sought to redefine the family. The employing of such euphemistic terms as "the brotherhood of man" and "the family of man" are meant to convey a soothing assurance with regard to the fundamental changes which are to be found in the family structure of the New World Order.

Women's Liberation And Abortion

Many unsuspecting women were duped by the feminist movement into believing that the only way to have total fulfillment is to have a job outside the home. While many women do have to work for economic reasons, those who buy the idea for its own sake often find their families' problems multiplied. The real goal of women's liberation is to "liberate" the women from their families. Traditional families (called "nuclear families" by the feminists) have been clearly earmarked for extinction by the People Planners.

According to *The Document: A Declaration of Feminism*:

> The nuclear family must be replaced with a new form of family where individuals live and work together to help meet the needs of all people in the society. With the destruction of the nuclear family must come a new way of looking at children. They must be seen as the responsibility of the entire society rather than individual parents. Children's lives should not be separated from society; instead, children should

begin to share in the life of society at an early age —on the one hand because the work they can do is useful and is the best way to learn, and on the other hand because this will teach them the interdependence of people in a collective society.

This is, of course, precisely the road the gangsters of the New World Order wish to travel. The One Worlders are not uncomfortable as an ally of the women's movement, because their ideas on so-called "social issues" are remarkably similar, if not identical. The feminists who constantly shriek about "equality of women" believe that the greatest "inequality" between the sexes is that women get pregnant and men don't. Their support of abortion is based on the belief that women should not be forced to endure any burdens that men haven't experienced!

Proponents of the New World Order side with the baby killers whole-heartedly. They see abortion as one way of achieving population control. Not only do they want to have the entire population under their thumb, they want to decide the exact number as well. In their opinion, the world is over-crowded and must be reduced. How is this reduction to be accomplished? A few of their favorite methods include: abortion, euthanasia, suicide, homosexuality and sterilization. So you favor none of the above as a way of reducing the population? They expected that. According to John D. Rockefeller III, appointed by President Nixon as Chairman of the Commission on Population Growth and the American Future:

The average citizen doesn't appreciate the social and economic implications of population growth and what it does to the quality of our lives. Rather than think of population control as a negative thing, we should see that it can be enriching.

The Rockefeller Commission stated: "In order to neutralize the legal, social and institutional pressures that historically have encouraged childbearing, as well as to equalize opportunities generally, we should eliminate discrimination based on sex by adopting the proposed Equal Rights Amendment." To "neutralize the pressures" of childbearing is paramount to the formation of a World Citizenry which is only to be concerned with the present; children are a link to the future!

Euthanasia And Other Measures

There is more to the anti-life stance of the One Worlders than their support of abortion-on-demand. The "achievement" of decreasing the population at the beginning of life via the abortion holocaust is just one way of curbing the population. An expansion on the idea, called euthanasia, is meant to include (or exclude) the elderly who supposedly have outlived their usefulness to society. The American Health Association states, ". . . euthanasia, mercy killing of individuals suffering from incurable and painful illnesses or disabilities . . . is an acceptable alternative to the unnecessary prolongation of life. Every precaution against abuse of this option must be taken, and the consent of the patient should be obtained *if possible*. For humanists, it should be remembered that the dead, being nonexistent, cannot regret being dead."

While it is true that the dead cannot regret being dead, it is safe to assume that some euthanasia victims may have regretted the way in which they became dead, particularly if it was not possible to obtain their consent at the time.

Abortion is legalized murder of the unborn; euthanasia is the proposed legalization of the murder of the elderly. Should it become too acceptable, what is to prevent the "acceptable" elimination of other people for whatever reason, be it racial, political, social or religious? Advocates of the New World Order actively promote such anti-life propaganda in order to robotize people into the idea that whatever is made legal becomes right.

Such is the case with homosexuality. Gay and lesbian rights are pushed by the futurists as another method of undermining the family. Since "marrriages" of the same sex cannot produce children, they are favored. Homosexuals are not born into their lifestyles; because they are recruited, their increase decreases the number of people willing to make the commitment to marriage and family. Without the continuence of heterosexual relationships, mankind as we know it will cease.

The deterioration of the family is the cause of the escalation of suicide, which is the third highest cause of death among young people. It should surprise no one that young people are resorting to suicide to end their pain and loneliness. Loneliness is not the result of being alone; it is the result of feeling empty inside and, in too many cases, that comes from the lack of a good family life.

The People Planners see the parents as incapable of raising their children to be perfect Citizens of the (One) World. Thus, it follows that they believe the sooner they get the children under their supervision, the better the chance to completely indoctrinate them. The concept of "social parenting" did not come about in America until the 1920s. Until that time, according to the Rockford Institute's publication, "Persuasion at Work," child rearing was the responsibility of each family. The 1909 White House Conference on Children said, "Home life is the highest and finest product of civilization."

Those were the good old days, before the New World Order sought to produce a generation of gender-free, cooperative children who were incapable of making moral judgments. This is why every negative force that now attacks the integrity of the traditional family, benefits those who would see a World Government built on its ruins.

Undermining Education

In the war of the New World Order, if the family is the main target, then education is its chief weapon of attack. The educrats of the future are the first to admit that the educational philosophies of today are the political policies of tomorrow. In his book, *A New Civic Literacy*, former Assistant Secretary of State for International Organizations and author of *Third Try at World Order*, Harlan Cleveland (CFR/TC) stressed the importance of education on the One Worlders terms when he wrote:

> The students in our public schools constitute, as my colleague Francis Keppel puts it, the nation's greatest and most attractive sucker list. Everybody who has anything to sell . . . would naturally like to get at this market of future American adults, and get at them as early in life as possible. . . . Those of us with global perspectives to sell may chafe at the sluggish reaction of American public education, but we had better first try to understand its profound and not illogical motivation.
>
> The education of the nation's adolescents must be superior to that of their parents. Part of this superiority must be an enhanced sense of the globe as the human environment. . . . All secondary school students should receive a basic global education. . . . Experimental activities should be undertaken to see to what degree formal learning experiences can shape the world views of Americans so as to make those views more compatible with (or at least resistant to) adjustments in behavior and attitudes necessary to cope more effectively with problems of global interdependence.

So there it is: education is no longer a process of learning. Instead, it is a series of "experimental activities" designed to shape the world view of Americans to insure that they will accept the *interdependence* of the New World Order.

Hitler's experiments on Jews in Germany during World War II caused America to be rightly outraged. Today, if mass experiments were to be conducted on dogs, cats, monkeys or whales, the animal rights crowd would be very vocal in their opposition and the Save the Whale Gang would be blubbering loudly! Yet, the most dangerous experiments are being done with the minds of children and it is being met by the majority of people with only yawns and silence.

The father of progressive education was John Dewey, an avowed socialist. His denial of God caused him to view man as nothing more than a biological organism molded by his changing environment. He believed that man changed as constantly as his environment and therefore saw no reason to teach children any absolutes, since they didn't exist. He redefined the purpose of education by saying, "Education, therefore, is a process for living and not a preparation for future living."

Dewey's foundation for turning students into nonthinking little zombies was made clear when he said, "We violate the child's nature and render difficult the best ethical results by introducing the child too abruptly to a number of special studies, of reading, writing, geography, etc., out of relation to his social life. . . . The true center of correlation of the school subjects is not science nor literature nor history nor geography, but the child's own social activities."

At Columbia University, Dewey surrounded himself with a group of young professors known as the Frontier Thinkers. While Dewey's influence was mainly in the area of teaching methods, the Frontier Thinkers, led by Dr. George Counts and Dr. Harold Rugg, believed in using the schools to build the New World Order. George

Counts' overall disgust for the traditions of the country were matched only by his loving appreciation of the Communist system. Having been to Russia, Counts knew that open revolution would not accomplish what he sought for the United States. It would be done best through the evolutionary process of education.

The main purposes of schools in early America were to teach children to read the Bible and to perpetuate the culture in which those schools existed. The purpose of today's schools, however, is to teach courses from an international point of view. As such, the socially unacceptable subjects have been replaced and textbooks have been rewritten accordingly, presenting a biased representation of both religion and traditional values. Thanks to the meshing of science, geography and history into one course—Social Studies—school students are denied a basic knowledge of this country's history and heritage.

World Government worshippers realized that they had no choice but to distort the teaching of history, since, as Archy Roosevelt wrote, "History, if accurately narrated, has a nasty way of exposing the evils of tyranny and its inevitable downfall; and socialism is a form of tyranny. The story of the decline and fall of the Athenian and Roman republics, truthfully told, has unpleasant analogies to the schemes of modern demagogues. The factual lessons of history had to be hidden under a fog of socialist mythology."

The National Education Association

In his book, *New Age Globalism*, Dr. Ed Rowe comments about the leading role the National Education Association plays in this promotion of teaching the New World Order. He reports that in June, 1976, the NEA's former presidents and then current chairmen of its Bicentennial Committee had this to say concerning educators and their role in relationship to the developing New World Order or global community:

It is with . . . sobering awareness that we set about to change the course of American education for the twenty-first century by embracing the ideals of global community, the equality and interdependence of all peoples and nations and education as a tool to bring about world peace.

Obviously, the NEA perceives education as a vehicle for capturing the minds of our school children and, through them, building the planned new globalist society of Planet Earth.

Dr. Rowe goes on to discuss the professional meetings conducted by the National Council for the Social Studies in which the "global perspective" is advocated among curriculum planners. In November, 1981, on occasion of the sixty-first Annual Meeting of this group, Dorothy Seaberg of Northern Illinois University delivered a 24-page paper stressing the need to "chart new directions" consistent with the "nature and purpose of the social studies":

Through a transdisciplinary view, the social studies interrelates all of the disciplines or systems of knowledge and shows the interconnections involved in the global or world system — in other words, the systemness inherent in the universe. Within the community of social educators, there is a growing consensus that the purpose of the social studies is to educate for participatory citizenship within the global system.

Seaberg goes on to urge social science curriculum professionals and teachers to take an active hand in "bettering the world" by moving "away from nationalistic and ethnocentric perspectives to a global view when analyzing issues and making decisions."

Considering the importance of education in achieving the New World Order, the opinion of the National Education Association is of utmost importance as it regards the concept of World Government and the role of teachers in it. This opinion appears as long ago as January, 1946 in an issue of the *N.E.A. Journal*. In an editorial entitled, "Teachers and World Government," editor Joy Elmer Morgan wrote:

> In the struggle to establish an adequate world government, the teacher has many parts to play. He must begin with his own attitude and knowledge and purpose. He can do much to prepare the hearts and minds of children for global understanding and cooperation. . . . At the very top of all the agencies which will assume the coming of world government must stand the school, the teachers and the organized profession.

Recruiting At Our Colleges

This indoctrination of students continues into the college and university level. Because many professors are Marxist-oriented internationalists themselves, there are no better training grounds for furthering the ideals of world government than our "institutions of higher learning." The selling of world government at the college and university level began in earnest when, as a 24-year-old undergraduate at Oxford, Cecil Rhodes wrote his first of seven wills and ordered that his fortune be used for, among other things, the building of a "foundation of so great a power as to hereafter render wars impossible and promote the best interest of humanity."

The establishment of the Rhodes Scholarships after his death made possible the selection of students who would then be subjected to special indoctrination at one of the colleges at Oxford University which, in turn, was necessary to bring about the Anglo-American unity Rhodes envisioned.

As England had her world government addict in

Cecil Rhodes, so the United States has her own in the person of Armand Hammer, chairman of the board of Occidental Petroleum. A capitalist in name only, and friend of Communists everywhere, Armand Hammer jumped at the chance to establish a United World College in the United States when the idea was presented to him by Louis Mountbatten and his nephew, Prince Charles.

The Armand Hammer United World College of the American West was established in New Mexico in 1982. On May 5, 1982, the *Los Angeles Times*, prior to the school's founding, said of Hammer, "He views the college as a place to train the future leaders of the world." And that is the goal of today's so-called "educators." By using education at all levels, the One World elite is training the future leaders of the world to forfeit their future in exchange for the New World Order.

From Our Pulpits As Well

While much has been accomplished through the betrayal of education, proponents of a One World Government have also made very skillful use of the pulpit to get their message across. Those in favor of world government resent the influence of the Judeo-Christian heritage and values upon our civilization, but it is important to remember that they are not against religion. Since they realize that their dream of a New World Order must be built on a religious foundation, they seek to replace traditional religions, Christianity in particular, with the religion of Humanism.

The severing of America's roots from her basic traditions and Christian beliefs has caused many people to have a blurred sense of moral concepts. As such, the replacement of God with Government has been and is being achieved through the orchestrated effort of mainstream denominational clergymen who preach what is known as the "social gospel."

Social gospel Christianity was developed by a Baptist theologian, Walter Rauschenbusch. Rauschenbusch, an avowed socialist, knew that his teachings would be rejected by the majority if they were understood. Therefore, he took it upon himself to give new meanings to already existing Christian terms which many of his unsuspecting followers believed were spoken directly from God himself.

For example, according to Rauschenbusch's "new" theology, "sin" described the injustices that can result from private ownership of property; "salvation" referred to the public ownership of all means of production; and "the kingdom of God" was the term meant for the established earthly Utopia as dreamed by the One Worlders. Because he viewed the glorious Utopia as a way to better provide for the people of the world, Rauschenbusch believed that the Church should be in the forefront of bringing this New World Order into existence.

Rauschenbusch was not alone in using the tools of the clergy to bring about his goal. Also dedicated to the World Government concept was Dr. Harry F. Ward. An identified Communist, Ward was also a professor of Christian Ethics at Union Theological Seminary where he sought to create ". . . a changed attitude on the part of many church members concerning the purpose and function of both the Church and Christianity."

What, then, is the chief purpose of the majority of mainline denominational churches which have become dominated by the One World thrust of both the National and World Councils of Churches? Following the dictates of the New World Order, many church leaders are as zealous as missionaries in their effort to replace the free nations of the world with a system of world government.

Because most people are naturally unsuspecting, it is difficult to associate any evil whatsoever with members of the clergy. After all, no one could seriously believe that priests and pastors would condone the slaughter of the innocent to bring about this so-called "Heaven on Earth." Yet, perhaps it is not entirely impossible to believe.

Consider the remarks make by South Africa's Bishop Desmond Tutu while appearing on the program, "The First Estate" on WNBC-TV in New York during his last trip to the United States. According to nationally syndicated columnist Lester Kinsolving, who is also an Episcopal priest, the host of the program, Dr. Russell Barber, asked Bishop Tutu, "Have you ever given any thought to the possibility that in the event of civil war in South Africa, blacks might be worse off than they are now?"

To which Tutu replied: "Yes, they (the whites) have the fire power, but we are the domestics. We take care of white people's homes. We cook their food and take care of their babies. Some of the domestics could be recruited and given a vial of arsenic. Who knows what would happen?" Winner of the 1984 Nobel Peace Prize, Bishop Tutu is supposedly a great man of peace. Yet, there he was on television hinting at the callous murder of white children.

It would appear that, with the exception of the fundamentalists, the majority of both Protestant and Roman Catholic churches have accepted the Ecumenism Movement's call for a One World Church. Of all religious leaders who are calling for a world religion, perhaps none is more surprising than Pope John Paul II. According to a special report in the June 20, 1983 issue of *Newsweek* titled, "Vision of a Socialist Pope," by senior writer Kenneth Woodward, the Pope favors the blending of socialism with Christianity. Included among the most revealing statements illustrating this preference: "What he did learn from the books was how to think like a Marxist as well as like a Christian," and "What the Pope seems to be calling for is a cooperative form of socialism. . . ."

Whether he realizes it or not, Pope John Paul II is playing right into the hands of the World Government gang. Don't think they don't appreciate it! It's like the song says, "Who could ask for anything more?" An example of this is found in the Pope's own words. As reported in the March, 1984 *Christian Inquirer*, while holding an audience on January 21, 1984 for forty delegates who attended an international meeting in Rome on the world economic crisis, arms spending and international security, Pope John Paul echoed the standard One World objectives when he said:

> Today the challenges and the problems which affect people everywhere transcend national and even regional boundaries. We would be deluding ourselves to think that some simple formula could be applied that would rectify the situation and restore a World Order of justice, fraternity and peace.

One World Government advocates want people to see themselves as "citizens of the world." Therefore, when a leader like the Pope suggests that today's problems are too complex to be handled by mere nations alone, patriotic nationalism is seen as an obstacle to finding solutions to the world's problems. While it may be "theologically acceptable" to the majority of the social gospel proponents, there is no biblical basis for such a position.

An Early Effort At World Rule

There's nothing new about the New World Order. Only the name has been changed to protect the guilty. The first attempt at World Government is recorded in Genesis 11, which states that, following the Great Flood, it fell on Noah and his sons to repopulate the earth. The end result was that there was one language spoken by all people, making it easy for everyone to agree on the building of a tower to Heaven.

God, however, was against this idea because He knew that completely self-sufficient people feel absolutely no need to rely on Him. To keep this from happening, He created different languages so that no one could understand anyone else. Thus, the tower project was abandoned and separate nations were established as people scattered around the world.

Nonetheless, One World enthusiasts don't quit easily. What was once known as the Tower of Babel is today known as the United Nations. Hopefully, one day, it too will cease to exist.

Civilizations not based on religious principles have very short survival spans. By attacking the family, education and religion, these New World Order advocates have attempted to control men physically, mentally and spiritually. Ultimately, it is a war for the world's freedom without which the world has no real future.

Chapter Eleven

The Spike in the Heart of America

"Some are members of the Party and some are not; but that is a formal *difference. The important thing is that* both serve *the same common purpose."*

— Josef Stalin in Moscow
February 9, 1946

Everyday, in millions of homes across America, a propaganda war is being waged against the minds of a largely unsuspecting public. This war is being conducted every morning in the daily newspapers, especially in such paramount publications of the Establishment press as the *New York Times*, the *Washington Post*, and the *Los Angeles Times*. It is waged every week in the major weekly news magazines, *Time* and *Newsweek*, and now, under its new management, *U.S. News and World Report*.

The American public is constantly being bombarded with salvos representing the "party line" of the Eastern "Liberal" Establishment in general and the Merger Maniacs in particular. It is heartening, however, to note that increasing numbers of Americans are becoming aware of the extent of the leftwing bias in the news media and are righteously angered by it.

Three years ago, a poll conducted by the *Los Angeles Times* surprised its editors with the revelation that only one American in three believes that reporters are fair. Another poll, conducted by the leftist *Washington Post*, found that fifty-three percent of its nationwide sample agreed with the statement that the major news media often cover up stories that ought to be reported.

Another important survey of public opinion was conducted by a Washington polling company, Finger-hut-Granados. This one polled people in the Washington area (not known for its pro-American leanings) to find out if they believe that the *Washington Post* tends to publish "made-up" stories. Only eight percent believe the *Post* never ran such stories, while sixty percent claimed that they were "rare." But a very significant twenty-two percent said they thought the paper ran "made up" stories at least some of the time, while three percent actually believed it ran them most of the time.

We enthusiastically applaud this increased public distrust of the Establishment media and hope the credibility gap continues to widen. But merely suspecting bias in the news one watches on the tube does not automatically insure that one is shielded from subtle propaganda, or is aware of important facts which the media moguls have chosen to suppress.

Soviet "Disinformation" In Our Media

Many Americans simply don't know who or what to believe. Too many others accept what they are told at face value. As a result, the American people, guileless and benevolent as they tend to be, are especially vulnerable to what Arnaud de Borchgrave and Robert Moss called "disinformation" in *The Spike*, a best-selling novel they co-authored in 1980. The book presented authentic details of the manner in which the Soviet KGB and Communist agents working for such Kremlin allies as Cuba and Vietnam secretly influence and manipulate the Western media.

In a sequel titled *Monimbo*, Moss and de Borchgrave provided a gripping account of the Soviet and Cuban roles in directing international terrorism. Although the information in both books was presented in fictional form, de Borchgrave emphasizes that the situations recounted in them are authentic. In fact, Mr. de Borchgrave, formerly Senior Foreign Editor for *Newsweek* magazine and currently Editor-in-Chief of the *Washington Times*, insists that the manipulation by the Communists of the American media establishment is continuing and is effective, especially in the area of disarmament and foreign policy.

Here is how de Borchgrave puts it:

> The Soviets spend $3-4 billion a year on disinformation operations throughout the Western world, about a thousand operations a year in our media—that's almost three disinformation stories a day. And, apart from that, the *Washington Post's* Ben Bradlee says that nothing so crass as Soviet disinformation ever gets into the *Post*. When he said that, I wrote an op-ed page piece for the *New York Times* in which I said that if a palpably fraudulent story like the Janet Cooke scandal can land the world's most prestigious journalism award, namely the Pulitzer Prize, I don't think it takes an overwhelming effort of imagination to figure out how more subtle forms of disinformation worm their way into the media on an hourly basis.

What exactly is disinformation? Disinformation, as defined in *The KGB and Soviet Disinformation: An Insider's View* by Ladislav Bittman, is "a carefully constructed false message leaked into an opponent's communications system to deceive the decision-making elite or the public." "Disinformation" is when the Soviets are able to plant false and damaging stories in the Western media and have them accepted as fact. According to de Borchgrave, this is happening an average of *three times every day.*

"Liberal" Bias Admitted

Now-retired ABC network anchorman Howard K. Smith gave a candid confession of "liberal" bias in the media in an article for *TV Guide.* Smith declared that network news bias is massive—beginning with the ideological composition of the news staffs, which are virtually all "Liberal." He confirmed that he and his colleagues in network journalism have "a strong leftward bias." Though Mr. Smith described himself as "left of center" and a "semi-socialist," his comments were prompted by his concern over the even more extreme views of some of his fellow newsmen who, according to Smith, were increasingly leaning to the anti-American world view of the New Left.

Howard K. Smith warned, for instance, that the self-proclaimed sophisticates of network news are seriously deluded about the intentions of the Communists. He explained, "Some [newsmen and commentators] have gone overboard in a wish to believe that our opponent has exclusively peaceful aims, and that there is no need for armaments and national security. The danger is unreal to many of them. But there is a kind of basic bias in the left-wing soul that gives the Russians the benefit of the doubt."

This tendency is well illustrated by the views of former CBS broadcaster Walter Cronkite. As longtime anchorman and managing editor of the "CBS Evening News," Cronkite became one of the most powerful influences in the national news game. In an interview with *Playboy,* he admitted that most of his media colleagues are "certainly liberal and possibly left of center as well." Indeed, he added arrogantly, "I think most newspapermen by definition have to be liberal. If they're not liberal, by my definition of it, then they can hardly be good newspapermen."

A detailed study of the content of CBS News, conducted by the Institute of American Strategy, found that on the issue of national defense, CBS gave more than sixty percent of its coverage to advocates of a weaker defense, and only 3.5 percent to those recommending a stronger America. When asked about these findings, Walter Cronkite shrugged the matter off by saying, "There are always groups in Washington expressing views of alarm over the state of our defense. We don't carry those stories. The story is that there are those who want to cut defense spending."

In other words, Walter favored a weaker America and was doing his part by suppressing the views of military experts warning about our deteriorating military strength. A clue to why he felt this way is suggested in his view of the nature of Soviet Communism. An interview with Walter Cronkite was published in the May Day 1979 issue of a Soviet magazine called *Literaturnaya Gazeta* and was subsequently reprinted in English in a publication called *Socialism: Theory and Practice.* The following is an excerpt from that interview, conducted by Vitali Kobysh of the Novosti Press:

KOBYSH: How can you agree with the idea that the Soviet Union menaces someone, that our people are preparing for war?

CRONKITE: If you watched my program every evening for several years, you must know that I never agreed with that, and do not agree.

KOBYSH: What do you think has to be done in order to establish full confidence between our peoples, to develop broad cooperation between our countries in all fields?

CRONKITE: I think, in the long term, the main thing is to dispel mutual distrust, suspicion, to be better informed and more tolerant. To the best of my ability I work in this direction. I know your country, your people. Shortly after the war, I lived for two years in Moscow as a UPI correspondent. I saw the legacy of the war and I will never believe in a "Soviet threat."

This of a totalitarian regime engaged in the most massive military buildup in history. While the Soviets were wringing all the propaganda they could from the interview with Cronkite, they were planning the invasion of Afghanistan. It is hardly surprising that viewers of CBS were never told the Soviet invasion of Afghanistan was accomplished in trucks and armored personnel vehicles manufactured at the Kama River truck plant which was constructed by U.S. industrial firms and financed by the Rockefeller-controlled Chase Manhattan Bank.

Some years ago, another admission of prejudice came from Fred Freed, an executive with NBC. Writing in *TV Guide*, he noted: "This generation of newsmen is a product of the New Deal. Those beliefs of the New Deal are the beliefs that news has grown up on. This is true of the networks, of *Newsweek*, of the *New York Times*, of all media. Men of like mind are in the news. It is provincial."

Confirming A Tilt To The Left

Pro-statist-internationalist-"Liberal"-left media bias exists over the whole range of issues and personalities. Statistical confirmation of this was presented in a major study published in *Public Opinion*. For this study, Robert Lichter of George Washington University and Stanley Rothman of Smith College conducted hour-long interviews with 240 of our nation's most influential journalists and broadcasters, representing the most powerful media outlets, including the *New York Times*, the *Washington Post*, the *Wall Street Journal*, *Time*, *Newsweek*, *U.S. News & World Report*, NBC, CBS, ABC and PBS. The findings of this scholarly study make fascinating reading.

The Lichter-Rothman survey revealed that our mass media are operated by a socially privileged class from upper-middle income homes. Ninety-five percent are white, seventy-nine percent are male, ninety-three percent are college graduates, fifty-five percent have postgraduate educations, and nearly half boast family incomes in excess of fifty thousand dollars. Geographically, two-thirds come from the quadrant of the nation extending from New England to Chicago's north shore. Only three percent come from the entire Pacific coast. Although fifty percent of those surveyed state that they have no formal religious affiliation, almost one in four was reared in a Jewish household, while only one in eight identified himself as a Roman Catholic.

Fifty-four percent of these leading journalists call themselves "Liberals." While this is a much greater percentage than in the general population, it is assuredly too modest a figure in view of the overwhelming "Liberal" bias in the media. Many "Liberals" now palm themselves off as "moderates." Only nineteen percent maintain that they are "Conservative" or "Right of Center."

On the issues, it is disturbing that these pressies credit the most obvious Marxist myths and propaganda. Half of them believe that guaranteeing jobs is a proper function of government, and sixty-eight percent think one of the purposes of government should be to bridge the gap between rich and poor through political programs that redistribute the wealth. This group also heavily favors "affirmative action" programs. The majority of them declared that poverty in the Third World is caused by the United States. More than half also claim to think that America's consumption of world resources is immoral and exploitive.

Is it any wonder that you never hear the mass media discuss Free Market economics as an alternative to the nostrums of Marxists, Keynesians and Monetarists? The mainstream journalist or commentator is simply ignorant of Free Market alternatives. Or opposed to them. On issues of sexual morality, the attitude of the newspeople is one of permissiveness. Only nine percent believe that homosexuality is wrong, and a full eighty-five percent support the "right" of sexual deviants to teach in public schools. Fifty-four percent see nothing wrong with adultery, with only fifteen percent saying they "strongly agree" that extramarital affairs are wrong. A huge ninety percent take the position that women have a "right" to abortion.

In terms of Presidential politics, the media elite are again dramatically out of step with the general population. They voted ninety-four percent for Lyndon Johnson to six percent for Barry Goldwater in 1964; eighty-seven percent for Hubert Humphrey to thirteen percent for Richard Nixon in 1968; eighty-one percent for Jimmy Carter to nineteen percent for Gerald Ford in 1976; and, in the landslide of 1972 when three-fourths of white America voted for Nixon (or at least against McGovern), this predominately white, male elite went eighty-one percent for the fanatic George McGovern! Figures on the 1980 election are not available, but you can bet that the media people did not favor less government and more individual responsibility.

Keenly aware of their own power, the aristocrats of the media want even more. Asked by Lichter and Rothman which groups they felt should rule America, the nation's top journalists surprised no one by naming themselves at the head of the list, followed by consumer groups, intellectuals, blacks, business, feminists and unions.

We see from all of this that our national press does not reflect the variety of America's ideological leanings and philosophical assumptions. The press and broadcasting elite share a single point of view — that of the Eastern "Liberal" Establishment. Little wonder that other viewpoints are systematically ignored and even suppressed.

Thomas Jefferson said, "If a nation expects to be both ignorant and free, it expects what never was and never will be." That's why honest reporting and exposure to alternative points of view are important. The news we see and hear helps us form our opinions. When we pick up a newspaper and read a story — or when we switch on the TV and watch the evening news — we are affected consciously and subconsciously. If we are given misinformation, or if relevant facts are left out, we are being manipulated.

The Power Of Television

By far the most vivid and the most powerful medium in the propaganda arsenal of the Eastern Establishment is television. The national television communications system extends into virtually every home in America. In 1952, only 19.8 percent of homes in the U.S. had TV sets; today more that 99.8 percent have at least one. The average American spends over twenty hours a week in front of a television set.

While newspapers and magazines have always reported on wars, riots, scandals, elections and other disasters, not even a majority of Americans reads these accounts — and fewer still read the editorial pages on a regular basis. Newspaper readers can turn quickly to the comic strips or the sports pages and avoid confronting the political news. By contrast, nearly everyone watches television.

Seventy percent of all Americans now rely primarily on television for their news, and over two-thirds of the U.S. population says it thinks television is the best way to follow candidates for national office. TV is unquestionably the most powerful medium in of all the mass media.

Television is an extension of the graphic arts and its appeal is more emotional than analytical. The emotional impact of both pictures and sound invites the need for action, drama and confrontation to hold the attention of the viewing audience. As NBC executive news producer Reuben Frank once advised his co-workers at NBC: "The highest power of television journalism is not in the transmission of information, but in the transmission of experience — joy, sorrow, shock, fear — these are the stuff of [television] news."

That is the key to understanding why TV is so useful for conditioning mass audiences. Scenes of rioting on campuses, burning and looting in the cities, plastic bags containing dead American G.I.s being loaded onto helicopters in Vietnam, a fictional account of a nuclear explosion — all seem very real on the cathode-ray tube, and they all compel *emotion* rather than analysis.

Because of the nature of the medium and its realism, moreover, TV news personnel want a story with *action*. After all, if nothing happens, where's the story? And what advantage would television have over print media? So desperate are TV crews that they sometimes stir up action when not enough is present for a good story. Indeed, they sometimes fabricate action of their own and make it into a media event.

Local television stations do not have the resources to produce their own national news programs; so, they confine themselves mainly to local coverage and rely on the major networks. The three big network corporations feed their propaganda news programs to approximately six hundred local "affiliated" stations. In addition, the networks own and operate their own key TV stations in the nation's largest cities, forming a media matrix which covers about forty percent of all TV households in America.

The Bias Of Television

Considering that there is a limit to the amount of information which can be jammed into the few minutes available for network news each night, we might wonder if anything of significance is left out. We might also wonder why the evening news programs of the three major networks seem so often to be virtual carbon copies of each other. And why is the point of view always the same on all three "competing" networks?

Thomas R. Dye, writing in *Who's Running America?*, accurately describes the situation as follows:

> Television is so important in mass socialization that diversity of views is avoided, and a single Eastern, liberal "establishment" interpretation prevails in all three network presentations. . . . Network entertainment programming, newscasts and new specials are designed to communicate established liberal values to the masses. These are the values of the elite; they include a concern for liberal reform and social welfare, an interest in problems confronting the poor and blacks, a desire to educate the ignorant and cure the sick and a willingness to employ governmental power to accomplish these ends.

An important technique in expressing this statist bias is the "selection" of news. A Princeton University study has concluded that "the mass media may not be successful in telling us what to think, but they are stunningly successful in telling us what to think about." Current "Liberal" issues such as opposition to the strengthening of national defense, vociferous concern for the poor and blacks, ecology, women's liberation, the anti-nuke protests and so on get mountains of coverage. Watergate received almost two straight years of attention. Yet other stories are ignored or played down. The Chappaquiddick tragedy involving Senator Teddy Kennedy was given only one or two weeks coverage, and was then barely mentioned, despite a closed judicial inquiry and the availability of witnesses to the drinking party which had occurred just before the accident.

Another technique is to present false alternatives, always ignoring Free Enterprise solutions. We were, for example, presented with several points of view on how to "reform" the bankrupt Social Security system; but the idea of encouraging a *private enterprise* solution, proposed by Senator Jesse Helms, disappeared down the Memory Hole.

Why this incredible uniformity of "Liberal" bias in the national news?

To a larger extent than most Americans realize, what they see and hear about their world is determined by a tiny, arrogant fraternity of privileged media elitists who work for the Columbia Broadcasting System (CBS), the National Broadcasting Corporation (NBC) and the American Broadcasting Company (ABC), all headquartered within a few blocks of each other in New York City. As Theodore H. White, a creature of the Left and a member of the Establishment's Council on Foreign Relations, once observed: ". . . the increasing concentration of the cultural pattern of the U.S. is in fewer hands. You can take a compass with a one-mile radius and put it down at the center of Fifth Avenue and 51st Street in Manhattan and you can have control of 95 percent of the entire opinion-and-influence-making in the U.S."

Precisely! ABC received a great deal of criticism last year when, in March, its "Nightline" program interviewed top Soviet propagandist Vladimir Posner and let him reply to President Reagan's televised speech on national security. Posner appeared immediately following the President, and no other spokesman was permitted to challenge the Soviet propagandist. This was too much even for Ben Bradlee, the very "Liberal" executive editor of the *Washington Post*, who said Posner's appearance was "inappropriate."

The episode may have backfired a bit, however. Pro-Soviet propaganda is always more effective when it comes from sources which are not identified as Soviet mouthpieces—such as the outlets of the American Establishment news media. But, as nationally syndicated columnist Joseph Sobran pointed out in his

March, 1986 editorial, "To my mind, the fascinating thing about Mr. Posner, and all the recent sophisticated Soviet spokesmen, is how much they sound like liberal Democrats, and vice versa."

So vulnerable is our "Liberal" Establishment media to being manipulated by Soviet disinformation that it becomes obvious to all but the most naive. There has been a long-standing rule of Soviet strategists that they try to advance Communist goals as much as possible through non-Communist hands.

A report on such Soviet strategy was cited on Page 19134 of the August 22, 1958 *Congressional Record*, inserted by the American Bar Association's Special Committee on Communist Tactics, Privacy and Objectives. This report states that Bjorke Dimitrov advised the Letterman's School of Political Warfare as follows:

> As Soviet power grows, there will be a greater aversion to Communist parties everywhere so we must practice the techniques of withdrawal; never appear in the foreground — let our friends do our work. We must always remember that one sympathizer is generally worth more than a dozen militant Communists. A university professor who, without being a Party member, lends himself to the interest of the Soviet Union, is worth more than 100 men with party cards. A writer of reputation or a retired general is worth more than 500 poor devils who don't know any better than to get themselves beaten up by police. Every man has his value, his merit, especially the writer who, without being a party member, defends the Soviet Union.

This approach has come to be known as "the Stalin Standard." It was Uncle Joe himself who said, "Some are members of the Party and some are not; but that is a *formal* difference. The important thing is that *both serve* the same common purpose."

The New York Times

What's black and white and read all over? Answer: The *New York Times*. It is The Important Paper for Important People Everywhere, and is the nearest thing in the United States to a national daily. Most Congressmen and Senators read it faithfully. It is found in all academic libraries and is read by more than half of this country's college presidents. Fifty copies of the *Times* go to the White House everyday. Over seventy Embassies in Washington subscribe to it, including the Soviet Embassy. It is even read by the comrades in Peiping, and thirty-nine copies are sent to Moscow. "A significance of the *Times*," Timesman James Reston (CFR) has written, "is its multiplyer effect. What appears in the *Times* automatically appears later in other places."

Concerning this multiplyer effect, columnist Alice Widener has observed: "It is a fact that most editors and newsmen on the staff of . . . *Time*, *Newsweek*, etc., and most editors, reporters and commentators at NBC, CBS and ABC take their news and editorial cues from the *New York Times*. Technically, it is a great newspaper; but it reports much of the news in conformity with its editorial policies."

One of the most damning indictments of the "Liberal" bias of the *New York Times* came from the late Herman Dinsmore. After serving thirty-four years on the news staff of the *Times*, including many years as its associate foreign editor and nine years as editor of its international edition, Mr. Dinsmore could no longer take the increasingly Leftist slant of the paper, and so he retired and wrote a book exposing it. In *All The News That Fits*, Dinsmore observed:

> The *New York Times* in more recent years has stated that it wants a balance of power in the world — as if it were possible to maintain such a thing. Editorially, it has freely criticized the United States while but sparingly finding

fault with Communist actions. The atttitude of the *New York Times* toward the Soviet Union has resulted in remarkable distortions in its news columns and in its editorial judgments.

Indeed, the *Times* has employed a number of reporters whose pro-Communist diatribes are notorious. Such men as Herbert L. Matthews (the CFR member who wrote that Castro was an *anti*-Communist!), Harrison Salisbury (CFR), Lester E. Markel (CFR), Ralph Parker and Walter Duranty spent the greater portion of their careers with the *Times* as side-show barkers for every Communist regime with a cage to rattle. Walter Duranty even received the Order of Lenin from Stalin for his propaganda efforts on behalf of Communism. Among other items, he spiked the whole story of the great famine which was going on in the Ukraine at the time he was correspondent in the Soviet Union during the 1930s.

The board of directors and top editorial staff of the *New York Times* are filled with members of the Council on Foreign Relations. They include among the directors William Scranton, Cyrus Vance and Richard Gelb; plus executive editor A. M. Rosenthal, managing editor Seymour Topping, assistant managing editor James Greenfield, editorial page editor Max Frankel and Frankel's deputy Jack Rosenthal.

The *New York Times'* policy of helping Communist or pro-Communist forces to overthrow existing regimes is a long-standing rule that goes back many decades. It was even openly admitted, albeit in very qualified terms, some twenty-five years ago.

On August 16, 1961, the *New York Times* ran this editorial: "You must seek to discourage anti-Communist revolts in order to avert bloodshed and war. We must, under our principles, live with evil even if by doing so we help to stabilize a tottering Communist regime, as in East Germany, and perhaps even expose citadels of freedom to slow death by strangulation." The comrades in the Kremlin must have loved that one!

We've mentioned the play by Herbert Matthews and others at the *New York Times* in creating and promoting Fidel Castro, who would bring "democracy" to Cuba. This same paper, and other U.S. media, participated in overthrowing another government a few months ago when it helped to destabilize the Marcos regime in the Philippines.

For example, the *New York Times* ran a devastating story just prior to the election claiming that Marcos' war record was a fabrication. As it turns out, it was the *New York Times'* story which was phony, not Marcos' achievements in World War II. Marcos' war record was exactly what he said it was. While he was winning medals in the Philippine jungles, the families of his rivals now in power were amassing a fortune by collaborating with the Japanese. In all the approbation that was heaped upon Mrs. Aquino by the Western media, this was not mentioned.

The *New York Times* was significantly involved in helping to overthrow Battista in Cuba and bring to power Fidel Castro. It was also heavily involved in conditioning Americans to abandon President Diem in Vietnam. It was a *New York Times*man named Sidney Shanberg who, when he was reporting from Cambodia, welcomed and wanted the Khmer Rouge to come in and take over; the result, as we now know, was the killing fields in which hundreds of thousands of Cambodians were slaughtered by the Communists.

It was a *New York Times* reporter named Alan Riding who helped to destabilize the government of President Somoza in Nicaragua by influencing public and congressional opinion to oppose Somoza and to favor the pro-Communist Sandinistas. The late Anastasio Somoza noted the following of Riding in his book, *Nicaragua Betrayed*: "Alan Riding admitted to me that he opposed my government and that he was a Socialist."

In one country after another, the *New York Times* has been involved in fashioning American foreign policy and handing whole nations of people over to the brutalities of Communism. Yet, after the revolutionaries take over after the fall of the old regime, things get infinitely worse than they were before. And the *New York Times* never apologizes or admits that it made any mistakes when it promoted the pro-Communists and gave bad press to the leader in power.

The Washington Post

The Washington, D.C. end of the Establishment's New York-Washington newspaper axis is the redoubtable *Washington Post*. What the *Post* prints is important as it is read by most Members of Congress. What the *Post* does *not* print is also important, and that fact is notorious. A longtime staffer at the Library of Congress once told us that fully half of the articles cited in congressional debate (not including additions in the *Congressional Record* appendix) come from either the *Washington Post* or the *New York Times*. Like its New York counterpart, the *Post* is infamous for its Leftward bias.

To illustrate the *Post's* incredible pro-left bias, consider the reporting of its Central American correspondent, Karen DeYoung, during the time just prior to the Sandinista takeover of Nicaragua. Her biased coverage of the revolution in Nicaragua indicates that she clearly included herself among those American journalists who, she said, were "very eager to seek out guerrilla groups, leftist groups, because you assume they must be the good guys." Indeed, she stayed with a secret Sandinista training camp in Costa Rica during the rebellion and became very friendly with the terrorists there.

Those who depended on Karen DeYoung's reports from Nicaragua were ill-prepared for the discovery that the revolution brought to power in Nicaragua a puppet regime of Castro and the Kremlin, which is trying to expand its own revolution to neighboring countries. It is clear that the Sandinistas have no intention of permitting Nicaraguans the degree of freedom they enjoyed under President Somoza. Yet, the media coverup of the atrocities and real human-rights violations of the Sandinista regime continues unabetted.

Again quoting from President Somoza's book, he went on to say: "Karen DeYoung and the *Washington Post* performed an excellent hatchet job on me. It's not just happenstance that every time there was a congressional hearing on Nicaragua, on that very same day, the *Washington Post* would carry an anti-Somoza article. This ploy, of course, was used to influence various U.S. Congressmen on that particular day."

In an eye-opening article entitled "What Is Wrong With The *Washington Post*?" which appeared in the October, 1985 issue of *Conservative Digest*, Reed Irvine of Accuracy in Media details several examples in recent years citing embarrassing chapter and verse about the "Liberal" prejudice in that paper. He recalls the role played by the *Post* in the debacle and bloodbath in Southeast Asia:

> The *Washington Post* shares with many others in the media a heavy responsibility for the tragic fate of Vietnam, Cambodia and Laos as a result of the surrender of those countries to the Communists in 1975. Having cheered on those who pulled the rug from under the Vietnamese and Cambodians in the spring of 1975, the *Post* was most reluctant to report the bitter consequences that it had helped bring about.
>
> A bloodbath of monstrous proportions began in Cambodia as soon as Pol Pot's Khmer Rouge took over Phnom Penh, but Kay Graham's rule that you have to tell your readers everything you know didn't apply in this case. Throughout 1975, 1976, 1977 and most of 1978, the *Post* refused to tell its readers about the horror taking place in Cambodia. . . .
>
> When one of the Cambodian escapees, Pin

THE SPIKE IN THE HEART OF AMERICA 211

Yathay, came to Washington in January, 1978 to tell the American people of his personal observations of this terrible holocaust, the *Washington Post* decided against running a story about his revelations. Its reporter, Elizabeth Becker, walked out of Pin Yathay's press conference, and a young lady who helped her with her coat says she heard her say, "Who needs to listen to this junk?" Becker denies making the remark, but there is no denying that she filed no story. She said she talked it over with the then national news editor, Laurence Stern, who agreed that no story need be done.

That is how important anti-Communist stories are routinely *spiked* at the *Washington Post*! Remember, to Karen DeYoung and others at the *Post*, the good guys are the left-wing guerrillas. In this connection Reed Irvine makes the following point:

Having helped these "good guys" achieve power in such countries as Vietnam, Cambodia and Nicaragua, the *Washington Post* has never admitted to any pangs of conscience for the misery that it helped inflict on the poor people of those countries. The *Post* weeps profusely for the oppressed of this world, but much more for those in South Africa than those in Mozambique or Angola, more for those in Somoza's Nicaragua than those in Ortega's Nicaragua, more for those in Chile than those in Cuba.

If our nation ever returns to rationality, the media giants in this country are going to have to answer for why they said next to nothing about the genocide and attrocities taking place at the hands of Soviet troops in Afghanistan every day, while they gave copious coverage each and every day to a motley band of "freezeniks" marching across the country in the so-called Great Peace March. This is only one example of the glaring double-standard which the "Liberal" Establishment uses.

A Final Warning

There are three words you can't say in the major media in this country. Those words are: "Communism is evil!" When President Reagan referred to the Soviet Union as an "evil empire"—which is what it certainly is by any objective standard of ethics—the media pundits squealed like a stuck pig. They attacked the President for endangering the "peace process" and Soviet-American relations. Like Neville Chamberlain, who appeased Hitler and proclaimed "peace in our time," today's one-world peaceniks are appeasing something even worse than Nazi-militarism—Soviet militarism and imperialism.

During the Geneva summit, Western media people fell over one another to portray Mikhail Gorbachev and his wife as "just like us" in the West. In fact, an objective appraisal of the record of Comrade Gorbachev shows that he is really a Stalin with a computer (and guess where the computer came from).

Americans must cut through the media curtain of misinformation and disinformation and get the facts about what is going on in the world; otherwise, they will not have a proper understanding on which to base their decisions and choices.

Always remember what Soviet tyrant Josef Stalin said regarding non-Communists who serve Communist goals: "Some are members of the Party and some are not; but that is a *formal* difference. The important thing is that *both serve* the same common purpose."

Keep this in mind when you read a vicious attack on some anti-Commuinist leader in one of our leading magazines or newspapers, or see distorted, one-sided coverage masquerading as televison news. The reporters and editors, whether they know it or not, *are* serving a "common purpose" with our enemies.

Chapter Twelve

How to Counterfeit —Legally

"It is apparent from the whole context of the Constitution, as well as the history of the time which gave birth to it, that it was the purpose of the Convention to establish a currency consisting of the precious metals. These were adopted by a permanent rule, excluding the use of a perishable medium of exchange . . . or the still more pernicious expedient of paper currency."

— President Andrew Jackson
Message to Congress, 1836

All roads to the New World Order lead through David Rockefeller's Chase Manhattan Bank and its allied money-center megabanks. It is a high-stakes game in which hundreds of billions of dollars, perhaps trillions, are involved. Also on the table of this international poker game is world control of manufacturing, commerce, transportation, and natural resources. You can see why the card sharks are attempting to rig the deck.

Before we peek at the international monetary game, let us examine the U.S. monetary system for a few moments. Because of the horrible experience with un-backed paper currency in the Revolutionary War, our

Founding Fathers were *hard money* (money based on precious metals) advocates. Thomas Jefferson wrote: "Paper is liable to be abused, has been, is, and forever will be abused, in every country in which it is permitted."

Records of the Constitutional debates clearly show that the Founders specifically *denied Congress the power* to print paper money. When Article I, Section 10 was debated, the Founders further barred the door on paper money. The original draft wording read only, "No State shall . . . coin money. . . ." Madison's account of what was said is brief. "Mr. Wilson and Mr. Sherman moved to insert after the words 'coin money' the words *'nor emit bills of credit, nor make anything but gold and silver coin a tender in payment of debts,'* making these prohibitions absolute. . . ."

"Not Worth A Continental"

To understand fully the actions of the Founders, we must examine the history of money. As Jefferson said, paper money has been abused in every country in which it has been permitted. Even in America, in the years just prior to the adoption of the Constitution, the Continental Congress issued bills of credit, which were nothing more than fiat money, or paper currency. The inflated paper currency imposed a cruel tax on the citizens, just as it has in all other countries, and they lost their fortunes. "Not worth a continental" describes perfectly the decline of that currency; by 1779 it was worth only one penny.

A further reason for the Founders' action was their desire to restrain the state governments from flooding the country with unbacked paper money. Josiah Quincy wrote to George Washington, "there never was a paper pound, a paper dollar, or a paper promise of any kind that ever yet obtained (became) a general currency but by force or fraud, generally by both."

Thus it was that on August 16, 1787, Section 8 of the Constitution was approved, specifically denying to Congress the right to print paper money, and on August 18, they framed Section 10 prohibiting the "friends of paper money" from going through the state legislatures.

Thus the Constitution is very explicit on the subject of money:

• Article I, Section 8: "The Congress shall have power . . . to *coin* money, regulate the value thereof. . . ." [Emphasis mine; note it does not say *print*. The clear intention was that *only* gold and silver coins would be used as money.]

• Article I, Section 10: "No state shall . . . coin money; emit bills of credit; make anything but gold and silver coin a tender in payment of debts. . . ."

That's pretty explicit, isn't it? Yet today, we have the kind of money system the Constitution prohibits. You may be searching your mind trying to dredge up the Amendment to the Constitution which supercedes precious metal backing of the currency and replaces it with a fiat (paper) system. *There is no such Amendment.* In 1913, Congress sold the farm, giving away its control over money to the privately owned Federal Reserve System. If you believe the Federal Reserve is a government body, as probably 99 percent of Americans do, check your phone book under U.S. Government and try to find a listing. It's not there.

Legal Counterfeiting

In our book *None Dare Call It Conspiracy*, we dealt extensively with the machinations behind the legalized theft of our monetary system. The best capsulization we have seen of this heist and subsequent establishment of our current system comes from economic historian, Dr. Gary North.

He tells the story of three counterfeiters who are discovered. The first one is a middle-class man who owns a cheap offset printing press. He has printed up 500 $20 bills and spent them into circulation. The second one is a U.S. government official. He works for the Bureau of Engraving and Printing. He has printed up a million $20 bills, and the government has spent them into circulation. The third is the Chairman of the Board of a multibillion dollar New York bank. His bank has loaned a billion dollars of fractional reserve bank money to Mexico's government-owned petroleum company, Pemex. The price of oil has collapsed, so Pemex can't pay its bills.

What happens to the three counterfeiters? The first man is convicted of counterfeiting and is sent to jail. The second man works until age 65 and is given a pension.

But what about the third man, the Chairman? Here is where it could get interesting. The third man goes to the nation's central bank, the Federal Reserve System, which in turn calls the Mexican government, which immediately prints up a Mexican bond for $25 million, which is then bought by the Federal Reserve System with electronic money created out of nothing. This Mexican bond then becomes part of the "legal reserve" which supposedly undergirds the U.S. monetary system. (This was made legal in the infamous "Monetary Control Act of 1980," against which only 13 Congressmen voted.)

The Mexican government sends the money to Pemex, which then remits $25 million to pay this quarter's interest payment to the New York bank. Three months from now, another $25 million will fall due. The Chairman of the New York bank gets a round of applause from the bank's Board of Directors, and perhaps even a $100,000 bonus for his brilliant delaying of the bank's crisis for another three months.

The $25 million then multiplies through the U.S. fractional reserve banking system, creating millions of new commercial dollars in a mini-wave of inflation. This scenario could really happen in terms of United States law. Is this system just? Would you say that the law respects neither the mighty nor the poor man?

Dr. North reports that people ask him, "If the present monetary system is so awful, how could it be made into something honest?" There are a lot of answers floating around. Dr. North poses a simple one. Because the one we have was imposed on us in 1913, and is anything but a free market system, he sees no reason for sticking with any aspect of it. But to know what needs to be done, you first need to know where the present system came from.

Founding Of The Fed

In late November, 1910, a private coach carrying some of the nation's leading bankers and a U.S. Senator pulled out of the Hoboken, New Jersey, train station and headed for Georgia. Their ultimate destination was Jekyll Island, which was owned by some of the richest men on earth as a hunting club. Membership in the club was by inheritance only.

On board that train was Senator Nelson Aldrich, the maternal grandfather of Nelson Aldrich Rockefeller. Also aboard was Henry P. Davison, a senior partner in the powerful banking firm of J. P. Morgan Co., Benjamin Strong (another Morgan employee) and a European expert in central banking, Paul Warburg. Representatives of two other major New York banking firms were also present.

The reporters who gathered at the train station were told nothing, except that the men were all going duck shooting. Six years later, Bernie Forbes, the man who founded *Forbes* magazine, reported briefly on the meeting, and most people thought the whole story was just a "yarn." Very little has been written on it since 1916. (Probably the most detailed account is chapter 24 of the highly favorable biography, *Nelson W. Aldrich,* by Nathaniel W. Stephenson.)

At that secret meeting, these men designed what became the Federal Reserve System, the central bank of the United States. As they were returning, they were met by reporters at the Brunswick, Georgia train station. Davison went to meet with them, and when he returned, he informed the group that "they won't give us away." They never did. The press never mentioned the meeting.

Senator Aldrich, a Republican, was the political middleman. His biographer relates this highly revealing information:

> How was the Reserve Bank to be controlled? The experience of the two United States banks, in our early history, pointed a warning. The experience of a lifetime spoke in Aldrich's unconditional reply. It was to be kept out of politics. It must not be controlled by Congress. The government was to be represented in the board of directors; it was to have full knowledge of all the Bank's affairs but a majority of the directors were to be chosen, directly or indirectly, by the members of the association.

Republican Aldrich did not succeed in getting his version of the central bank through Congress in 1911 and 1912, but Democratic President Woodrow Wilson got a very similar version passed in late December of 1913. Thus, in the year of the income tax was also born the Federal Reserve System, our nation's central bank.

The Federal Reserve Bank is the most powerful insurance company in the United States, and possibly the world. Its function is to control the money supply of the U.S., inflating or (hardly ever) deflating at will the total money supply. It was created, the founders promise, in order to eliminate "panics," as recessions and depressions were called in those days. The results:

- The "panic" of 1920-21
- The Great Depression of 1929-39
- The recession of 1953-54
- The recession of 1957-58
- The recession of 1969-70
- The recession of 1975-76
- The recession of 1981-82

The Fed was also created, we are told, in order to supply a so-called "elastic currency" to meet the seasonal needs of business. This "elastic currency" has stretched into the hundreds of billions, ever upward. What it was *really* created for was to prevent the bankruptcy of any major commercial New York bank, and other major banks around the country.

The Fed was also created to supply funds to keep a bank panic from spreading to the major banks. The key phrase is "supply funds"—a synonym for *inflate*.

Who Owns The Fed?

The Federal Reserve Bank is a privately owned corporation whose shares of ownership are held by the member banks. It is quasi-public, in that the President of the United States appoints the members of the Board of Governors of the Fed, but the directors of the 12 regional Fed banks, and especially the powerful New York Federal Reserve Bank, are not appointed by any political body. There are nine directors of each regional Federal Reserve Bank; six are appointed by local bankers and three by the Board of Governors of the Federal Reserve System.

Can the government tell the Fed what to do? The answer is yes, says Dr. North, if Congress and the President are agreed about what to do. If there is disagreement over monetary policy—and there usually is—then the Fed does pretty much what it wants. What the origin of the Fed indicates is that the Fed does what the major multinational banks want.

The government allows the central bank, legally a private organization, to manipulate the money supply of the United States. The central banks of every nation possess this same prerogative. Why do the governments tolerate it? Because they always need money. The central banks stand as "lenders of last resort" to the government.

The government pays interest on the Treasury bills held by the Federal Reserve. It amounts to about $15 billion a year these days. At the end of the year, the Fed sends back about 85% of this money to the U.S. Treasury. It keeps 15% for "handling." The Fed has *never been audited* by any agency of the United States government. The Fed's officials have resisted every effort of any Congressman or Senator to impose an audit by the Government Accounting Office.

The U.S. money supply is totally regulated by decisions of the Board of Governors of the Federal Reserve System. The Fed establishes the "reserve requirements" of the commercial banks. The Fed buys or sells U.S. Treasury bills (U.S. government debt certificates). When the Fed buys, it increases the money supply (multiplying because of fractional reserves). When it sells, it deflates the money supply (shrinking by this same multiplication number). But, it never sells for more than a few weeks. It is almost always buying. It is almost always inflating.

Thus, the American business cycle ("boom and bust") is controlled by a handful of men who are not responsible to the President or the Congress, except in those rare instances when the Legislature and the Executive agree completely and press their decision on the Fed.

How The U.S. Lost Its Gold

An important point to note here is that the Fed owns the entire U.S. gold stock. Legally, there is no "United States" gold stock — there is only the Fed's gold stock. It is stored, not in Fort Knox, Kentucky, but at 33 Liberty Street, New York City, New York. The U.S. government has always sold its gold to the Fed, beginning in 1914.

Where did the Fed get the money to buy the gold? It created it, of course. In short, it *counterfeited* it—but it's legal.

Dr. North reminds us, also, that in 1933, the U.S. government outlawed the private ownership of gold. It bought all the gold it could forcibly collect from the public, paying the going price of $20.67 per ounce. Then it sold it to the Fed at $20.67 per ounce. The next year, the government raised the price of gold to $35 an ounce. Net profit to the Fed was 75 percent. This raised the legal reserves for banks, and the money supply zipped upward by 30 percent between 1933 and 1935.

"No," you say to yourself. "It couldn't be true. The government confiscated our gold in 1933 so that a private corporation owned by the member banks could buy it at a discount? Impossible!"

If you are one of these skeptics, pick up a copy of any Friday edition of *The Wall Street Journal*. Somewhere in the second section (they always shift it around) you will find a table called *Federal Reserve Data*. Check the listing under Member Bank Reserve Changes. There you will see a quotation for "Gold Stock." It never changes: $11,090,000,000. They don't sell it, and it's kept on the books at the meaningless arbitrary price of $42.22 per ounce.

Whose reserves? Member banks. Who holds the title? The Federal Reserve System. Who owns the Federal Reserve? Member banks. This leads to the conclusion that if you're going to become a counterfeiter, you might as well be an audacious one. The backyard operators risk going to jail—central bankers don't.

The structure and operation of the giant banks is one which has long divided and confused Conservatives who are in basic agreement on most subjects. The Ayn Rand Libertarians and the GOP elephant worshippers have long put the international bankers on marble pedestals and praised them as the backbone of the Free Enterprise system. Dogmatic "Liberals" and labor-union activists tend to view them as stereotypical Republicans, while the academic cliché has it that bosses of the international banking operations are reluctant progressives.

New World Order opponents do not see these operators as the bedrock of capitalism, but as its blood enemies. They view Big Government and Big Banking as Siamese twins involved in scratching each other's back and mutually lining their pockets, while building up the size, scope and power of Big Banking and Big Government. Libertarians generally ascribe this to a combination of greed, hostility to competition and fear that without manipulation, ignorant and destructive monetary policies will be introduced by venal politicians and power-hungry bureaucrats.

Your author believes that these are all factors, but that at the highest levels, there is a great deal more involved. He contends that banking elitists are working with other elitists in government, the media, the academy and the labor unions to establish an all-powerful government, first at the national level and then internationally, under the control of the inner party of the New World Order.

This is not to say that the friendly local banker who lends you the money to buy a washing machine on eighteen easy payments is a conspirator or a Machiavellian. He is almost certainly an honorable professional going about the business of making sound loans. Your local banker may be a "Liberal" or a Conservative. More than likely he describes himself as a "moderate" and is more interested in his golf score than in monetary philosophy. If you query him about the gnomes of the Federal Reserve and their leverage over the American economy, chances are you will find that he has never given these matters a thought.

The point is that one does not compare David Rockefeller of the vast Chase Manhattan Bank with his counterpart at the Cattlemen's Bank of Elephant Breath. The latter is trying to make a living, while the former is out to create a New World Order. It should be understood, however, that banking enjoys a unique and privileged position unmatched by any other industry. A bank is quite simply a money factory. No other industry or private institution has the privilege of manufacturing money. And one can hardly think of a more bountiful monopoly to be bestowed by the political powers that dispense bank charters.

The Banking Lobby

We are led to believe that the big international bankers are staid, careful and conservative. They are in fact wheeler-dealers who promote loose Keynesian money policies. They want money made available through Federal Reserve "stimulation" to lend at interest to the public, the government and the corporations. This is, of course, inflationary. As a matter of fact, this increase in the money supply *is* inflation. The deficit checkbook money takes on value only by depreciating the value of all the other money—including yours—which is already in circulation. Politicians run deficits which are monetized by banks that in turn make loans based on credit extended by "the Fed." That is the carburetor of inflation.

You can see why the banking crowd and the politicians have what is commonly known as a "community of interest." Even the *New York Times* admitted on December 22, 1977, that in the opinion of many Senators and Representatives, as well as congressional staff, Washington lobbyists and other officials, "The nation's banks exert an influence over Congress and the Federal Government [which] surpasses the power of any other regulated industry." The *Times* quotes a lobbyist identified only as the "dean" of the fraternity as stating: "The bank lobby can almost certainly stop anything it does not want in Congress." The power of the banks, reports the *Times*, rests on an intricate political and financial structure that has many elements.

The bankers' lobby has grown in sophistication as well as size. The American Banking Association, for example, has for many years had a system of "contact bankers" who could be called upon to reach a Senator or Congressman with whom they had developed "personal ties." William Lunnie, an ABA spokesman, says: "This has all been computerized now. We can activate just those who have some kind of relationship with House or Senate members we want to reach on a given issue. We very seldom have to mobilize the whole list." What Mr. Lunnie is saying is that the money fraternity can turn the heat on key legislators to keep adverse legislation bottled up in Committee or to lobby for the passage of foreign aid and other appropriations which create business for the big banks.

The *New York Times* reports of the regulatory system:

> The operations of the three principle agencies — the Office of the Comptroller of the Currency, the Federal Deposit Insurance Corporation and the Federal Reserve — are funded by the banking industry itself, and thus are subject neither to the usual Congressional appropriations process or to audits by the G.A.O. And bank regulators, who insist that public criticism of bankers could lead to a damaging loss of confidence in banks, carry out their supervision with little oversight, and with a secrecy almost unknown in other parts of the Federal bureaucracy, outside the intelligence agencies.

Not surprisingly, the banking lobby concentrates its largesse on those in a position to be more helpful. Seventeen members of the House Banking Committee have been the recipients of gifts from the bankers' political action committees. According to public records of the Federal Election Commission, the campaign committees of twelve current members of the House Banking Committee obtained loans totaling $80,193 for 1976 elections. The reports also show that, as of September 1977, the campaign committees of six of the twelve Banking Committee members had not repaid their loans at the time the Committee was considering legislation strongly opposed by almost all banks.

So those overseeing the Paper Aristocracy are being financed by those whom they are supposed to regulate. Admittedly, this is not an unusual situation. Members of the House and Senate Labor Committees accept huge contributions from the AFL-CIO, but that does not make the situation any less dangerous. The situation is made worse by the fact that the key positions in the bureaus charged with direct regulation and examination of the banking industry are held by former bankers. This is hardly akin to appointing a "former" coyote to guard a herd of sheep, but it does raise questions.

For many years, we have pointed to the unparalleled influence the money magicians of Manhattan have over the Executive branch of the federal government through the Rockefeller family's Council on Foreign Relations. Every major banking institution in the country is represented in the CFR. While the *New York Times* is prepared to complain about the influence of the big banks on the Congress and the federal regulatory agencies, it says nothing of the power the banking biggies have in the White House.

Because of the unique conjugal relationship between the bankers, the regulators and the politicians, our banking system has become a huge money machine, ripping off the whole economy. The Constitution specifies that money shall be gold or silver. If that held true, there could be no mass manipulation of the financial system and no need for stern regulation.

The Coming Bank Panic

Even the prospect of nuclear warheads raining down from the skies probably carries with it no more fear for Americans over fifty than collapse of the banking sys-

tem. The thought calls up the nightmare of 1933 and
conjures visions of long lines in front of banks as tellers'
windows are slammed down in front of enraged depositors waving passbooks recording their now-worthless life
savings. For many decades it seemed that such scenes
had disappeared with raccoon coats, nickel cigars and
the Pierce Arrow.

One of the most successful of the New Deal reforms,
we were assured, was the establishment of more
stringent regulation of banks and creation of the
vaunted Federal Deposit Insurance Corporation. Now,
for the first time since the days of Herbert Hoover, the
possibility of a general failure of the U.S. banking system is a topic of concern in the mass media and along
the Potomac.

Until this year, such discussions were reserved to the
doughty little band of newsletter writers catering to the
antediluvian gold bugs with the high button shoes and
spats. You know, the ones who go about repeating that
"a" is "a," two plus two are four and other pre-Keynes-
ian homilies and platitudes.

Now, just as it did through the booming Twenties,
the banking system is once more painting us all into a
corner. Whether this an unintentional upset or a deliberate setup is currently provoking considerable debate.

David Rockefeller is apparently confident that, even
if there are problems at the bank with money running
short in the meantime, the taxpayers can be made to
step in and ease the strain. Rockefeller thinks Chase
Manhattan has a friend in you. And his power in Washington is beyond question.

It is possible that we may have an old-fashioned,
deflationary crash in the style of 1929. During that period, the Federal Reserve, following eight years of pump-
ing up credit and (therefore) the stock market, pulled
the plug and threw the country into deflation. These policies were carried on for several years and the money
supply was actually contracted by one-third, despite the

fact that "the Fed" had been established for the avowed purpose of preventing such a deflationary crunch.

Apologists for the Federal Reserve claim that the money managers choked in the clutch and that it was all an unfortunate accident. That is hogwash! As Professor Murray Rothbard has proved in his book, *The Great Depression,* it was about as accidental and impromptu as the Rose Parade. But it is doubtful that such a scenario could be repeated today. In the 1930s, very few people understood what was happening. Now, thanks to widespread educational efforts by Conservatives and Libertarians, there are too many people who are familiar with the actual causes of the Great Depression to get away with playing that scene again.

Most Free Market economists and financial analysts believe the approach this time will be the exact opposite. Professor Antony Sutton, author of *The War On Gold,* maintains: "A general banking collapse could be caused by huge foreign loan defaults, major corporations filing bankruptcy, foreigners pulling their funds from the banking system, a war in the Middle East, a major bank becoming insolvent or a large city or state going broke.

"If the crises come one at a time, I think the Washington bureaucrats can handle them. They can handle a Penn Central, a New York City, a Franklin National Bank if they are not simultaneous. They will do it by simply creating the liquidity necessary for the bailout. This is inflationary, but it will at least hold the system together. But, if there should be multiple crises at the same time, a chain reaction or a domino effect, the problem could get out of hand."

Economists and analysts believe that the strategy of the New World Order bankers and their allies in Washington is to get out from under by cranking up inflation and wiping out their debts with the printing press, as Germany did after World War I—crushing the frugal German middle class and bringing on Hitler. As one European central banker put it, "The dollar is going to be asked to die for its country." The 1940 dollar is now worth twenty-four cents. It is heading for a value equal to a Roosevelt dime, a Jefferson nickel, and ultimately perhaps a Lincoln penny.

What happens if we do get multiple simultaneous crises which produce a bank panic? What happens to all those bank accounts which, as they say in the ads, are "insured by an instrumentality of the United States Government?" The FDIC's reserves are miniscule in comparison to what it would need in a panic. But psychologically the existence of the FDIC insurance programs helps millions of people sleep better at night.

Certainly the FDIC can protect depositors if a small or medium-sized bank goes over the falls of bankruptcy. But there is no way it can pay off from its reserve funds in the event of a nationwide catastrophe. What would it do in case of a crash? Most likely government would simply print the cash needed to bail out the banks and other financial institutions. Perhaps giant Air Force transports will be flying thousands of tons of freshly printed paper money all over the country. The result will be instant runaway inflation as the people dump cash to get into hard goods before the money further depreciates. A Big Mac could cost you fifty dollars in Federal Reserve notes . . . or one real silver dime.

The Monetary Control Act

On March 28, 1980, the House and Senate passed the most revolutionary banking law since the creation of the Federal Reserve in 1913. Three days later, Jimmy Carter signed the Depository Institutions Deregulation and Monetary Control Act into law. Despite the far-reaching consequences, you probably read very little about this new law in your local newspaper. And, if the report did creep into your local tabloid, what appeared on the wire services was strictly a sanitized, Little Red Riding Hood version.

One part of the bill which could be very popular with

the public is that the Federal Deposit Insurance Corporation now insures savings accounts to $100,000 instead of a mere $40,000. But, as the *Wall Street Journal* points out, the FDIC has only $1.22 in its coffers for every $100 in liabilities. With the stroke of Jimmy Carter's pen on March 31, he increased the liabilities of the FDIC by a staggering $75 billion. The idea, of course, is to convince savers that they have nothing to fear but fear itself. The FDIC is 1.22 percent reality and 98.78 percent wishful thinking. The *Wall Street Journal* described how this strategy could backfire:

> The situation is "even worse than it looks," worries Jack Guttentag, a senior banking professor at the University of Pennsylvania's Wharton School. If the FDIC ever had to use any "significant" amount of that kitty to pay off depositors of any major bank, he reasons, the public would come to realize how little was left and might well pull enough out of other banks to cause "a shambles." His recommendation: eliminate the "mischievous" reserve fund altogether, so that no one would be panicked into thinking that it is all that stands between him and a chain reaction of collapses.

Somehow, we don't see Congress going for this suggestion.

One of the most significant aspects of the Act is that it puts all depository institutions, not just national banks, under the control of the Federal Reserve System. For all intents and purposes, all the state banks in the country have been put under the jurisdiction of Paul Volcker and the Federal Reserve System. National banks had been dropping out of the Federal Reserve System because of the interest-free reserves which the Fed required.

From now on, the Fed will dictate policy to all savings institutions. After all, if you are going to have a funny money system where the money is not backed by gold or silver, but by the promises of politicians, bureaucrats and bankers, you eventually have to have one money dictator to make sure that everyone creates money out of nothing in approximately the same amounts.

Opening The Floodgates

The other hidden features of the new law — the ones that the media ignored — made it clear why the Fed must control all financial institutions. When the likes of the *Wall Street Journal* and *Business Week* start sounding like Howard Ruff, you know that the Big Money Boys in New York and Washington are very nervous. Today, the depository institutions are so interlocked that the domino theory applies to banks, savings and loans, and other thrift institutions. The Money Crowd can't afford a chain reaction of collapse.

It has been officially decided that the banking system is not going to be allowed to go broke. Instead, as Dr. Gary North observes, "the dollar is going to be allowed to go broke."

Banks get in trouble because they "borrow short and lend long." Most of their deposits can be pulled out on short notice, but their loans may not be repaid for many years; so banks are inherently not liquid. In normal times, this does not matter, as the number of people making withdrawals is matched by those making deposits. But, we are not talking about "normal times" in the future; we are talking about highly abnormal times.

So, the bankers are interested in stopping runs on the banks by making sure they have plenty of cash with which to meet any emergency. The new banking law does this in several ways. Now that all depository institutions must meet the Fed's reserve requirements, they also have access to the Fed's loan window. The Fed can serve as the "lender of last resort" to all savings institutions. The government has billions of dollars in cash stored up and in the case of an emergency, C-141s will be hauling fresh new greenbacks all over the country.

The new law also lowers the reserve requirements for banks so they can pump out more newly created credit to keep bad loans afloat, so they won't collapse the system. The law also allows the Federal Reserve to suspend all reserves for 180 days. This means that every bank would have the equivalent of its own printing press under these circumstances. The printing press will actually be "the lender of last resort."

The law also eliminates the requirement that the Fed have collateral for Federal Reserve Notes (currency) held in the vaults of the Federal Reserve Banks. This will enable the Fed to print, for the first time, unlimited quantities of Federal Reserve notes and store them in their vaults.

It also expands the definition of collateral to include any asset the Federal Reserve Banks may purchase or hold in their Open Market operations. This will enable the Fed to put more Federal Reserve notes into circulation and effectively lower reserve requirements.

And, in order to keep you from getting to your safety deposit box, where you may have cash, coins or other hard assets, the Comptroller of the Currency is empowered to impose selective banking holidays, city by city, state by state, without any approval of Congress.

We do not wish to cause panic. On the other hand, ostriches tend to get kicked in the tailfeathers. Allen's rule Number One for financial survival is: "Never be last in line when there is a run on the bank." Rule Number Two is: "Never believe a politician who says we have nothing to fear but fear itself and that prosperity is just around the corner."

Chapter Thirteen

Banking on the New World Order

"The evidence is compelling that reconsideration of the world monetary system is overdue. Therefore, national economies need monetary coordination mechanisms and that is why an integrated world economy needs a common monetary standard, which is the best neutral inflationary coordinating device. But, no national currency will do—only a world currency will work."

— President Ronald Reagan
At the Spring, 1983 Economic
Summit, Williamsburg, Virginia

At the 1983 Williamsburg summit, the Establishment press described everything from the gracious colonial ambience of old Williamsburg to how well President Reagan got along with other world potentates. But it failed to report one crucial piece of news, an item which should have merited headline treatment: The fact that the Reagan Administration had pledged the United States to contribute another $50 billion to the Rockefeller-dominated International Monetary Fund! While the American press either missed or deliberately covered up this shocking commitment, the secret promise made headlines in the *London Financial Times*.

Why were the Americans kept ignorant of this move? Simple enough. If hard-pressed Americans had learned that their standard of living was to be reduced to prop up corrupt socialist regimes overseas and to bail out the big money-center banks, their spirit of self-sacrifice might have proved very thin indeed. In fact, an enraged public might just have blackjacked a timid Congress into flushing the whole scam.

The expansion of the U.S. contribution to the International Monetary Fund is part of a scheme for bailing out the huge international banks that have overextended themselves by making high-risk loans to Communist and Third World governments. Conceived in 1944 by Communist agent Harry Dexter White and Fabian Socialist John Maynard Keynes, the IMF acts as the FDIC of the world and funnels bailout funds to debtor governments which, all together, now owe Western banks and Western governments over $1 trillion. The Big Banks have simply arranged for the U.S. taxpayers to "socialize their risks" by picking up the tab for bad loans. To facilitate this shift of the "Old Maid" from the private banks to the public treasury, the U.S. is asked again and again to increase its aid of the IMF.

Free Market economist Murray Rothbard notes that this "is really only a facade through which the Federal Reserve can flood the world with counterfeit dollars. The Keynesians are delighted by this step toward the achievement of their dream of a world central bank. Ideally, such a bank would print a world money unit which would be used by all nations. Since there would be no balance of payments problems or other checks associated with the abuse of an international currency, the world bank could print money forever — that is, there would be no check on world inflation."

By going to a One World currency and a world central bank, the One Worlders can avoid the nasty problems which characterize our present system of free-floating and competing national fiat currencies and fluctuating exchange rates—problems which result from governments and central banks debauching their currencies at different rates of inflation. If everyone had to use the One World fiat currency, it is reasoned, uneven monetary debauchery would not occur. There would be no currency markets—everyone would experience uniform inflation, and all currency would become equally worthless. Hallelujah!

Americans are being ripped off by this New World Order redistributionist game. For every foreign government which is bailed out of its current debt obligations, there is a price to be exacted—and that price is charged to all holders of dollars via a shrinking of their purchasing power. In any case, our liquid capital is being pillaged. Though the process may be arcane and obscure to many of its victims, it is nonetheless theft. The banking "Insiders" expect us to pay and pay and pay.

A New International Economic Order

In an attempt to account for their continuing poverty, lack of development, and need for more loans, the leaders of the Third World nations promulgate a notion called "neocolonialism" or "economic imperialism." According to this facile rationalization, they are poor because the Western "capitalist" nations are affluent. This view, which is half-baked Leninism, is akin to concluding when we see a fat man standing beside a thin man that the fat man got that way by eating food belonging to the thin man. A call for redistribution of fat makes about as much sense as the call for the New International Economic Order.

But believe it or not, a demand for a New International Economic Order is now the *official* policy of most of the world's governments—including our own! Such a demand was formally propounded in the "Declaration on the Establishment of a New International Economic Order," pushed through the United Nations by Third World and Communist representatives, and adopted by the General Assembly on May Day of 1974. This Declaration has gained increased importance in recent years with the growing debate over the foreign debt crisis.

Calling for nothing short of a global Welfare State, the NIEO Declaration proposes that "the prevailing disparities in the world be banished. . . . " Three measures for attaining this are outlined in the manifesto. First, there must be a transfer of wealth from the industrialized, developed countries to the lesser-developed countries. Under the proposal, both technology and financial assets will transferred — at no charge, of course.

Second, the Declaration calls for and encourages policies of nationalization by Third World governments. It even describes this confiscation of foreign-owned private property as an "inalienable right"! Third, while it demands capital infusions from America and other Western nations, it encourages the erection of "protectionist policies" (read: trade barriers) against imports from the developed countries. Thanks, guys.

These proposals for a New International Economic Order and the Big Banks' scheming for a bailout fit together like a hand in a glove. The cruel irony in the whole charade is that the real effect will be to keep impoverished Third World counrtries in perpetual and ever-deeper indebtedness. How will they ever get out of debt if they have to borrow more and more funds just to pay interest on previously assumed debts?

While an orderly bailout of the Big Banks is being politically balanced on the backs of the American taxpayers, the debt-crisis jugglers have to cope with each problem case as it arises. There is always the possibility of a disastrous fumble. The best laid plans of rats and the New World Order can go astray. After all, these conspirators are fallible human beings and not omnipotent and omniscient gods.

Until their safety net is fully in place, the last thing the bankers want is to have to write down these Third World loans, which they are currently carrying on their books as performing assets. Hence, the necessity of pretending that the loans are good. According to the *New York Times*, loans by the nine largest U.S. banks to only three Latin American governments — Brazil, Argentina, and Mexico — amount to 113 percent of their total equity. These are the BAM countries — when they can no longer pay the interest on their debts, the whole scheme will go BAM!

The banking establishment depends on the Federal Reserve to play a key role in the planned bailout by providing the necessary liquidity to the international redistributive agencies, such as the IMF. David Rockefeller and his pals need someone they can depend on to oversee the arrangement. That is why Paul Volcker, a nominal Democrat and former vice president for David's Chase Manhattan Bank, was reappointed by President Reagan for a second term as Federal Reserve Chairman. Volcker, who is very chummy with BIS president Fritz Leutwiler and other European bankers, received solid support from Europe's central bankers for his reappointment.

Toward A One World Currency

The organized drive toward a New World Monetary Order is not a recent happening. It has long been the goal of naive dreamers and conspiratorial schemers. A centrally-managed fiat currency is a crucial element in the push for One World Government. As Mariner Eccles, then governor of the Federal Reserve Board, declared in 1944: "An international [fiat] currency is synonymous with international government."

Karl Marx, in his *Communist Manifesto*, called for "Centralization of credit in the hands of the State, by means of a national bank with state capital and an exclusive monopoly." He was recommending a monopoly in counterfeiting — a central bank — as one of the means for socializing the world. Lenin observed that instituting central banking amounted to accomplishing ninety percent of what is necessary to establish socialism.

As I have noted, the ultimate monopoly would be a World Central Bank with the ability to issue its own fiat currency as a world money. And a single fiat currency for the entire world is the goal toward which socialistic monetary reformers are aiming. They are of course eager to adopt whatever stopgap measures they can get to move the world closer to their goal. As these schemes break down, calls for a common international or regional currency become more and more insistent.

A glimpse of how that future may be achieved occured in an article entitled "A Monetary System For The Future," published in the Fall 1984 issue of the CFR house organ *Foreign Affairs*. In that article, New World Order financial architect Richard N. Cooper offered the following bold proposal:

> A new Bretton Woods conference is wholly premature. But it is not premature to begin thinking about how we would like international monetary arrangements to evolve in the remainder of this century. With this in mind, I suggest a radical alternative scheme for the next century: *the creation of a common currency for all of the industiral democracies, with a common monetary policy and a join Bank of Issue to determine that monetary policy.*" [Emphasis in the original.]

Obviously, this goal of a world fiat money is no trivial pursuit on the part of the banking Insiders.

Richard N. Cooper is a professor of international economics at Harvard University. He served as Under Secretary of State for Economic Affairs during the Carter Administration, a regime well-known for its disastrous monetary and foreign policies. In 1972-1974, he held the position of Provost at Yale. Author of *The Economics of Interdependence* and other works, Cooper favors both collectivism and internationalism. This is not surprising. He is an active member of the Council on Foreign Relations and the Trilateral Commission, both organs of the Rockefeller-dominated Eastern "Liberal" Establishment.

Of course, this is not the first time Establishment planners have openly advocated a world currency. There was another plan by Professor Robert Triffin (CFR) of Yale University back in the 1950s. In 1973, for another example, John P. Young, former director of the U.S. State Department's International Finance Division, offered a proposal at the Claremont International Monetary Conference, claiming that "there is no satisfactory alternative" to a single world currency "to supplement and eventually replace" all national currencies, including the dollar.

Another such scheme was advocated by Byron L. Johnson, an economics professor at the University of Colorado who had, as a member of the Eighty-sixth Congress, served on the House Banking and Currency Committee, and had previously worked among the giveaway artists of the Agency for International Development in the early Sixties. In the October 1971 issue of *War/Peace Report*, Johnson enthused:

> A new world currency, which should be authorized by the UN, could strengthen world institutions. Articles 57 and 63 of the UN Charter provide a legal basis by which the Economic and Social Council could begin the process, and invite alternative by the General Assembly, to develop an agreement whereby the IMF becomes, in effect, a central bank and a source of support for the UN. and its specialized agencies. Control of the amount of world currency must be in the hands of the IMF so that monetary reserves will be created for the purpose of promoting the orderly growth of world trade.

And there have been many other serious world-money schemes—the Stamp Plan, the Bernstein Plan, the White Plan (which proposed to enumerate the world fiat in "unitas"), the Keynes Plan ("bancor") and others. All these proposals envision a world fiat currency that would be issued by a world central bank, a sort of Federal Reserve for the planet. In almost all, the nucleus for this bank is seen as the International Monetary Fund.

Beginning With World War II

Planning for a New World Order and its concommitant One World currency began in earnest during the Second World War. Members of the elitist Council on Foreign Relations were busily engaged in planning the post war world even before Tojo's boys made their Sunday morning visit to Pearl Harbor.

In several recommendations during the late 1930s and early 1940s, the War and Peace Studies groups of the CFR proposed that several international institutions were required to "stabilize" the world economy after the cessation of hostilities. One such proposal, first advanced in July 1941, for example, stressed the need for worldwide financial institutions to begin "stabilizing currencies and facilitating programs of capital investment for constructing undertakings in backward and underdeveloped regions."

The idea was to set up a system after the war which would launch a global redistribution of wealth from productive Americans to the perpetually needy socialist dictatorships and Communist regimes.

The Council's own records show that during the last half of 1941 and in the early months of 1942, the CFR was already formulating plans for remaking the world. These recommendations were forwarded to F.D.R. and the State Department, where the CFR's agents were already assuming top positions of authority. Treasury advisor and CFR operative Jacob Viner wrote a memo proposing what would later turn out to be the IMF and

World Bank. The note stated, "It might be wise to set up two financial institutions: one an international exchange stabilization board and one an international bank to handle short-term transactions not directly concerned with stabilization."

A world meeting of bankers, bureaucrats and government planners was called by President Roosevelt to convene in July of 1944. Officially called the United Nations Monetary and Financial Conference, this historic occasion is generally referred to as the Bretton Woods Conference because it took place at the famed New Hampshire resort in Bretton Woods. That was the birthplace of the International Monetary Fund and the postwar monetary system which has since become less and less stable.

The Two Chief Conspirators

The Bretton Woods Conference was dominated by two individuals, one from Britain and one from the United States. *The American Banker* for April 20, 1971, in a monograph history of the IMF, reports:

> The main architects of the [International Monetary] Fund were Harry Dexter White and John Maynard Keynes (later Lord Keynes) of the American and British Treasuries. . . . Keynes had written about a world central bank as early as 1930, while White had been instructed by the U.S. Treasury only a week after Pearl Harbor to start drafting plans for an international stabilization fund after the war.

John Maynard Keynes was the darling of the British Fabian Society, the gang of socialist conspirators who had taken over and wrecked Great Britain. An aggressive homosexual, Keynes also promulgated a queer brand of economics which, among other things, strongly encouraged unrestrained government spending and deliberate budget deficits as a cure for inflation-caused recessions. Politicians and bureaucrats were delighted.

Harry White was a bird of an even more crimson hue. While all the standard histories of the IMF fail to mention it, Harry Dexter White was at once a member of the Council on Foreign Relations and a dedicated Soviet agent. Having taught economics at Harvard University, White had moved into various positions of importance in the U.S. Treasury Department where he carefully laid out plans for a new world monetary order. Others working in the Treasury Department with White who were later identified under oath as Communists were Harold Glasser, Irving Kaplan and Victor Perlo.

On November 6, 1953, Attorney General Herbert Brownell revealed that Harry Dexter White's "spying activities for the Soviet Government were reported in detail by the FBI to the White House . . . in December of 1945. In the face of this information, and incredible though it may seem, President Truman went ahead and nominated White, who was then Assistant Secretary of the Treasury, for the even more important position of executive director for the United States in the International Monetary Fund." White had help from his comrades.

In his 1954 book *The Web of Subversion*, Professor James Burnham observed: "From its beginning, and before its beginning, the International Monetary Fund has been closely encompassed by the web of subversion. . . . The technical secretary of the Bretton Woods Conference was Virginius Frank Coe. Coe became the principal administrative officer of the International Monetary Fund, the secretary, at a salary of $20,000 a year." This was the same Mr. Coe who had been identified under oath as a Communist agent by both Elizabeth Bentley and Whittaker Chambers. Coe later traveled to Red China where he was in the employ of Comrade Mao Tse-tung as an economic advisor.

Another of White's assistants at Bretton Woods was William L. Ullman, who, like Coe, took the Fifth

Amendment when presented with the evidence and asked if he were a Communist spy.

For three weeks, Keynes, White, Coe and thirteen hundred delegates had labored in New Hampshire to hammer out details for formation of the IMF. According to the *American Banker* monograph, "Keynes wanted his international central bank to have power to create its own money," and proposed to call this world currency "bancor."

While agreeing with Keynes that a centrally managed world fiat money was the ultimate goal, Comrade White was more cautious. He knew the dangers of going too far too fast, recalling how the Senate had kept the United States out of the internationalist trap known as the League of Nations in the aftermath of World War I. The wily Communist was concerned that the Senate would scuttle so obvious a move toward One World government. The proposals for the new international institutions were made to seem moderate as White and his planners judged every proposal by its chances of gaining congressional approval.

At the same time, the Establishment's drumbeaters in the mass media cranked out massive amounts of propaganda to support the Bretton Woods *coup*. Typical was an article in *Collier's* for June 2, 1945, modestly entitled "Bretton Woods or World War III." The drumbeaters were crusading in earnest.

A World Paper Standard

In 1945, Congress bought the whole United Nations/ IMF/World Bank package. It is true that the Establishment New World Order leaders sponsoring all of this did not get the full-blown world currency that they wanted; but they saw half a loaf as halfway to getting the whole bag of bread. They knew that, just as when they created the Federal Reserve in 1913, it was most important to establish the framework into which more power could later be poured as it became available.

The Bretton Woods agreements never intended that the signatory countries return to a gold standard. As a matter of fact, John Maynard Keynes, the fairy god-father of the IMF system, boasted that he and White had created "the exact opposite of a gold standard." A new gold-exchange system has been established, but this time only the U.S. dollar was to be the key reserve currency to which all others would be linked.

The IMF was to stabilize the world monetary situation by holding exchange rates among the various national currencies more or less constant. Of course, it didn't work out that way. Nations were inflating at different rates. Sooner or later, one that is inflating at a greater rate than another has to devalue its currency in terms of the other currency. Between 1947 and 1971 there were over one thousand full or partial devaluations under the Bretton Woods system. But if the IMF failed to achieve stable exchange rates, what was it actually doing? Economic historian Dr. Gary North offers the following answer:

> It gave speculators the opportunity to make very high profits or losses during major devaluations. It gave IMF bureaucrats very high-paying jobs. It got them out of Uganda and into Washington, D.C. which even today is a pretty good deal. It gave Keynesians more time to foul up the various national economies. It provided the illusion of stability in between major devaluations. It made price controls temporarily respectable. After all, if price controls can work in international monetary affairs, why not elsewhere? So the IMF no doubt benefitted some people—the planners, their philosophical supporters and these speculators who had inside information preceding major devaluations and revaluations. It certainly helped central bankers, at least to the extent that the IMF did keep

some currencies fixed in line longer than they
would have been fixed had the excuse of the
IMF been absent.

A little inside information on forthcoming devaluations can be very helpful when placing one's bets in the
international currency casino. The New York megabankers and the allied multinational corporations behind Rockefeller's CFR—the organization which drew
up the blueprint for the IMF in the first place, have ben-
efitted richly.

Unlike the old classical gold standard which prevailed
before World War I, the Bretton Woods house of paper
lacked the automatic checks against domestic inflation
provided by gold. The U.S. Government and the Federal Reserve embarked on a deliberate and escalating
post-war policy of megaspending and accelerating monetary inflation, thus exporting inflation worldwide. The
rules of the Bretton Woods game required Western
European countries (many of which were pursuing a relatively "hard money" policy) to keep piling up dollars in
their reserves and using this increasing base further to
inflate their currencies and expand credit.

As America's increasing levels of inflation in the
1950s and 1960s reduced the purchasing power and value
of the dollar, European governments (led by France)
began more and more to exercise their option of
redeeming their piles of dollars for gold at $35 an ounce.
From the early Fifties, gold flowed steadily out of the
U.S. and into the coffers of foreign governments and
central banks. But foreign dollar claims were many
times the gold reserves held at Fort Knox in the U.S. It
would be impossible to redeem all the Eurodollars that
might be presented. America was running out of gold.

Despite intense arm-twisting by the U.S. to keep
European governments from redeeming the dollars that
had been accumulating in their central banks, the Bretton Woods scheme began unraveling in the late 1960s.

Finally, on August 15, 1971, at the same time he imposed a wage-price freeze in a vain attempt to hide the effects of currency inflation, President Nixon brought the Bretton Woods gold-exchange standard to an end by slamming shut America's gold window. For the first time in its history, the U.S. dollar was totally irredeemable, even by foreign governments. This was a *de facto* declaration by the U.S. Treasury of bankruptcy.

In effect, our government did to the rest of the world in 1971 what it had done to its own citizens in 1934.

As the Bretton Woods system broke apart, the U.S. Government tried to pretend that the dollar didn't need any link to gold to give it value, and that gold was unimportant. Massive gold sales had been made in the attempt to keep the price of gold at the official level of $35 per ounce. America had lost more than half its gold reserves. The foreign central banks and wealthy New World Order planners who gobbled up gold at the artificially low price of $35 enjoyed a terrific bargain. They had literally been allowed to loot Fort Knox.

Another Step Toward A World Currency

The New World Order banking elite have certainly not forgotten their aim of a fiat currency for the world. They planned for the day when gold would be unlinked and replaced by the centrally managed paper. In 1970, the IMF created out of thin air something called "Special Drawing Rights" (SDRs) as a step in that direction. The SDR is an abstract unit based on a so-called "basket of currencies" which is a weighted average of several major fiat currencies. Since January of 1981, this basket has consisted of the U.S. dollar (forty-two percent), the Deutsche mark (nineteen percent), and the yen, pound sterling and French franc (at thirteen percent each).

The SDR is still a long way from being a true world currency and the IMF is not yet a central bank for the world. But they do provide a nuclear precedent for such a global money monopoly. And, with a world currency at their disposal, the Rockefeller-led Establishment New World Order group could permanently rig the international commodity markets and dominate national economies by controlling the availability of money to debt-ridden governments.

David Rockefeller was not only the Chairman of the Council on Foreign Relations, but also founder of that klatch of One World planners called the Trilateral Commission. The latter's Task Force Report, titled "Toward A Renovated World Monetary System," states:

> A renovated system needs to place the new Special Drawing Rights (SDRs) in a position of primacy among reserve assets. SDRs, properly managed, can provide for adequate and controlled growth in world liquidity. Under the system of exchange-rate parities that we envision, all currencies, including the dollar, would be convertible to SDRs at a fixed but alterable price. The United States would be expected to finance any payments deficits by drawing on its holdings of Special Drawing Rights.

Which brings us back to Richard N. Cooper writing in the Fall 1984 issue of the CFR journal *Foreign Affairs*. Cooper is not, of course, a gold man. He tells his CFR readers:

> Exchange rates can be most credibly fixed if they are eliminated altogether; that is, if international transactions take place with a single currency. But a single currency is possible only if there is in effect a single monetary policy, and a single authority issuing the currency and directing the monetary policy. How can independent states accomplish that?
> They need to turn over the determination of

monetary policy to a supernational body, but one which is responsible collectively to the governments of the independent states. There is some precedent for some parts of this type of arrangement in the origins of the U.S. Federal Reserve System, which blended quite separate regions of the country, and banks subject to diverse state banking jurisdictions, into a single system, paralleling the increasingly national financial market.

Similarly, we will need a world monetary system that parallels the increasingly global financial market. It will probably not be possible, even within the time scale envisiaged here, to have a truly global Bank of Issue [world central bank]. But that will not be necessary either, and it may be possible to have a Bank of Issue which serves a more limited group of democratic countries, and which can serve as the core of an international system.

Well, there you have it. By going to a One World currency and a world central bank, the would-be world monopolists can avoid the nasty problems associated with our present system of competing national fiat currencies and fluctuating and uncertain exchange rates — problems which result from governments and their central banks debauching their currencies at different rates of inflation. If everyone had to use the One World fiat currency (or electronic credit/debit unit), we are told, uneven monetary debauchery would not be shown up as it is now in the daily currency markets. In fact, with only one currency, there would not be any currency fluctuations, there would not be any currency markets (except black markets, of course) and everyone would experience uniform inflation.

In short, Richard N. Cooper of the CFR wants to let the New World Order planners do to the world what the

Federal Reserve has done to America. It amounts to a gigantic mechanism for ripping off the productive nations. Marx and Lenin would love it.

What The Future Might Hold

In a free market, the government does not force the taxpayers to underwrite the investments of any business or individual. Businessmen are free to take their own risks and either succeed or fail — with neither hindrance nor assistance from government. But we do not have Free Enterprise today; we have *privileged* enterprises for those conspiring elites who use political interventionism to keep out potential competitors and to obtain favors and monopolies.

If the Insiders are successful in achieving a world monopoly in money, energy and agricultural resources, then everyone who uses these things will depend on the globalists for survival. And, again, the whole takeover operation will have been guaranteed by Uncle Sam — which means, the U.S. taxpayers.

Will the United States be dictated to by an international monetary authority? Will we soon be taking yet another giant step toward the New World Order by going to a new currency? What will be the signs to look for?

Well, unless it can be stopped by fierce political opposition, look for a currency call-in at some future date. It would occur not long after a second "Betton-Woods-type conference" in which some plan will be debated and adopted to try to achieve fixed exchange rates through the artificial means of "cooperation" and "coordination" among the monetary policies of each nation's central bank according to a central plan — or perhaps to go directly to some form of "bancor" or common currency unit.

The transformation of the currency will be a gradual process, to avoid undue suspicion among the grass-roots citizens. One of the main excuses for the currency call-in will be to counteract counterfeiters and to help control the criminal element such as drug dealers who deal in large quantities of cash. The various bills will probably be in different colors and perhaps metal threads will be woven into them so that large amounts of currency can be detected by metal detectors such as those used at airports.

Informed sources believe that the new currency a few years from now will have blank spaces on the bills. Other currencies in other countries already have this feature. The space could then be printed over with the international currency number or designation. Sound hare-brained? Of course! But they are going to try it, anyway! And that's only part of the story.

So that the New World Order Big Brother can monitor everything you do, a "cashless" society is being experimented with. This experiment has already begun in several cities both here and abroad. In Singapore, for example, not all cash has been removed from circulation. But major stores have installed electronic fund machines, and the use of cash to buy things is actively discouraged. Many workers now receive their salaries by electronic transfer to their bank accounts. People are also being encouraged to pay their monthly bills electronically.

If you use a major bank credit card, such as VISA or MasterCard, you may have noticed that some systems both approve your credit *and debit your account* in the same transaction. In other words, as your charge is being processed at the local gas station, a computer thousands of miles away debits your account and credits the vendor's account. Welcome to the world of electronic payments!

The monetary problems in the world today stem from the fact that money is under the control of central banks chartered by national governments; the solution is to remove politics from monetary matters—and to expose the conspirators who are involved with both.

The first U.S. coinage act (April 2, 1792, Chapter XVI, Section 19) has never been repealed. It provides the death penalty for anyone who debases U.S. gold or silver coins.

Come to think of it, that's not a bad idea!

Chapter Fourteen

Say "No!" to the New World Order

"Other misfortunes may be borne and their effects overcome. If disastrous wars should sweep our commerce from the ocean, another generation will renew it. If it exhausts our treasury, future industry will replenish it. If it desolates and lays waste our fields, still, under a new cultivation they will grow green again and ripen under future harvests.

"But who can reconstruct the fabric of demolished government? Who can rear again the well-proportioned columns of Constitutional liberty? Who can frame together the skillful architecture which united national sovereignty with state rights, individual security and public prosperity?

"No; if these columns fall, they will be raised not again."

— Daniel Webster

Now that we know exactly who the enemy is and how he is working, what do we do about it? How do we stop the One-World socialists and the whole New World Order crowd, now that we understand their game plan?

Well first, we must set up a clamor and a holler, to

make the country and the world know that there is something called "The New World Order." We must make them see that this "something" means the end of their freedom and independence, the end of their religious liberty, the end of their children's future—the end of every civilized value and tradition that we have known for nearly 6,000 years. Then we will win—because the American people do not want "The New World Order"; they just don't know about it.

In the past, the New World Order has been treated as merely another one of the issues. Instead, it should serve as the name for *all of the issues*. You don't have to speak of conspiracies and plots. You just have to say "New World Order"; that is enough to identify and indicate conspiracies and plots.

We must focus attention on the *New World Order* as *the three words* that best describe the root cause and common denominator or our problems. We must expose the New World Order and then say "NO!" to it. Or, putting both parts together, we get the succinct, definitive slogan, "Say 'NO!' to the New World Order." It would be represented by a logo that looks like this:

Notice that this doesn't say a word about abortion, or the Equal Rights Amendment, or gun control, or prayer in the schools, or marijuana, or the Panama Canal, or any of the issues. No, if you started with that, it would be much less effective. Most people don't get very excited about most of the issues. They think they apply to someone else, not them. That's why the phrase —New World Order—can be so effective. They haven't heard of it before and they are at least curious.

That is why I have become convinced that fighting each issue, no matter how significant and important it may be, is not enough. Yes, the issues must be fought. But we can be much more effective fighting them *if we put them in context*.

Before we fight any issue, we must *name the game*. We must show the entire deck — the New World Order. That is what I mean by naming the game: identifying the battle *in context*.

What happens when we name the game? When we identify what we are fighting as the New World Order? The American who never felt part of the battle before suddenly realizes that this does concern him — that this is not just a debate over a narrow issue, but a debate over whether he lives or dies.

That's the key. It's not life or death for the *unborn baby* that concerns us now (although that's one of the key issues). It is life or death for the *born adult*. It is life or death for every American, for the millions living in what's left of the Free World, and for the hundreds of millions who have been enslaved.

Let me put it another way. We are not being sold out because of abortion, or the Equal Rights Amendment, or the Panama Canal, or nuclear freeze, or Zimbabwe, or whatever. These are only *elements* of the drive to create a New World Order. It is conceivable that we could win a decisive victory on one of these elements . . . and still lose our freedom, because we did *not* defeat the New World Order.

We are being sold out by the One-Worlders in government and the banks, and their allies in the media, education, the foundations, etc. That is the enemy we face; *that* is what is responsible for all of the issues that concern us.

Their goal is not just to win on abortion, disarmament, or whatever; their goal is to bring about a one-world socialist state called the New World Order. *That* is what we must stop.

The New Constitution Con

In view of what we've revealed in this book, you may well ask: the Merger Maniacs seem so close to attaining their New World Order, why haven't they brought it into being yet? There are several reasons; chief among them are the following three:

1. The U.S. Congress and the America people are just not ready to swallow the New World Order yet. Not enough Americans have been brainwashed into thinking of themselves as Citizens of the World. More propaganda is necessary.

2. There remains some residual nationalism within the nations of Europe. Germans still think of themselves as Germans and French still think of themselves as French, despite the loose cooperation which exists under the label of European Economic Community (EEC).

3. The United States Constitution, even as ignored and forgotten as it is by most people and the judicial system, still stands as an important formal roadblock to the New World Order. This is especially true of the first ten amendments, the Bill of Rights. It would be impossible to impose a socialist world state without overriding the guarantees built into our system of government by our Constitution. The U.S. Constitution is incompatible with the proposed New World Order, so it must be scrapped.

How? That's where the Constitutional Convention comes in. The last Constitutional Convention that was held in the United States was supposed to look into improving the Articles of Confederation (under which the United States operated until 1789), but, instead, wound up giving the fledgling nation a whole new constitution, with expanded powers for the central government. The old Articles of Confederation were totally abandoned.

The New World Order fanatics want to replace what's left of our Constitution with a *new* constitution, one which will be much more compatible with the Great Merger.

We've already discussed the Declaration of *Inter*dependence, composed by historian Henry Steele Commager and promoted by the World Affairs Council of Philadelphia. Another aspect of the movement toward a New World Order is the push for the adoption of a new constitution, with models which invariably dispense with such important principles as the checks and balances featured in the original, not to mention the betrayal of individual rights in favor of the bogus notion of "human rights" granted by the state.

The promoters of the new constitution want to destroy the separation of powers between the legislative and executive branches. They want to have, instead, an executive dictatorship run by unelected bureaucrats. The powers of Congress would be greatly reduced and restricted under this plan. It would give the controllers more centralized power through which they could manipulate our society for their collectivistic ends.

During the 1960s, the influential Center for the Study of Democratic Institutions, a front for the Ford Foundation, put forth a "Constitution for a United Republics of America." The Center, then headed by Paul Hoffman (CFR) and Robert M. Hutchins (CFR), also came out with a grandiose "World Constitution." Both documents were written by Fabian New Dealer Rexford G. Tugwell.

What kind of political system would we have if the United States adopts this Constitution? The fifty states would be replaced by ten regions. The President would be elected to one term lasting for nine years. The members of the Senate would be appointed by the President and their appointments would be for their lifetimes. There would be two vice-presidents — one in charge of "general affairs" and one in charge of "internal affairs."

The wording of the Newstates Constitution has been very carefully considered to provide as many loopholes for the government to expand its powers as possible.

Under A New Constitution . . .

The key point of the new system would be that it would entail an even greater centralization of power at the apex of the Executive Branch of government. The President would have virtual dictatorial authority. Many of the individual rights and constitutional guarantees from arbitrary governmental intrusions into our lives would no longer be recognized and protected. For example:

The constitutional right to a trial by a jury of your peers will disappear. A judge will decide what kind of trial you will have and whether or not you will have a jury at all to hear your case. You might even have an adversarial trial. That is, you are assumed guilty and you must try to prove your innocence (sort of like with the IRS today).

Freedom of religion will go out the window, to be replaced by the privilege of worshipping or not worshipping as you please — until the government decides to withdraw that privilege. Remember, a right cannot be revoked, but government-granted privileges can be.

Private property rights would be diluted into nothingness. The new constitution states that no property can be taken from its owner without conpensation. The compensation is to be determined by the government. Who is to say, for example, that the government couldn't confiscate your house and give you one dollar in "compensation"?

The right to bear arms, another traditional American freedom guaranteed under our current Constitution, will be gone under the new system. Totalitarian dictatorships always reserve the right to bear arms to its own officers and deny this to the citizen.

If such a document is adopted as our new constitution, as the result of a Constitutional Convention initially called to examine the proposed Balance-the-Budget Amendment, it will likely be under the pretext of doing something decisive about an economic crisis — a crisis that can only occur because of previous unconstitutional acts of meddling and usurpation by our present bunch of political leaders.

In other words, the Merger Maniacs will sell the new constitution during a time when the U.S. will be in the midst of a severe economic crisis, such as runaway inflation, by claiming that the problem could be solved or better managed if only the President were given more direct authority over the economy. We must remember that when the government has the power to control our economy, it has the authority to control our lives and livelihoods. That is a dangerous power which would mean the end of freedom in the U.S. and dash hopes for enslaved people in the rest of the world.

The scheme for a new constitution is backed by a myriad of New World Order groups and groupies including the American Academy of Political and Social Science, the League of Women Voters, the UAW, the NAACP, the Urban League, the National Council of Churches, Common Cause, the Rockefeller, Ford and Carnegie foundations, and the Council on Foreign Relations and Trilateral Commission. Hail, hail, the gang's all here!

More recent drumbeater organizations pushing for the new constitution have been formed to join in the movement. The Committee on the Constitutional System is a group of some 200 very prominent individuals from government, business, banking and academia, led by C. Douglas Dillon (CFR) and Lloyd N. Cutler (CFR/TC).

At the time of this writing, 32 of the required 34 states have passed resolutions calling for a Constitutional Convention to consider the Tax-limitation, Balanced-Budget Amendment. If Establishment forces should gain control of such a convention, they would be able to do much more than merely contemplate the so-called balance-the-budget amendment proposal. If such a constitutional convention cannot be stopped, the

American people must make sure it is not stacked by members who do not care for our current U.S. Constitution. Eternal vigilance is, indeed, the price of liberty.

Putting The Pieces Together

We must say "NO!" to any tampering with our Consitution.

Does the "Say 'NO!'" program really work? Yes, it does! Time after time, people ask, "What does it mean, the New World Order?" And then we tell them. They listen because they are receptive. And they're shocked because they have never heard this before. *And they don't like what they are hearing!*

The simple truth is that *no* American wants to lose his country and his freedom; he just doen't know both are being stolen from him. We're going to tell him!

For many years, we in the Americanist cause tried to tell the American people about the New World Order and have met with only mixed success. Now, it is coming out in the daily news. Witness such books as Joseph Finder's *Red Carpet* and the works of Professor Antony Sutton. There are even articles in *Readers Digest* and the *New York Times.*

People can now see on television or read in their morning paper details of what we have labored for twenty-five years to tell them. All they need is the key, to put the pieces of the puzzle together. They see the effects of the New World Order crowd everywhere; now, we must reveal the manipulators behind the scenes.

In other words, the pieces of the puzzle are no longer hidden; they are out on the table. They are in the headlines. So, much of our educational job is eased. But, the most important and crucial job is now pending. That is to show that these pieces of the puzzle go together to make up the New World Order.

It is not enough to oppose aid to Red China, or missiles to Russia, or steel to Romania, or Soviet pipelines, etc. We must show that this aid and these issues make up the game plan for the New World Order. Then we must convince enough of our fellow citizens that the establishment of the New World Order means the end of their freedom and liberties.

Our main job is to put the pieces together; and that's what the three magic words—New World Order—accomplish. Without knowing anything about it, the average person automatically realizes that it is a program of some kind; and programs have to be planned and implemented by people. Programs put together by people in secret are conspiracies. That's how simply and effectively these three words do their job.

The American Freedom Movement

The key is to make the three words—New World Order—visible. And that is where the American Freedom Movement comes in. Members of this new organization will use this phrase at every opportunity. We'll get envelope stickers and put it on letters, checks, envelopes and elsewhere.

We'll put it on bumper stickers on our cars. We'll get it on billboards across the country. We'll run it in advertisements, use it in speeches and casual conversation. We'll raise it on talk shows and write about it in letters.

All the activities of the American Freedom Movement should be directed at this one central theme—exposing every American to this phrase again and again.

"Say 'NO!' to the New World Order."

"Say 'NO!' to the New World Order."

"SAY 'NO!' TO THE NEW WORLD ORDER."

When enough Americans know what is meant by these three words, New World Order, the battle will be over and we will have won. We will, quite literally, have saved freedom in this country.

When General Douglas MacArthur was pinned down on the tip of Korea and about to be pushed into the sea, he didn't try to fight his way back up the peninsula with only dim hope of victory and the prospect of a fearful loss of life. No. He looked over the situation, identified the enemy's weakest spot, and *attacked*. He did an end-run and struck at Inchon. It was one of the greatest feats in military history and it won the war — even though his victory was later lost in Washington.

That is what we are proposing now: An end-run that strikes at our enemy's weakest spot. The New World Order is our Inchon, our target for attack.

The American Freedom Movement must focus exactly and directly on the "Say NO!" program. Those of us who are at present the most informed on the New World Order will be the ones to tell the American people about it.

The New World Order must be made an issue. We must make it an issue because the mass media manipulators certainly will not until they are forced to. We must turn up the fires of public opinion to such a degree that every Congressman and Senator will have to take a stand for or against the New World Order. As Senator Everett Dirksen once observed, "When I feel the heat, I see the light." The American Freedom Movement is going to put the politicians' feet to the fire. Then they will feel the heat; and they will see the light.

There is no excuse for those of us who do know about the New World Order to sit back and do nothing. That assures defeat for us and victory for totalitarian socialism. If we do not take strong, positive and imaginative action *now*, we will lose and suffer the tragedy which will ensue. America will be gone and the Free World will fall to the One-Worlders and their Communist enforcers. Why let that happen when victory can be so sure and so complete? We are so close to a victory — and at the same time, so close to defeat if we do not act with courage and intelligence.

We have the plan, the strategy for victory. We need contributions of time, money and effort. But we will no longer be hitting our heads against a brick wall. Our efforts will not be in vain. Every day, many Americans are waking up to what is taking place. It is becoming more and more obvious to any who will see and think. By focusing on the New World Order and its underlying purposes and fallacies, we can achieve victory and save America and our precious freedoms.

What You Can Do

What can you do? Join or form a local American Freedom Movement committee. If you need assistance in locating or starting one, contact the American Freedom Movement at P.O. Box 2686, Seal Beach, California 90740. We'll rush the necessary information to you.

The American Freedom Movement will provide its local leaders with a great deal of autonomy and opportunity for initiative. We will not create a stifling bureaucracy which inevitably smothers activity, a mistake so many other organizations have made. Yes, we'll provide guidance, materials and training. But the stress will be on local control and local autonomy.

The only control we're interested in is making sure that our name and purposes are not subverted by infiltrating agent-provocateurs, racists or hate mongers with their own axes to grind. This is protection for ourselves and our other members. The enemy does not play the game according to Hoyle. Any effective organization will be targeted by chaos-creators attempting to take local groups off on tangents or inciting feuds to divide the local membership. However, strong local leadership should be able to spot and handle these situations.

While the American Freedom Movement will be decentralized in its general organizational structure, headquarters will provide a number of services to its local committees. Among the tools we will use and assistance we will provide will be straight-forward handbooks and guides on such topics as:

• How to organize and recruit new members.
• How to build good public relations and raise funds.

- How to establish effective media relations.
- How to use radio call-in "talk shows" to best advantage.
- How to get the most out of letters to the editor and petitions.
- How to use posters and bumper stickers to spread the word.
- How to conduct informative forums and seminars.
- How to set up and manage book and literature tables.
- How to organize successful speaking engagements.
- How to encourage increased internal education among members.
- How to develop local speakers to address service clubs and other community organizations.
- How members can benefit from training in debate techniques.
- How to develop a patriotic network with other groups.
- Other techniques on how to maximize your influence and win support.

The above tools and "how to" tips and techniques are only a few of the things that the American Freedom Movement plans to do for its local organizations and activists. This list is far from complete; it's meant only as an indication of the kind of assistance that will be available.

Spread The "Say NO!" Slogan

The American Freedom Movement will also publish a monthly newsletter, which will go out to all of its members. The newsletter will contain information on the latest activities of the New World Order. It will also stress positive success stories of the **"Say NO!"** program in action. This will provide inspiration and ideas for local committees. There is no need for each committee to re-invent the wheel. We must share our successes and failures and out of that, synthesize the most productive program.

We intend to make the **"Say NO!"** theme a part of the American lexicon. We will put the slogan on billboards, bus benches, radio and TV spots, T-shirts, posters, bumper stickers, badges, lapel pins, match books, business cards, playing cards, envelope stickers, drinking glasses—every place you and we can think of. We're going to hammer this phrase home until it is familiar to every citizen in the country.

The more the phrase is used, the more it will be used. We anticipate that the **"Say NO!"** slogan will be copied in dozens, and then scores, of other places. Since imitation is the sincerest form of flattery, we'll be flattered, I guess, when Madison Avenue starts saying, "Say no to bad breath—wash your mouth with Listergargle." Or "Say no to cavities—brush your teeth with Crestodent." There will be "Say no to drugs" campaigns, "Say no to drunk driving," "Say no to AIDS."

But everytime the phrase is used, it will remind people of the origin of the slogan—**"Say 'NO!' to the New World Order—Keep America Independent."** Repetition will burn this slogan into the minds of the entire population. Then we will say to Congress, "Say NO or you GO!"

Speaking of politics, I have—as you might suspect —a few thoughts on what we must do to reform the mess in Washington.

1. In every election year, let us do our utmost to see that only patriotic Americans—not eastern establishment internationalists or welfare state pinkos—are elected to every available office. As George Washington said, "Let only Americans stand guard tonight."

2. Compel Congress to impose a total embargo on all trade with and aid to all Communist governments.

3. Compel Congress to rebuild our defense forces as rapidly as possible, and regain mastery of sea, air and space.

4. Stop letting spies and traitors, disguised as UN officials, roam our country at will. Restrict UN officials to the UN compound and their residences, while at the same time working to disband the organization.

5. Work toward some form of a gold standard and honest money.

6. Adopt as a platform some slogan similar to that of the late Sen. Henry Cabot Lodge, Sr., the Senator who was so instrumental in keeping us out of the old League of Nations: "I am an American . . . I can never be anything else but an American . . . and the United States is our last and only hope, for if the United States stumbles and falls, freedom and civilization everywhere will go down in ruins."

That was a powerfully effective message then. It will serve us well again today.

I am convinced that if we act forcefully, with purpose, intelligence and determination, we will win this epic struggle. The "Say 'NO!'" campaign (and our enemy's boldness) has made it much easier for us to oppose and expose him.

Let us seize that opportunity now. If we do not act, we will not win. It is that simple. I hope you will resolve to join us in the battle, and work with us until victory.

Epilogue

Bloody Footprints in the Snow

Can we stop the New World Order juggernaut? After all, it has behind it the full force of the financial Establishment, their puppets in the mass media, and the increasingly frightening military might of the Soviet Union. They have money, momentum, Machiavellian plans and the aura of legitimacy. Right now, on our side, all we have is the gut feeling in millions of people that something is wrong. Many are not sure just what is wrong or why, but they do know that something is rotten.

What were the odds against the success of the American Revolution against the New World Order of its day, the British Empire? Astronomical! About all the patriots of 1776 had going for them was courage and determination. In Connecticut, the flag proclaimed, "Don't Tread On Me." In New Hampshire, the flag carried the motto, "Live Free Or Die!" Benjamin Franklin announced, "We must all hang together or surely we shall all hang separately."

In 1777, George Washington had lost *every single battle* against the New World Order's Britanic army. At Christmas of that year, the remnants of his starving army huddled in the snow. Those brave men wanted to be home with their families, and needed to tend their farms and businesses. But instead of surrendering in despair, our forefathers went on the offensive and *attacked*.

Washington marched his rag-tag army down to the Delaware River. Many of his troops had no shoes or boots. You could follow the army by the bloody footprints in the snow. Yes, *bloody footprints in the snow.* After crossing the Delaware, the Americans attacked the British soldiers with a vengeance. Washington's resulting victory at Trenton saved the American Revolution and paved the way for victory and independence.

Those men were willing to pay a fearsome price for freedom and liberty. They knew that freedom is not free; it has its price. As Winston Churchill said:

> If you will not fight for right when you can easily win without bloodshed; if you will not fight when your victory will be sure and not too costly; you may come to the moment when you will have to fight with all the odds against you and only a precarious chance of survival.

And that masterful orator and inspiring leader then described an even more terrible choice:

> There may even be a worse case. You may have to fight when there is no hope of victory, because it is better to perish than live as slaves.

We don't have to perish, and we don't have to live as slaves. In the past, whenever America was in danger, its people were willing to pay any price for victory. Whether it was at Guadalcanal, Bastogne, the Chosin Reservoir, or some miserable rice paddy in Vietnam, Americans were willing to pay in blood to oppose tyranny.

Today, it is not necessary to go that far or sacrifice that much. We are not asking for anybody's blood. The New World Order can be stopped before it comes to that. But we *are* asking you to *remember those bloody footprints in the snow.*

At the battle of Midway, as American torpedo planes were being annihilated by Japanese Zeroes and anti-aircraft fire, a stunned Japanese admiral remarked in shocked amazement, "These Americans die like samurai." He had been taught to believe that Americans were too soft and self-indulgent to fight. Seconds later, while the Japanese who proclaimed they were building a New World Order in the Orient had their guns trained on the torpedo bombers, American dive bombers came screaming out of the sky and the pride of the Japanese Navy, the carriers which had attacked Pearl Harbor, were a blazing mass of twisted metal. Pearl Harbor was avenged. As the song of the day said, "Praise the Lord, and pass the ammunition."

The American Freedom Movement intends to be the dive bombers against the New World Order. Predecessor groups and organizations have already served as the torpedo bombers. We intend to sink the New World Order or, to change the metaphors, to sever the head of the snake or put a bullet in the brain of the octopus. We intend to be a terrible swift sword against the enemies of freedom, justice and humanity. A modern-day Thomas Paine, to use the 1986 vernacular, might say, "This is no time to play ostrich."

Can you look in the mirror, or look into the faces of your children or grandchildren, and say that you were too busy to become involved, or whimper that it might be bad for business? Are you not willing to give your time and money when our Founding Fathers pledged their lives, their fortunes and their sacred honor to oppose the New World Order? Our National Anthem closes with the question, "Does that star-spangled banner yet wave o'er the land of the free and the home of the brave?" If we are not brave, *soon we will not be free.*

This country wasn't founded by moral cowards, and it won't be saved by moral cowards. We echo the sentiments of John Paul Jones, when asked by the New World Order if he was ready to surrender; he thundered back, "I have not yet begun to fight!"

We need you and we need you *now*. Once again, freedom is not free; it costs time, money and effort. Slavery is free.

It may take Divine Intervention to save this country. Many of us believe it was Divine Intervention which, against incredible odds, founded this country. But Divine Intervention will not come from just praying and certainly not to people who are too apathetic to care. It will come the old-fashioned way—only if we earn it. We have to prove we are willing to earn it with our own bloody footprints in the snow, with our own dive bomber attack on the New World Order.

So, we say to you, get on board or get out of the way. The Americans are coming!